THE GUN DIGEST BOOK of 9mm HANDGUNS

Second Edition

By Steve Comus

DBI Books, Inc.

ABOUT OUR COVERS

Efficient. That's probably the best way to describe both the subject cartridge and the SIG Sauer handguns shown on our covers.

On the left is the SIG Sauer P226, the full-size member of the trio. Available in double-action/single-action or double-action only, this handsome pistol has an overall length of 7.71 inches, weight of 26.5 oz., barrel length of 4.41 inches and a 15-shot magazine (20-shot optional). It can be had in blue, nickel or K-Kote finishes, depending upon the shooter's needs. Hundreds of law enforcement agencies have adopted the P226, and the FBI has chosen it for its elite Hostage Rescue Teams and SWAT units.

At right is the 9mmP P228, a reduced-size and compact sidearm designed for concealed carry or off-duty roles, but equally capable of front-line work. It, too, is available with double-action/single-action or double-action only trigger modes, but has a rounded trigger guard, 3.86-inch barrel, with an overall length of 7.08 inches, and weighs in at 26.1 oz. Like the P226, this gun is offered in blue, nickel or K-Kote finishes. Despite its compact size, the P228 has a large 13-shot capacity magazine.

Center stage is the SIG Sauer P225 with double-action/single-action trigger. Also compact, it has a 3.86-inch barrel, overall length of 7.08 inches and weighs 26.1 oz. This model has a squared trigger guard and 8-shot magazine capacity, which allows a slimmer grip for smaller hands. Originally designed for the West German police, this is the most widely issued police pistol in Europe. It also has achieved immense popularity in the U.S.

These three 9mm SIG Sauer handguns represent some of the finest technology available in the shooting sports world today. That they happen to be extremely efficient at performing their tasks just adds icing to the cake.

Photo by John Hanusin.

EDITORIAL DIRECTOR
Jack Lewis

ART DIRECTOR
Rueselle E. Gilbert

PRODUCTION DIRECTOR
Sonya Kaiser

PRODUCTION COORDINATOR
Russ Thurman

COPY EDITOR
Julie Duck

PHOTO SERVICES
Ben Delaney

PUBLISHER
Sheldon L. Factor

Produced by

GALLANT CHARGER

OUTDOOR GROUP

ISBN: 0-87349-149-1

Library of Congress Catalog Card Number: 86-071043

CONTENTS

INTRODUCTION

From the moment Jack Lewis proposed doing this book until it the final word was typed, a host of people became involved to varying degrees. Each literally made the entire project possible. To all, a hearty thank you!

Rather than attempt to list all of the names of the people who helped out (that would be done only at peril of inadvertently omitting one or more to my supreme embarrassment), it seems more fitting to recognize the kinds of assistance which made it all happen.

Thousands of hours of range time go into the collecting of data for a book such as this, and there is no way the author could have done it all himself. Thanks, guys, and a special tip of the hat to Mike Raahauge who never hesitated to provide a place to shoot.

Without ammunition, this tome would have been impossible. Gratitude goes out to CCI, Federal, Hansen, PMC, Remington, Sure Fire and Winchester for assistance with loaded ammunition. Also helpful with components were CCI, Hercules, Hornady and Turners Outdoorsman.

On the firearm front, chapters within the book witness the assistance of the many makers and marketers of guns which fire 9mm cartridges. Thank you all for that.

Also, we could not have done detailed range work without basic gear like the Oehler 35P chronograph or the Ransom Rest which were pressed into service repeatedly.

No single writer can do it all. Some segments of this book were the efforts of others who are recognized experts in the various specialties. Add to their input all of the efforts of the staffs at Gallant/Charger Publications and DBI Books, and the list begins to grow beyond belief.

Yet all of that effort, if not channeled and focused — indeed, at times even ramroded — never could have jelled into a singularly identifiable work. Thanks, Jack.

Shooters throughout the gun world ultimately comprise the army of book-buying gun buffs who really make this possible. I sincerely hope the information contained herein is both helpful and informative, entertaining and worthwhile.

Before closing, however, I must recognize — even salute — a German soldier whose identity I've never known. He carried a P-35 into combat and relinquished much more than the pistol that day. It was his handgun which introduced me to the world of 9mm. So, in the end, there was a beginning.

Good shooting to all,

Stephen F. Comus

CHAPTER
One

HISTORY & THE
9mm

Is This Truly The Cartridge People Love To Hate?

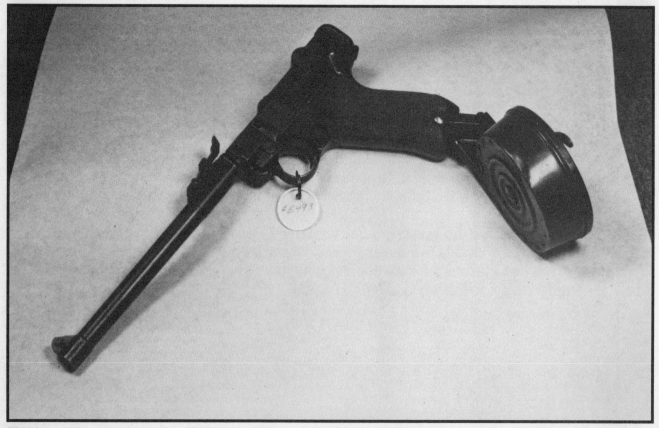

This interesting 9mm Luger is a DWM 1916 artillery model with snail drum magazine. Many of the firearms featured in this chapter and others are available from Sam Fowler Gun Room, 964 N. Tustin Ave., Orange, California, 92667.

This special 9mm Luger was one of 250 manufactured in the 1970s by Mauser. It is called a 1902 Cartridge Counter.

THE 9MM IS more than just another cartridge. It is an institution around the globe. Through common usage and over a period of time, some specific items become generic, representing entire classes of entities. So it is with the 9x19mm pistol cartridge. Both praised and vilified, this relatively petite round is referred to by a number of different names. The most common is the 9mm Luger (named for the handgun design in which the cartridge made its debut shortly after the turn of the last century). The cartridge is also known as the 9mm Parabellum (meaning, loosely, to guard against war).

In terms of numbers, the 9mmP, as it shall be called from now on in this work, has no equal in the world, save, perhaps, the .22 rimfire, when it comes to handgun cartridges and the firearms made to shoot them. Other cartridges have come and gone during the 9mmP's 90-plus-year presence. Arguably, the 9mmP is far from perfect, or even the best handgun cartridge ever designed. But it must have something going for it, or it would have died out long ago — with some of the "better" rounds which failed to pass the test of time.

In this work, the totality of the 9mmP will be inspected, discussed, dissected and explored. Close attention will be given to precisely what it *can* do, and exactly what it *cannot* do. With universal application has come no small degree of misuse, to say nothing of applications beyond design parameters. It is when the incredibly efficient 9mmP is tasked beyond itself that it gets a bad rap. However,

when the good guys, bad guys and all the Average Joes between find themselves owning and shooting the 9mmP, it definitely is doing a lot right.

To appreciate this wonder of 20th Century handgunning fully, it is necessary to start at the beginning — to take a closer look at the times and situations into which the 9mmP was introduced. The year was 1902, and the pistol in which the cartridge was introduced was the semi-auto designed by Georg Luger. More about the Model 1902 Luger pistol later, but for now, focus is on the cartridge itself.

The 9mmP embodies all that the 20th Century is, was — or ever will be. It defines an era in which humans went from initial powered flight to the moon, and beyond. The 9mm's development was concurrent with that of things like the automobile and electrification of the entire world. Consider that the 9mm is one year senior to the M1903 U.S. military rifle and its cartridge, the .30-03 (which, when the neck was trimmed back a bit, became the venerable .30-06 Springfield, considered by many to be the finest centerfire rifle cartridge ever developed).

In 1902 when the 9mmP came upon the scene, there were only 45 states in the United States (Oklahoma didn't become the Sooner State until 1908, and New Mexico and Arizona didn't join the fold until 1912. Of course, Alaska joined the Union as a state in 1959, followed by Hawaii the next year). Henry Ford was still trying to put together a viable automobile company when the 9mmP was introduced, but he wasn't able

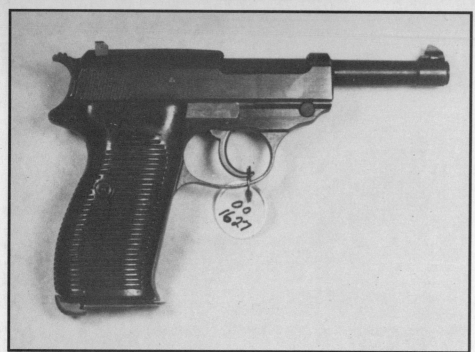

This is a superb specimen of a Walther AC 45 P38.

This Erfurt arsenal 1918 Luger is an excellent example of an early model 9mm military issue officer sidearm.

The Walther P38 was built to meet the demands of military operations. It was the first DA military pistol.

to line-up the initial $100,000 capitalization for the Ford Motor Company until the following year — 1903. It was to be a full decade later — 1913 — when Ford introduced the production-line form of automobile manufacturing.

Apache Indian Chief Geronimo was still alive and well when the 9mmP was introduced (he died seven years later in 1909). Many of those who had signed-up to fight with Teddy Roosevelt and his Roughriders were still serving-out their initial military enlistments then. Imagine that there were still quite a few American Civil War veterans who were active shooters when the 9mmP was introduced.

Or consider this: It wouldn't be for another year that Orville and Wilbur Wright would make their historic flight at Kitty Hawk, North Carolina (Dec. 7, 1903). A scant 10 years before the 9mmP came along, both the 7mm Mauser (7x57mm) and

.30-40 Krag (.30 U.S.) smokeless powder military rifle cartridges were introduced. Unveiled the same year as the 9mmP was the .33 Winchester cartridge, introduced as a smokeless powder loading for that company's then-most-successful Model 1886 lever-action hunting rifle.

But perhaps most notable was the fact that when the 9mmP was born, the cartridge against which it would come to be judged so often wasn't even a gleam in John Browning's eye. Browning introduced the .45 ACP in 1905. By then, the 9mmP was already an adopted military round, having been accepted by the German navy in 1904. The 9mmP subsequently was adopted by the German army in 1908 (with the P-08 pistol), and that was a full three years before the .45 ACP became a military cartridge. It was adopted in the Model 1911 Browning-designed pistol which became known in many circles as

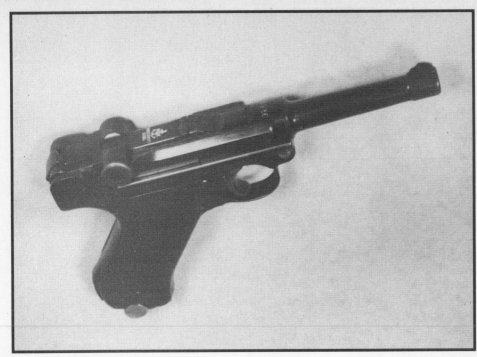

Here's a valuable collectable. The 1936 Krieghoff Luger in 9mm is a rare find today.

This Walther P38 byf 44 was produced late in WW II.

Rushed through production late in WW II, the P38 byf 44 lacked the fit and finish of earlier production models.

the Colt .45 Auto.

Enough of the history lesson. Suffice to say that when the 9mmP was born, the world was a vastly different place. With that in mind, this little cartridge is, indeed, a wonder. That it would survive and even flourish during its eighth and ninth decades is strong testimony to its validity. If anything, the country which first adopted it as a military cartridge was largely responsible for its jerky, if not rather retarded, proliferation around the world. Being the pistol cartridge of a country which lost the two biggest wars in the world this century can tend to put a damper on popularity. But when something works, it will not be denied. So it is with the 9mmP.

Ostensibly, there is nothing mysterious about the 9mmP. Fully loaded, it is only slightly more than an inch long. The case, at .754-inch in length, features a neck diameter of .380-inch. The rimless case starts out at .394-inch at the "rimless" rim, and is .391-inch in diameter at the rear of the case body itself — tapering ever so slightly to the .380-inch width at the mouth.

That means it is a rather simple, straight-forward design. In traditional handgun terms, the 9mmP is a relatively high-intensity cartridge which throws out service weight bullets at slightly more than the speed of sound. That's right. It's a supersonic round which was a fact of life before powered airplanes were invented.

Actually, through the years, there have been a number of 9mm pistol cartridges, some only civilian in nature, but others having had some sort of military career. Most notable among them is the .380 Auto, a cartridge designed by John M. Browning in 1912 (aka 9mm Browning Short). In 1903,

Above, the Model 1896 Broomhandle Mauser 9mm. This firearm was among the first military 9mm pistols to be used during wartime.

Right, this is a Husqvarna Model 1940 Lahti 9mm. It's another example of a pistol used during WW II.

Browning introduced the 9mm Browning Long, hence, the motivation to call the .380 Auto the "short." And, there were others: the 9mm Glisenti, 9mm Steyr and 9mm Mauser. Among these others, the .380 Auto is the only one besides the 9mmP to be manufactured widely and used significantly as the 20th Century comes to a close.

There are many theories as to why the 9mmP made it big. And, since there is no absolute authority on the matter, one person's guess is as good as another's. Perhaps it is simply because it works and works well. But what makes it work?

Everything in the gun world involves levels of acceptability. For example, few people ever go varmint hunting with an elephant rifle. It would work, but the weight of the firearm, the recoil, noise and expense preclude such usage. It is simply not

considered acceptable. By the same token, elephants are not hunted with .22 caliber rifles, but varmints are.

Between the extremes are bore diameters which seem to be best suited for most people. For example, in rifles, the .30 caliber is accepted generally as the largest bore size that most shooters can handle well. For shotguns, the 12 gauge rules supreme because it seems to the largest bore diameter which can be handled well by the majority of shooters. And during the last part of the last century and the first nine-tenths of this one, handguns with bore diameters in the mid-.30s have been more or less universal. In the United States, it was a revolver round called the .38 Special (.357-inch diameter). In most of the rest of the world, it was the 9mm (.355-inch diameter).

More than any other kind of firearm, a handgun needs a

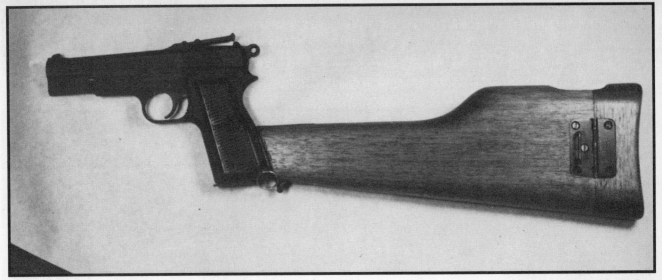

Above is a P-35 (Browning Hi-Power) made in Belgium for issue to German troops during WW II. The wooden stock also serves as a holster.

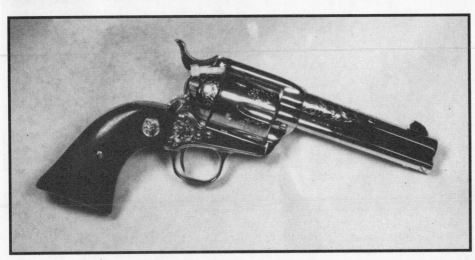

Left, the 9mm has been chambered in nearly every type of handgun. This is a Colt Single Action Army.

series of interdependent qualities to be universally "usable" by people who come in many sizes, shapes and strength levels. Handguns chambered for cartridges in the mid-.30-caliber range can be built in convenient sizes and weights. And, the resultant recoil of all but the "magnums" is also tolerable in this size cartridge. Hence, the 9mmP had the important basic specifications going for it right from the start.

The overall length of the 9mmP is ideal. Semi-auto and full-auto firearms to shoot it can be designed easily, and they can be extremely efficient in the process. Speaking of efficiency, the 9mmP makes total use of the relatively small amount of powder it takes to fuel it. Even from a military perspective, the 9mmP is a winner. Logistics are aided by ammunition which takes up relatively little space. The 9mmP is a winner on that front, as well.

So, the 9mmP fills the needs for which it was designed. However, as much as it is a total winner in and of itself, it has inherited a darker image over the years when compared to other handgun cartridges which were designed to do things other than those for which the 9mmP was intended. Also, the 9mmP has found itself thrust into the midst of controversies which are totally foreign to its role.

For example, it has been in vogue traditionally to pit the 9mmP against the .45 ACP. In such contexts, the 9mmP definitionally loses on all but two fronts: magazine capacity and supply logistics. Part of that comparison seems to find its way into the "knock down" discussion. Again, the 9mmP will not knock down a full-grown, adult human being. Neither will the .45 ACP. But because the .45 ACP's paper ballistic characteristics come closer to accomplishing that mythical quality, the 9mmP becomes the cartridge many shooters love to hate.

More recently, the 9mmP has been compared to the .40-caliber new kids on the block: the .40 S&W and its predecessor, the 10mm Auto. Given the availability of the new generation of bullets for handguns, the actual differences in tactical performance are more imagined than real.

And so it goes. The 9mmP is a total winner, or a total loser, depending more on the mind set of the person considering the question. That is fine. Because wherever the 9mmP fits into a particular discussion or argument, there are basic, bold face facts of life.

There have been more 9mmP firearms and ammunition made and used in the world than any other kind of centerfire handgun or load. And, the popularity continues to grow, despite all-out challenges by other cartridges. The final answer is that if the 9mmP is the most popular form the world has known ever, then it is a definitional winner. This book takes a close look at many of the the guns and loads which have helped make and keep the 9mmP on top.

HISTORY CONTINUES WITH DON MITCHELL'S P-08 STAINLESS UPDATE!

Author fires Mitchell Arms P-08 Luger. The stainless steel remake is faithful to the original German military pistol.

THE LUGER P-08 pistol was the launching pad which made the 9mmP cartridge a factor on the world scene during the early days of the 20th Century. Now, as that same century draws to a close, there is an American rebirth of both the handgun and the ethic which for millions of shooters always has defined the 9mmP. It is called the Mitchell Arms American Eagle version of the legendary Pistol Parabellum P-08 (Luger).

To a degree, the Mitchell Arms Luger might be considered

The Mitchell P-08 has the natural pointing dynamics inherent in all Luger pistols.

as nothing more than a stainless steel clone of the original. However, that simplistic view would be doing a disservice to what is emerging as one of the planet's great 9mmP handguns. It is the author's opinion that Mitchell's incarnation of the legendary design goes far beyond being faithful to the original design. It simply is a better pistol.

More about the pistol and its performance later. First, it is important to put everything into a proper historical perspective. In a way, Mitchell's P-08 brings it all home — it takes the entire ethic full-circle and completes the theme.

For example, the P-08 is an evolutionary example of what happened when a basic design by Hugo Borchardt was improved upon by Georg Luger. Borchardt, who worked for Winchester during the late 1800s, had designed a pistol bearing his name which was one of the very first of the autoloading pistols of the world.

A full century later, Don Mitchell returned the concept to the United States, and began making and marketing his version of the P-08 in stainless steel.

How faithful to the original P-08 design is the Mitchell?

Field-stripped, the Mitchell P-08 shows the simplicity of the basic Luger design.

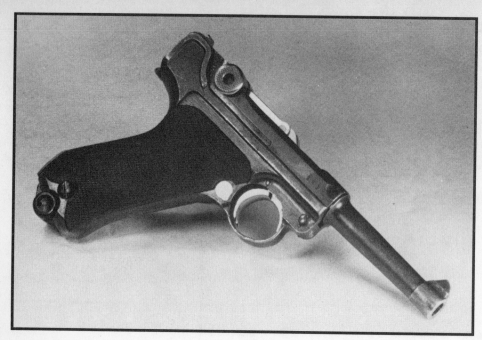

This original 1917 Luger has several stainless steel parts from the new Mitchell.

The stainless steel sideplate and trigger on this Luger are from a Mitchell pistol.

Close enough that the stainless steel parts for the Mitchell P-08 can be fitted into an original German military handgun. In fact, Mitchell did exactly that with one of his own well-worn originals. It was a pistol made in 1917, and Mitchell replaced the toggle linkage, trigger and trigger side plate with some of his new stainless steel parts. The pistol shoots. However, it might be noted that the original not only fails to shoot as accurately as the new Mitchell offering, but it also will not feed as wide a variety of ammo as reliably as the new gun. It is important to note that the reason the original hybrid will not feed ammo as well has nothing to do with the new parts. It has to do with the unaltered feed ramp which simply did not allow the use of many different kinds of loads.

The new Mitchell Lugers are dimensionally very close to the originals (identical, except for the use of American types of measurements like threads on screws and bolts and that sort of thing). This means that the originals and the new Mitchells feel the same in the hand, and offer the same natural pointing characteristics which made Lugers so popular through the years.

Like the originals, the new Mitchells are magazine-fed, recoil-operated, closed-bolt, striker-fired, semi-auto pistols. The safety system is the same as on the originals — with the safety lever located on the left rear side of the frame. When pushed to the rear, the lever puts the pistol on "safe." When forward, it is in the "fire" mode. Incidentally, there is a slight difference between the original and the new Mitchell which is apparent when the pistol is put into the safe mode. On the original, the word "GESICHERT" appears on the frame, while no lettering appears on the Mitchell.

Wooden parts are the same on originals and the new Mitchells. Wood grips are fully checkered, and there are wooden bases on both types of magazines.

A couple of other minor differences noted between the new Mitchell and the 1917 hybrid appeared on the rear of the pistol. The lanyard ring featured on the original is not present on the

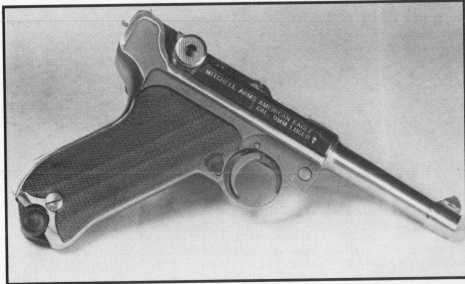

Above, a Mitchell stainless toggle linkage has been installed on this 1917 Luger. Left and below, this is the Mitchell Arms American Eagle Model. Each of the Mitchell firearms is stamped with the year it was made.

Mitchell, and the grip strap at the bottom of the frame, although having the same contour, is not cut to accept a shoulder stock, as is the original. Certainly, there were more differences among the many variants of the originals than these slight differences between these two pistols represent.

Both examples tested for this chapter were of the four-inch barrel "army" persuasion. Of the many original variations, four-inch versions were used by the army, six-inch-barrel models were navy propositions, and then there was the artillery model with its eight-inch barrel. The magazines on the originals and the new Mitchells hold seven rounds, and the magazines are interchangeable.

Original Lugers have carried with them the stigma of being finicky when it comes to the ammo they will digest well. In fact, many of the function problems encountered when shooting the originals occurs when the loadings are milder than the original military spec loads which, compared to some American fodder, are considered quite hot.

For the Mitchell P-08, contemporary commercial loads are suggested. The maker states: "You must use factory new

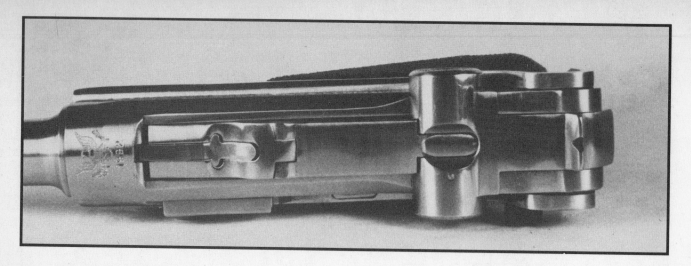

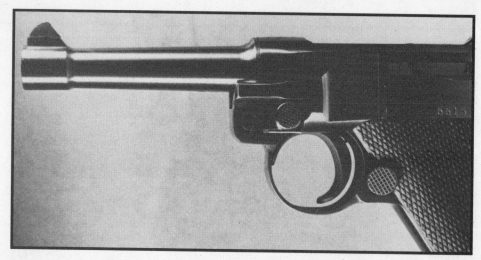

Above and right, the new Lugers from Mitchell Arms have a smooth, fine finish.

ammunition only; no reloads. Your gun is designed to function best with American-manufactured 124-grain full metal jacket ammunition. This ammunition is also called military ball, ball, or hardball. Any of the above ammunitions will result in the most trouble-free operation."

The admonishment against the use of reloaded ammo is standard in the industry during the 1990s. Most manufacturers advise against the use of reloads for a number of reasons, including legal considerations which might arise if improper handloads are used and cause some sort of problem. But the concern goes further. Improper handloads also can cause function problems, which can tend to make the firearm look like it is not as good a shooter as it would be with new factory ammo.

For the workout here, the author fed the Mitchell P-08 a diet of diverse loadings, including the suggested 124-grain FMJ variety. There were no function problems with any full-house factory loads. However, it might be noted that there also were no problems with any of the 115-grain factory ammo used, nor with any of the 147-grain factory loadings fired. In fact, Winchester's sub-sonic 147-grain hollow-points produced the best and most consistent groups through the Mitchell P-08.

Testing also included the use of forbidden handloads. Again, no function problems, and groups were equal to those produced by factory ammo. Although the Mitchell cycled some of the lighter handloads that originals will not digest, the author cut back a half-grain from one of the basic lead bulleted reloads, and that was just enough to cause one intentional malfunction. What all of this seemed to indicate was that the Mitchell will handle any full-power loading with aplomb. And, it will handle a wider variety of loadings and bullet configurations than will its predecessors. However, as is typical of the Luger action design, light loads can cause cycling malfunctions.

Sights on the Mitchell P-08 are identical to those on the originals. The front sight is an inverted V type which is drift adjustable for windage, and the rear sight is a fixed V-notch built into the rear toggle link. These are combat sights, and not meant for accurate target work.

Accuracy achieved from the bench with the Mitchell was typical of any Luger. The sights are the most limiting factors, and they simply do not lend themselves to precision bullet placement. Groups at 25 yards with all ammunition were similar in size and configuration. They ranged from three inches with the Winchester 147-grain hollow-points to four inches with the "worst" of the other loadings. That is consistent. Groups typically were concentric, and for the author the gun shot a couple of inches high and about an inch to the right at 25 yards. That's pretty good for an "out of the box" proposition with a wide variety of loads.

All Mitchell Arms Lugers are built here in the U.S.A.

One factor rang out loud and clear, however. When all of the shooting was done, every bullet hole was within a six-inch circle at 25 yards! What that means is that every single bullet fired in a lengthy range session would have hit the same six-inch target every time. For a combat setup, that is incredible. In all, nearly 500 rounds were fired.

Shooting the new Mitchell P-08 even feels just like doing it with one of the originals. The author never has been a serious collector of Luger pistols. However, he has been a frequent shooter of them, having run tens of thousands of rounds through Lugers over the years. This was mostly in the late 1950s and very early 1960s when such handguns routinely were thrown-in with multi-gun deals to make the overall price right. At that time, the author traded, bought and sold Lugers at about every gun show. Typical prices for P-08s in good working order or better at that time were $25 for the army model and $35 for the artillery model. A wooden holster/shoulder stock for the artillery model at that time commanded an added $15, and some of the navy models went for as much as $50. At such prices, and with such a large supply of pistols on the market which had been brought back by World War II GIs, it was common to have a Luger involved in a gun deal for some other totally unrelated type of firearm, like a Winchester Model 12 shotgun or Model 1873 rifle.

The trigger pull on the Mitchell P-08 felt somewhat better than the average military-issue originals. It was a smooth, rather spongy pull. The sponginess is due to the mechanism, and was also typical of the originals. However, the letoff of the trigger on the Mitchell is somewhat cleaner than on most of the originals the author has fired over the years.

There is a classic Luger "feel" when a cartridge is fired through a P-08. It is quite sharp and sends the muzzle skyward violently. This characteristic precludes really fast firing of the model. This phenomenon occurs, because of the design which puts most of the bulk and weight of the pistol squarely into the palm and extending over the top of the hand. The barrel is relatively short and light.

Ejection is the same on the Mitchell as on the originals. This means the empties are sent skyward with force sufficient to launch them quite high into the air. The extractor is also the same, which means that it also doubles as a visual and tactile loaded chamber indicator. That's handy. What it means is that

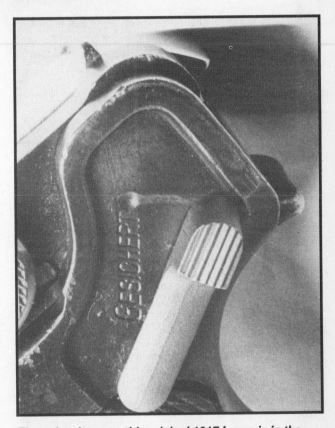

The safety lever on this original 1917 Luger is in the safe position, showing the German word "Gesichert."

when there is a cartridge in the chamber, the extractor sits higher through the top of the bolt, and it can be spotted with the eye or felt with the finger.

Other functioning and firing procedures and techniques also are the same on new or old P-08s. The action is locked open after the last shot has been fired. To close the action, it is necessary either to insert a loaded magazine and then pull the toggle action back enough to unlock the bolt stop, or simply remove the empty magazine, pull back on the toggle system and lower it forward on an empty chamber. There is no

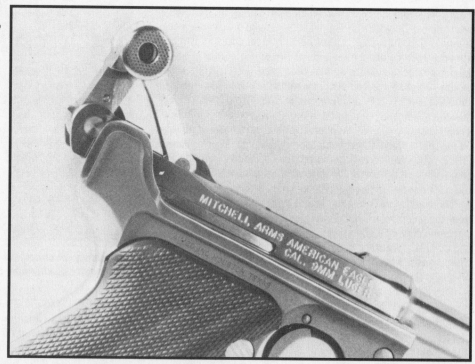

Above, the action of this Mitchell Luger is closed. At right, the action is open, showing the toggle linkage at its most rearward position.

separate slide release button or lever.

Although the Mitchell owner's manual does not suggest field stripping for routine cleaning and maintenance, the Mitchell P-08 disassembles and reassembles the same way as do any of the originals.

After assuring that the pistol is not loaded, allow the action to close on an empty chamber. This assumes the magazine has been removed. While pushing the barrel/slide assembly rearward a fraction of an inch, rotate the take down lever on the left front of the frame clockwise 90 degrees. The trigger side plate, located on the left side of the frame just above the trigger, can then be removed. This allows the slide, complete with toggle

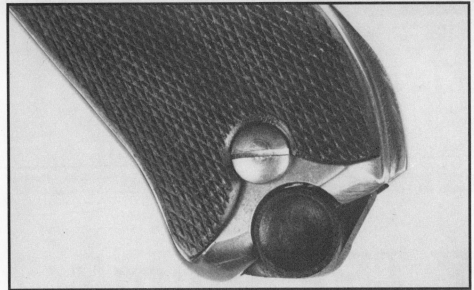

The new Mitchell Lugers even have checkered walnut grips and walnut magazine base just like the German originals.

linkage, to move forward and off the frame. By removing the through-bolt at the rear of the barrel/slide group, the toggle linkage can be removed. Further disassembly is possible and obvious, but necessary only when there is a need to replace a damaged or broken part. There is no need to disassemble the pistol further for any sort of normal maintenance or cleaning. Reassembly is the reverse process, and there are no surprises in doing so. It is a simple, straight-forward design.

The Mitchell stainless steel P-08 is called the "American Eagle" version, because there is an American Eagle atop the front of the action. This is similar to some of the original "American Eagle" Luger variants. Below the eagle, the date of manufacture is shown. On the test pistol, it was 1992. It was common for original P-08 pistols to have the date of manufacture indicated in the same place. For example, on the original hybrid used, the date is 1917, indicating World War I vintage.

All of the fit and finish on the Mitchell P-08 was superb. Couple that with the lasting qualities of stainless steel, and this is a very appealing, serious handgun that literally can last several lifetimes.

It may be rare for a clone to surpass its predecessors, but the author feels that the Mitchell P-08 is a much better all-around handgun than were its ancestors. So, as a complete handgun, this is a real shooter that doesn't have to sit in a vault as part of a static collection. But there is more.

As this writing was being completed, there were repeated rumors that a sizeable supply of original Lugers would be imported to the United States from the former Soviet Union where they had been warehoused when they were liberated at the end of World War II. Condition of these pistols was fabled to range from like new to clunky.

Should such a supply of surplus Lugers become a reality on the domestic market, Mitchell Arms may find itself extremely busy just manufacturing replacement parts for the many well-used pistols included in the deals. That would represent a benefit that shooters of the '20s and '30s following World War I, and the shooters of the '50s and '60s following World War II did not have — a reliable supply of high-quality new replacement parts to keep the old war veteran firearms in operation. During the previous periods, shooters were pretty well stuck with cannibalizing other Lugers to get the parts to

Just behind the date on this new Mitchell is the Luger's extractor. It also serves as a loaded chamber indicator.

keep the others operating.

Regardless what happens on the surplus front, one factor is certain: Mitchell Arms has come up with a total winner in its American Eagle version of the legendary P-08 pistol. Yes, the entire ethic has now come full-circle, and shooters are the beneficiaries in the process.

Both the P-08 and the 9mmP cartridge are living proof of the validity of each individually, as well as of both as a combination. It is nice when things work out so cleanly.

CHAPTER
Two

WHY THE 9mm?

This Cartridge Holds A Specific Position In The Overall Picture

The 9mmP is the world's most common centerfire handgun cartridge. Even if manufacture of the handguns and ammo stopped, there would be plenty around for a long time. Here, a Browning Hi-Power is literally awash in a sea of 9mmP.

Unlike peas in a pod, the 9mmP (left) is different from the 9x21mm (center) and .38 Super. The added length of the 9x21mm and the .38 Super cases allow them to be loaded safely to major power for target work.

Two 9mmP pretenders are the 9x21mm (left) and the .41 Action Express (center). With the same head size, they function well through the same action designs.

AT NO time during its 90-year career has the 9mm Parabellum faced such a serious and potentially life-threatening series of attacks as it sees right now. Yet, there is no reason to believe the venerable old cartridge can't — and won't — continue to thrive on the world scene.

The 10mm/.40-caliber assault upon the 9mm's status has been relentless and is growing. Favor of the fatter cartridges by certain major law enforcement agencies, of course, has played the major role in this saga. However, the relative fatness of another cartridge never has put a crimp in the 9mm's style. If the bumblebee-shaped .45 ACP couldn't do it, why is there any reason to believe the in-between .40 will fare any better?

After all, a couple of decades ago there was a major movement, both within the shooting sports industry as well as law enforcement circles, touting the then in-vogue .41 Remington magnum cartridge. Proponents pointed out that the powerful .41 magnum was much bigger and better than the traditional .38 Special, yet not so user-brutal as the thundering .44 Remington magnum cartridge. It was seen as the ultimate compromise when it came to size and power. Like most compromises, it fizzled dramatically. In-between in the gun world just never seems to cut it. Now, the 10mm/.40-caliber auto blitz is on, again challenging the established status quo.

On the surface, there are actually a number of reasons for one to suspect the various .40s might be formidable foes for the 9mm, but reality is more than skin deep, and surface fears need not go any further. The secret to understanding the entire phenomenon of cartridge acceptability and success is to recognize that there is room for a lot of different things in gundom, and that the .40s have their place, as well.

Without being deliberately disrespectful, it would be safe to say that if cartridge design and development were left to law enforcement gurus alone, the world probably would still be stuck with the .38 Special and the .380 ACP as defensive/

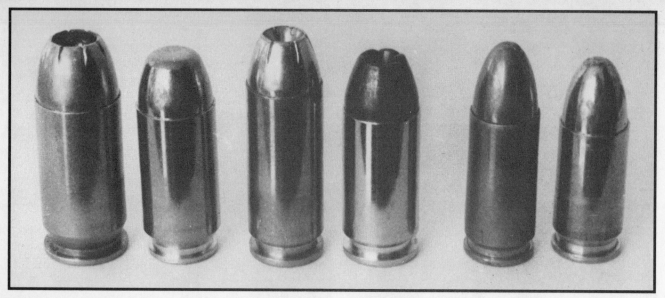

Many cartridges would like to steal the 9mmP's thunder. There are agruments for and against each round. The 9mmP (right) stands quietly. The others are (from left) the .45 ACP, .41 Action Express, 10mm Auto, .40 S&W and 9x21mm.

offensive handgun options. The sun in gundom neither rises nor sets on those who wear badges for a living, but law enforcement can — and, at times, does — have meaningful input. That is what the industry is witnessing to some degree now with respect to the 10mm Auto and the .40 S&W cartridges.

In the sometimes confusing arena of law enforcement agency endorsements of cartridges, it probably would be safe to suggest now that had the .40 S&W cartridge come along first, the 10mm Auto probably would not be a factory-loaded option.

To comprehend the situation fully, one must go back to the beginning. In that beginning, there was the .45 ACP and the 9mmP, and there were those who insisted the two cartridges should be cast into roles of Cain and Abel, or David and Goliath. In short, depending upon who was doing the arguing, one was good and the other was bad. The discussions never did include an allowance that both might have legitimate uses.

The big .45 ACP was characterized as the stopper by its proponents who argued — sometimes vehemently — that the 9mmP was a puny pretender to the throne of legitimacy. Conversely, proponents of the 9mmP argued that the round's comparatively higher velocity, coupled with the ability to produce handguns with much higher capacity magazines, more than outweighed any edge the .45 might have on the killing front.

Such arguments were definitionally moot, because each side had reached its conclusion before any debate was allowed

The Bren 10 launched a mania for 10mm/.40 caliber handguns in the late 1980s, early '90s. Oddly, by the time the ammunition was available, the gun was not.

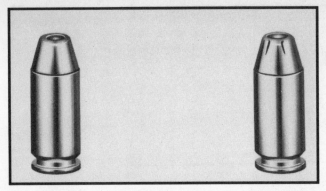

The .40 S&W is a challenger to the throne of the 9mmP. Many law enforcement agencies have embraced the .40.

Remington's .40 S&W, 180-grain carries a jacketed hollow point bullet that's rated at 936 fps at 50 yards.

to begin. Hence, there never could have been an effective argument, regardless of what the actual facts might suggest.

Interestingly, though, the traditional arguments involving the .45 ACP versus 9mmP were at least based on the assumption that full-size firearms were to be used for comparison. By full-size, one means the full military configuration and heft.

Given the relatively minor role handguns actually have played in the activities of the militaries of the world during the lifetimes of active shooters today, it prompts one to wonder why there could be such a debate launched in the first place. But, there is a romance surrounding the ethic of handguns, making them the objects of intense love/hate relationships, both within and outside the shooting industry.

For militaries, a lot of things are relatively easy to decide. One of them is the size of the handgun. The reasons are relatively simple. Militaries can be — and usually are — arbitrary in their approach to anything. Beyond that, militaries have the luxury of adopting equipment based on its performance and not necessarily upon its carrying convenience. Hence, the official military sidearms, regardless of chambering, have tended to be on the full-bodied side.

But when more and more of the law enforcement agencies in the United States decided they should switch from revolvers to autos, gun companies found pay dirt and were going to waste no time going for the mother lode.

All of a sudden, previously academic concerns became quite real. Whether a particular design would fit a wide range of hand sizes, for example, was of paramount concern. Magazine capacity was another big item. With a .45 ACP, there was no possibility of having it both ways. With the 9mmP, it was not only possible, but relatively easy.

However, the largely misunderstood concept of "knockdown" power reared its ugly head. What everyone seemed to want was a cartridge which would deliver the potent punch of the .45, yet offer the size flexibility in handgun design and the high magazine capacity afforded by the 9mmP. The .40 caliber size seemed to offer the best of both worlds, and that concept remains the chief selling point in favor of the .40s today.

Everyone did not just leap headlong into the .40 caliber arena, however. Like most things in gundom, the matter was approached slowly and methodically. In fact, the first seemingly serious thrust came not from the scaled-down school of thought in handgun design, nor from the rocket scientists-turned law enforcement handgun experts. Instead, it came from the then wide-open paramilitary/survivalist crowd which demanded a handgun cartridge with more punch farther downrange than the .45 ACP could ever offer, coupled with the flat trajectory at that distance which had always been enjoyed by the 9mmP.

What started out as high hopes for a Southern California company of the Eighties turned out to be gundom's version of the chicken-and-the-egg proposition.

Although officially "manufactured" from 1983 to 1986 by Dornaus & Dixon Enterprises in Huntington Beach, California, the Bren Ten handgun really never got off the ground. Pick just about any alleged corporate ailment normally afflicting new and innovative firms, and it was alleged at some time or other that it was the reason for the virtual non-existence of the Bren — a well made, robustly designed autoloading handgun.

At first, there were prototypes of the Bren on special display at the SHOT (Shooting, Hunting, Outdoor Trades) Show. Excitement soared, but alas, no commercially made ammo was available. Eventually, Norma in Sweden made the 10mm Auto ammunition, but by then the Bren guns no longer were being made.

Colt capitalized on the situation, and merely reconfigured the trusty old 1911 design to handle the 10mm ammo. Presto, the Delta Elite was born. A quick move at that juncture ensured there would be guns to shoot all the ammo that suddenly was available for guns which didn't for the most part exist, until the Delta Elite came along.

But, frankly, not much ground had been gained overall, because the gun was exactly the same size as the traditional .45 auto, and included the relatively low capacity necessitated by the in-line cartridge stacking of the magazine.

The downrange performance of the 10mm Auto cartridge, however, did capture the imaginations of many shooters, including some of the larger law enforcement agencies. With such interest, there soon were to be other companies hopping onto the 10mm bandwagon. Some agencies even adopted the cartridge, but then a strange thing happened. Scholars among

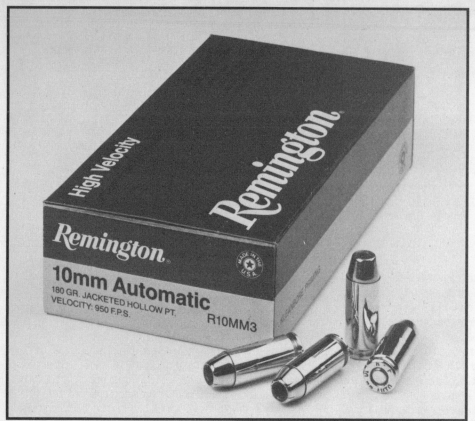

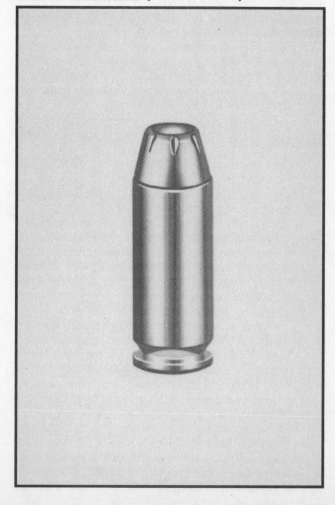

Left and below, this 10mm automatic cartridge from Remington has a 180-grain jacketed hollow point bullet.

armorers saw the full-house 10mm cartridge as too much of a hot-rod. What needed to be done, they opined, was to slow it down, make it subsonic and all would be right with the world.

Was it not the blistering downrange ballistic performance which justified this cartridge's existence in the first place? Never mind trivialities. These gurus demanded less muzzle blast/flash and all that sort of thing. Hence, there came to be the sheep-in-wolf's-clothing sub-cartridge — a 10mm Auto loaded to sub-sonic velocities. Never mind that the .45 ACP always had been a subsonic proposition which had been available all along in handguns of the same general size and weight, with almost the same magazine capacity.

The marriage may have been made with 10mm, but it wasn't quite consummated yet. During this same general era, there was another upstart cartridge which was having problems on the acceptability chart. It was called the .41 Action Express which began life on the competition front, with some real Yankee ingenuity involved.

The .41 AE was born with the kiss of death. It had a rebated rim. That means the rim diameter is less than the case body diameter. Rebated rims were nothing new. They were simply not universally appealing. Witness the underwhelming "successes" of cartridges like the .284 Winchester, the .425 Westley Richards, the .500 Jeffery or the 11.2x72mm Schuler.

But the .41 AE phenomenon is a necessary element in understanding the four-oh mania. Its rebated rim is the same size as that of the 9mm. What this meant for the custom target gun trade was that available 9mm handguns could be retrofitted to shoot .41-caliber bullets, thus raising the power potential out of the same general length package. Although this idea may have had some sort of merit, it was blown out of the water

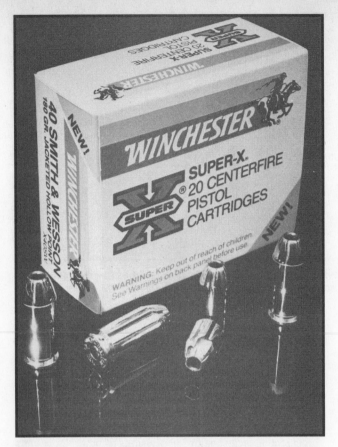

When the .40 S&W captured a following with shooters, Winchester introduced their version of the cartridge.

THE 9MMP:

Factory loadings for the 9mmP focus primarily upon three bullet weights at more-or-less "accepted" velocities. There is the 115-grain loading at 1160 feet per second and 345 foot-pounds of energy at the muzzle. Also, there is the 124-grain loading at 1120 fps/345 foot-pounds, and the 147-grain loading at 975 fps/310 foot-pounds.

The .40 S&W

Two bullet weights dominate the .40 S&W scene. One is the 155-grain loading at 1140 fps/445 foot-pounds and the other is the 180-grain loading at 985 fps/390 foot-pounds.

The 10mm Auto

Three bullet weights have made the biggest news on the factory-loading front. They are the 155-grain loading at 1325 fps/605 foot-pounds, the 180-grain loading at 1030 fps/425 foot-pounds and the 200-grain loading at 990 fps/435 foot-pounds.

The .41 AE

A typical factory loading for the .41 AE is a 180-grain bullet at 1000 fps/400 foot-pounds of energy.

The .45 ACP

Although the .45 ACP has been factory-loaded and handloaded with a truly wide range of bullet weights, the 230-grain loading is the classic which set the pace. It generally is loaded to 850 fps/369 foot-pounds. Other common loadings include the 185-grain bullet at 950 fps/370 foot-pounds and the 200-grain bullet at 940 fps/392 foot-pounds.

What does all of this really mean? The answer to that question depends totally upon who is talking. However, the actual energy churned-up by all of those loadings (with the exception of the 155-grain 10mm Auto loading) falls within a 100-foot-pound window; there is only a 100-foot-pound spread in actual energy. That's not much.

It is easy to envision the difference among them all. Simply take a 100-pound bag of flour and drop it from one foot above the floor, take a 50-pound bag of potatoes and drop it from two feet up or take a 25-pound bag of shotgun shot and drop it from four feet above the floor. That impact is the total difference represented in the common loadings for all of these various cartridges — and that's not impressive. So much for the "knock-down" syndrome.

This should come as no great surprise because of the parameters within which such handguns and their ammo must fall. For example, they dare not create so much recoil as to jump out of a normal person's hand when shot, and they dare not create so much noise as to instantly deafen the user when no ear protection is worn. Hence, if the gun and ammo have to be limited to "manageable" levels, then so, too, does down-range performance.

That puts the argument right back to square one. Within those performance levels, which of the trade-offs are most important? Is it better to have more magazine capacity at the expense of bullet diameter? After all, when conventional bullets are discussed, bullet diameter in handgun loads over-

when two major manufacturers decided to come out with their own version of the ultimate compromise.

As all of this was going on, the light bulb turned on in the heads of some folks at both Smith & Wesson and Winchester (Olin) ammunition. If updated specifications for law enforcement applications called for loading-down the 10mm Auto, why have the cartridge case so long? When downloaded, there was air space in the case which accomplished nothing.

Enter the .40 S&W cartridge. For practical purposes, it is nothing more or less than a 10mm Auto short. But there are factors here which could almost be considered clandestine. The length of the .40 S&W cartridge put it right back into the 9mmP ballpark with regard to gun design factors like slide travel, feeding and all the related timing considerations implied there. These were all proven quantities.

Smith & Wesson and Winchester had come up with the ultimate compromise for the traditional warring parties. Depending upon how one wanted to view the situation, they had developed a fat 9mmP or a skinny .45 ACP — a wonder cartridge which was supposed to offer the best of all worlds. It had more punch than the maligned 9mmP, yet could be offered in handguns with greater magazine capacity than the fat .45.

In fact, for perceived American law enforcement needs, the .40 S&W very well may have hit that perfectly harmonious chord. A close look at the ballistic performances of the various cartridges in question reveals the facts.

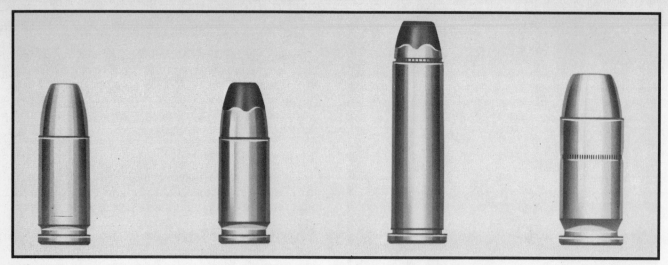

For comparison (from left), here are Remington's ammo in 9mm Luger +P, 115-grain JHP; the 9mm Luger, 140-grain SJHP (practice round), the .357 Magnum, 125-grain SJHP (medium velocity) and .45 automatic +P, 185-grain JHP.

rides most other concerns when it comes to effectiveness on the target when that target is live tissue. Certainly, high tech bullet designs expand the performance possibilities for any and all of the cartridge sizes, but in the final analysis, judgments are made more on subjective criteria than objective data.

In as little as a tenth of the time the 9mmP has been around, the .41 AE has come and, essentially, gone. The 10mm Auto, in half that amount of time, has gone from a rising star to a rather mediocre seller. The only meaningful challenge to the 9mmP from the 10mm/.40-caliber pretenders at this time is the .40 S&W.

For all of the fanfare accompanying the .40 S&W cartridge and handguns to shoot it, however, general public acceptance during these early years of its existence gives one cause to take pause and assess the situation more closely.

Regardless the merits of the .40 S&W or its parent, the 10mm Auto — and they have totally measurable merits — there are bedrock facts of life extant in the real world with respect to their effects on the 9mmP.

Although they may fill niches left open in the cartridge line-up at the time of their introductions, neither of the 10mm/.40-caliber rounds is about to replace the 9mmP. For that answer, simply view the history of the 9mmP.

The 9mmP grew up on the tough side of town, so to speak, having had its vocal detractors almost since birth. Yet, it has thrived as no other handgun cartridge on the face of the earth! Why? The answer is so simple and obvious as to be obscured.

The 9mmP is large enough to have a sufficient quantity of the right stuff to get most jobs done, yet it is small enough to fit into designs that feel good to hands around the globe. At the same time, it is more user-friendly to any logistics application. Put another way, it is a snappy cartridge that can be shot by almost anyone, and anyone can physically carry a lot of cartridges.

At this point in its career, the 9mmP has mountains of inertia going for it. With the mega-millions of firearms chambered for it, and the mega-billions of rounds of ammo spread all around the planet for it, the 9mmP would continue to be a popular cartridge even if tomorrow all manufacture of 9mmP firearms and ammo ceased!

As for either of the .40 caliber cartridges replacing the 9mmP, even on the American law enforcement front, don't hold your breath. There are a number of facts of life at play here, as well. One such factor is the ever-increasing terminal performance of some of the new bullet designs which literally make the 9mmP an enhanced cartridge.

But there is another undeniable factor, as well. Call it the "bottom line" or whatever; it is dollars and cents. Law enforcement agencies, being subdivisions of umbrella government agencies, are saddled with incredible budget restraints.

Since much of the law enforcement transition from revolver to auto happened when the 9mmP was the overwhelmingly favored choice over the then-only-viable-option .45 ACP, and before either of the .40s came along or were established, many of these agencies now use the 9mmP as their official cartridge.

To re-equip the troops with something else would be a most costly move, one that many agencies and/or politicians simply could not or would not allow. And they would have a convenient argument for those who would question how they could continue using an "inferior" cartridge like the 9mmP.

No single cartridge is the best bet for everything in every situation. Even the .45 ACP lacks the "knock-down" power of the 12-gauge shotgun, and the 9mmP itself lacks the flat trajectory and downrange punch of the 7.62mm NATO round. Obviously, then, compromises have to be made somewhere. It then becomes a question only of degree.

Oddly, there is a left-handed factor which would potentially lessen some of the effective internal arguments in favor of replacing an agency's 9mmP handguns with ones to handle either of the .40s. One of the major arguments against revolvers and in favor of autos when departments were eager to change was that the criminals possessed significantly more firepower, because they were using the autos.

At last check, criminals — lumped under the banner of murderers, drug dealers, rapists and robbers — were using none of the .40s in significant numbers. They still were "stuck" with the 9mmP combos.

For 9mmP detractors, however, there is light at the end of the tunnel, still. Over the past few years, the .45 ACP has been experiencing a largely unexplained re-birth or, at least, an

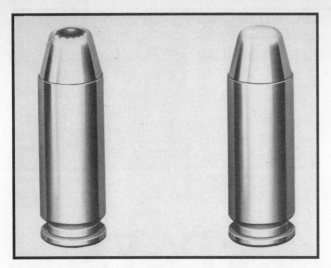

These are two of Remington's 10mm automatics: the 170-grain hollow point (left) and 200-grain metal case.

awakening in sales and use among the ranks of citizen shooters. What does this mean?

Maybe it's time to rekindle the old .45 versus 9mm debate. And, as was mentioned earlier in this chapter, that debate is decided in the minds of those participating even before data is inserted. And so it goes. There are newcomers, but the old argument is still alive and well.

There are a couple of like-diameter pretenders to the 9mm throne, as well. However, they merit comparatively little attention in the big picture. One is the .38 Super, the other the 9x21mm. Both enjoy a degree of popularity among some of the target-shooting disciplines.

Sadly, the .38 Super has been around for decades and ignored emphatically through the years. It is a true performer, but for some reason just never captured the imaginations of many in the gun world.

The 9x21mm is quite a bit newer, having been developed in an effort to sidestep governmental regulations in Europe which addressed the need for civilians not to own guns and ammo which also are used by the military. Hence, all it took to bypass regulations and still have a cartridge which would work in standard 9mmP handguns (after a chamber job or new barrel) was to lengthen the case by two millimeters.

It didn't take long, however, for some of the target blasters in the United States to start checking-out this longer 9mm. A longer case meant a bit more powder capacity — and that meant more power.

Through the years, the 9mmP came close but just wasn't quite enough to make what has been termed major power for some kinds of matches. It could be loaded hot and make it, but pressures were high enough that it was essentially banned for such purposes.

That same phenomenon was responsible for today's limited interest in the .38 Super, because that cartridge could be heated up to perform better. This may have been handy, but the 9x21mm was even handier — and it could knock right on that power level door everyone was wanting.

No doubt the 9x21mm will be around for a while, but don't expect it to be a major factor much beyond specific target applications. In street terms, there isn't enough tactical difference to justify a change from the long established 9mmP.

Suffice it to say that well placed bullets from any of the cartridges in question are far better bets than badly placed bullets from all of the others combined. All are potentially lethal, and all are potentially inert. It really depends upon how any particular one is used in a specific situation. There simply is no one "right" answer to this age-old question, and so long as the 9mmP exists, it will be included in the discussion.

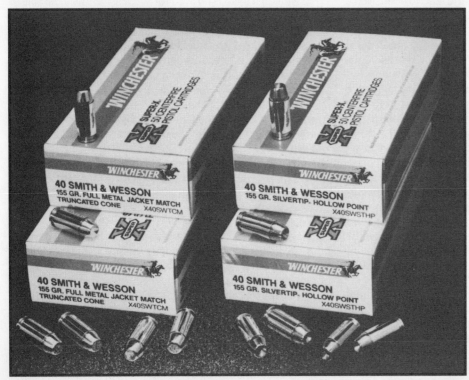

In late 1990, Winchester added two new loads to its .40 Smith & Wesson line. At left is the 155-grain, Full Metal Jacket Match and on the right is the 155-grain Silvertip Hollow Point.

CHAPTER Three

THE 9mm STAYS AT HOME

As A Home-Defense Gun, Its Faults Seem Outweighed By Advantages!

AMONG CIVILIAN shooters, the 9mmP plays its largest role as a home-defense/self-defense proposition. In fact, it is in this context that some of the most serious questions of life need to be answered if one is to have insight into whether something is right or not.

Elsewhere in this book, the 9mm's military and law enforcement roles are investigated. And, since the cartridge was invented as a military round, one would think it would be in this arena that it fits best. Perhaps, but don't bet on it.

Whenever discussions of equipment arise in the military or law enforcement context, there is a major factor at play which is totally missing on the civilian or home front. It is the matter of standard issue firearms, uniformity and all that sort of thing.

Frankly, individuals have infinitely more choices than do those in uniform, regardless what the uniform happens to be. Yet, traditionally it has been common for civilians to take their lead in firearms choices from both the military and police.

Although there is a left-handed sort of connection between uniformed and civilian firearms choices, informed procurers realize the ultimate choice should be based on the specific intended use or uses, not on whether some other person or agency has seen merit — or lack thereof — in a particular cartridge, firearm or combination of the two.

What this means is that when civilians decide what sort of firearm they should acquire and maintain for self-defense — which will be assumed here to include home-defense — the number and extent of options are seemingly endless.

For example, equipment intended to be used solely in a defensive role need not have any credible offensive character-istics. This means that a home-defense firearm need not be good for assaulting an enemy installation, nor for shooting through barricades.

Although there is no need for a defensive tool to be able to perform offensive activities, it doesn't mean that a firearm/cartridge combination which may have been designed for assaults is not also credible in a defensive mode.

For home-defense/self-defense, there is no particular need for concern about the size or weight of the rig, so long as it can be handled fluidly by the owner. And, there is no need for a rig to be particularly concealable, as might be of concern for undercover law enforcement officers. Hence, when opting for a home-defense firearm/cartridge combination, the field is literally wide open.

If such is the case, then why not opt for a 12-gauge shotgun and be done with the matter? Certainly, the 12-gauge is among the best tools for home-defense in a number of ways, but nothing is perfect and all-inclusive. So it is with the 12-gauge shotgun.

So what is really important, and what is not, when it comes to choosing a firearm/cartridge combination for home-defense? Further, where, if at all, can the 9mmP fit into this picture?

Finding that answer is not difficult for each individual, but it does require a logical investigation of facts and options. The most important factors and decisions have nothing to do with the firearm or cartridge at all. They have to do with the shooter himself or herself.

The concept of acquiring and maintaining a firearm for

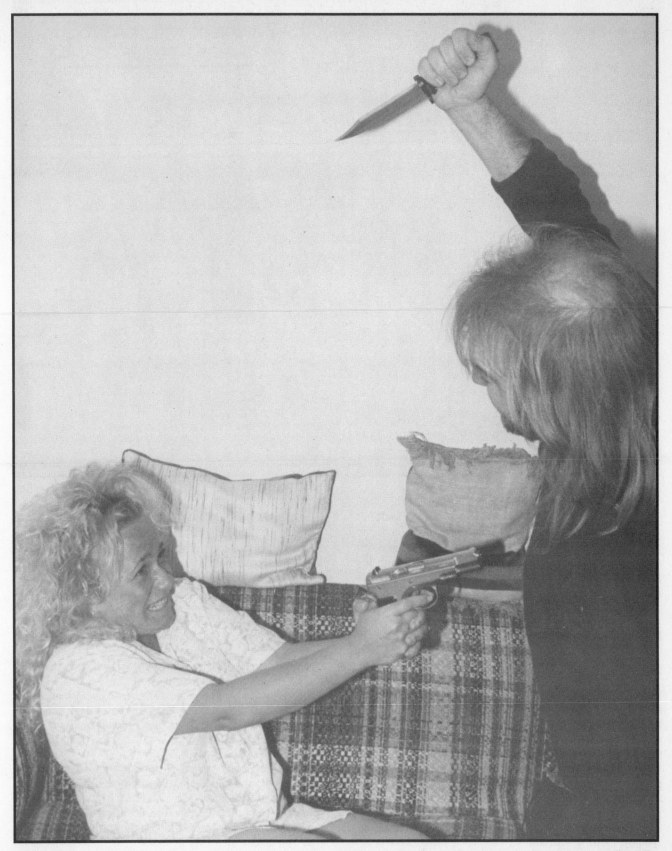

Violent criminal attacks in the home are usually up close and personal. In such situations, the handgun must fit well enough to point and shoot quickly. Fast follow-up shots from a 9mm semi-auto like this CZ-75 can make a difference.

If a person awakens to find an intruder in the room, a double-action 9mm auto can be put into service immediately.

home-defense is moot if the person in question lacks the ability or resolve to pull the trigger at the moment of truth. For people who are not prepared mentally to drop the hammer, it is better not to consider any firearm as a viable option. In fact, opting for a firearm at all can be deadly for them. They are the people who find themselves facing criminal attack, hesitating to take action and then having their firearms taken way by the criminals who often use the citizen's firearm against him or her.

So the first, and pivotal, question is as personal as anything in the world can be: *Can I look an attacker in the face and pull the trigger?* There is nothing macho involved here, and no one has to worry about looking or feeling like a wimp or superperson, depending upon the answer to the question. It can be asked solely in the mind of the individual, and answered without anyone else ever knowing what it is. If the answer to the basic question is yes, then a totally logical discussion about defensive firearms and cartridges can take place — and have meaning.

Ironically, most people are incapable of answering that specific question with authority. In fact, it most often is better to focus upon those who answer the question negatively. Yes, those who realize up front that they really couldn't pull the trigger are fortunate in a strange sort of way. They need not be

concerned about a defensive firearm, because they would not use one at the moment of truth, even if they had one in hand.

The majority of people fall somewhere in between. Most might have personal problems pulling the trigger in most situations, yet are probably capable of dropping the hammer under other conditions. It is because of this single phenomenon that the choice of a personal defense firearm is so unique to the individual in question.

Yet, it is important to point out that, when needed, any firearm is better than none at all, assuming it actually is used when needed. So, gunowners who maintain firearms for sporting, recreational or collection purposes have defensive potential within reach, even though they may or may not ever consider them as such — except and until they might be used in panic when danger arises.

Those who have a predisposition to pull the trigger can make an informed choice easily and rather quickly. Those who know they couldn't drop the hammer know they are better off pursuing some other form of defense/escape. It must be stressed strongly here that firearms never should be considered as implements of intimidation. They never should be considered as things with which one "scares" an intruder or attacker. When any firearm is brought into a confrontational situation, it is of the most serious nature possible. Briefly,

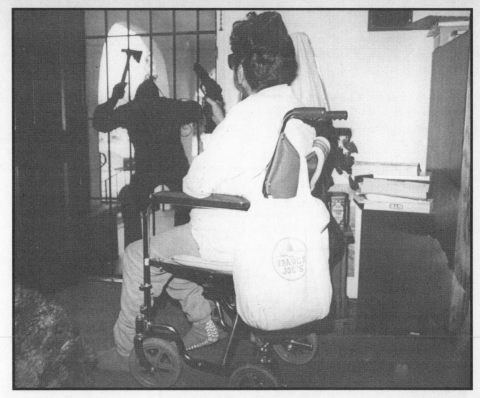

Some suggest homeowners try to flee violent invaders. However, some people, like those physically disabled, cannot escape quickly. In such cases, a high capacity 9mm gun can save a life when an attacker breaks in.

never ever inject a firearm into a confrontation with the idea that its presence alone is going to resolve anything. By definition, such misuse of a firearm will not result in harm to the intruder or attacker, yet very could lead easily to the demise of the individual who produced the firearm in the first place.

Discounting those who know they can pull the trigger and those who know they cannot, the majority of people are doubtful. Yes, when they or members of their family are threatened with deadly force, they "could" react in a way which would result in them pulling the trigger. Yet, under almost all situations, they would not fire at another human being. For them, a 12-gauge shotgun is not a terribly good choice for home-defense. Shotguns are relatively large and

long, they are comparatively difficult to swing and shoot in the confines of residences and they are extremely loud when fired inside.

Likewise, centerfire hunting rifles make relatively bad home-defense choices, if for no other reason than the fact that shooting one in a home is likely to cause permanent and total hearing damage to the defender, regardless what happens to the intruder/attacker. Also falling into this less-than-optimum category are the high performance "magnum" handguns with full-house loads in them. Granted, all of these kinds of rigs will accomplish the job, and some of them dramatically so. But in the final analysis, they are less than ideal.

Conversely, does it then mean that something on the low end of the power scale is the better choice? Perhaps, perhaps

Any peaceful neighborhood can turn into a nightmare if a violent criminal decides to break into one of the homes.

not. That question can be answered more fully later. But having discounted some of the lesser choices in home-defense firearms/cartridges, it is proper to investigate what factors might be truly important in making a choice.

Relatively few individuals need to use a home-defense firearm on a regular basis. This means that most firearms intended to be used solely or primarily for home-defense will spend most, if not all, of their time in an inert mode — just lying around.

Hence, some degree of thought needs to be applied to the storage of a home-defense firearm, since it will be in storage much longer and more often than it ever will be used. Safety is a primary concern of everything involving firearms. Hence, it is proper to consider the safe storage of a home-defense firearm. This means the gun must be readily available if and

when it is needed, yet secure from access by unauthorized people, including children. In fact, many states now have statutes which address this situation specifically, and have established felony sanctions for those who allow minors to get their hands on firearms. This is serious stuff. Even without such criminal sanctions, it is advisable to keep firearms out of the hands of those too young or too irresponsible to handle them properly.

When considering such matters, handguns — as a classification of firearms — offer a number of conveniences. They take up less space, and they can be secured in smaller containers which can be kept out of sight in a wider variety of areas around a home.

There are a host of security devices on the market which either keep a handgun out of reach, or make such a firearm inert. These come in the form of locking boxes and miniature vaults, locks and the like. Many of these containers feature multiple-button locking devices which can be opened in the dark, using the "feel" of their raised buttons to allow the owner to know which ones to push — and in what order. They can keep unauthorized hands off a firearm, yet allow almost instant access to the gun should the owner need it. They are totally worthwhile. Locking devices also come in a variety of forms, and they make the gun inert, yet can be removed quickly if the gun needs to be used in a hurry.

Having established the inherent convenience of a handgun, there are some important considerations when deciding what kind of handgun/ammo might be best for specific situations. For example, will the handgun be used only by the owner, or might someone else in the household, like a spouse, also possibly use it? Here, we get into the tactical performance arena.

It doesn't matter how much lead is launched into the air at an attacker, nor how large and potentially lethal the bullets are if the target is not hit. A bullet in the air is relatively meaningless, and often can create more problems than it ever could have solved. Hence, whoever might find himself or herself using a home-defense firearm should know how to use it properly, and should be able to hit the target with it. In handgun shooting, the fit and feel of the gun in the hand are

Above, the smaller 9mmP (left) is often chided when compared to the .45 ACP. Yet, with the right bullets, like the PMC/Eldorado Starfire (left), it can be a true home-defense cartridge. Right, high performance ammo like Winchester's Black Talon makes the 9mm come alive, notably in automatics like the CZ-75.

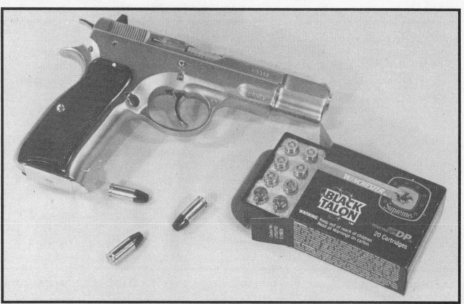

Hornady offers factory-loaded 9mmP ammunition that features the company's XTP high performance bullets. The round is an outstanding choice for home-defense.

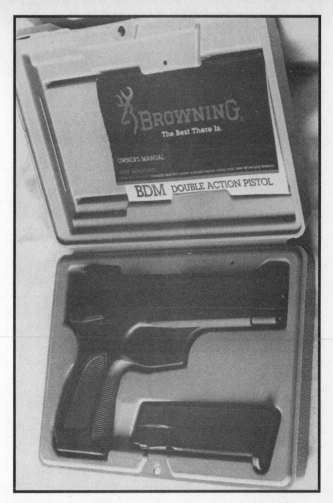

Many 9mm handguns are supplied in a lockable box, like this Browning BDM in 9mmP. The box keeps the gun handy, yet out of the hands of unauthorized people.

primary factors contributing to accurate hits.

If only the owner will ever use the home-defense firearm, then proper size of the firearm is dictated solely by that individual's hand size, upper body strength and preferences. However, if more than one person might use the firearm, then the gun has to be small enough not to be too large for the smallest person who might use it. In real world situations, large hands and strong people can handle smaller firearms better than smaller and weaker people can handle larger firearms.

Any discussion of tactical performance presumes some degree of familiarization and practice. It is during such sessions that many well intentioned gunowners make gigantic mistakes. In any form of shooting, perceptions (mental images) mean more than most actual factors. The subjects at hand here are noise and recoil. These two factors act in interdependent ways to cause flinching at least, and hesitation to fire at most. It is self-defeating for a person to maintain a firearm for self-defense if that person is intimidated by the gun.

Unfortunately, the perceptions of both noise and recoil are exaggerated on the range. Hunters are quite aware of this phenomenon. A powerful centerfire hunting rifle may "kick" severely when they sight-in at the range before a hunt. Yet, when they shoot at an animal during the hunt, they are unaware of recoil at all. So it is when the discussion involves home-defense firearms. Too often, shooters are so intent on impressing a family member with the power of a firearm that they cause their students to be intimidated by the very implement which is intended to help save their lives. Hence, a home-defense firearm should not be so loud, nor kick so hard, that any of those who might use it would hesitate to do so, simply because in the back of the mind, there is the memory of pain or intimidation.

So what does this mean so far? If a home-defense handgun has to be physically small enough to be handled well by the smallest of hands which might use it — and if it cannot recoil violently enough to intimidate the user — then most, if not all, of the big, large-bore handguns are less than ideal choices.

But what about stopping power? Is that not important when considering the advances of an intruder or attacker? Yes and no. The subject being discussed here is not casual, nor particularly sociable. The use of deadly force never is to be taken lightly, nor incompletely.

The concept of "knock-down" power when used in the discussion of handguns often is misunderstood. Virtually no firearm which can be fired when held in one hand has the brute force actually to knock down an attacker. What is often interpreted as "knock-down" power is nothing more than the target's muscular response to instant trauma.

Granted, it really doesn't matter precisely what causes an attacker to hit the floor, so long as it happens. But the real object is to stack the deck in favor of the attacker hitting the floor. A number of factors beyond brute force come into play in the equation — and actually may be much more important in the end.

What is the actual goal of the gunowner should the home-defense firearm be pressed into service? First, the gunowner wants to stop any and all aggression. After that, concerns can be listed in a diminishing order of importance which is fairly easy to establish.

In matters involving firearms, bullet placement is the trump card in all situations. Good placement of a bad bullet is

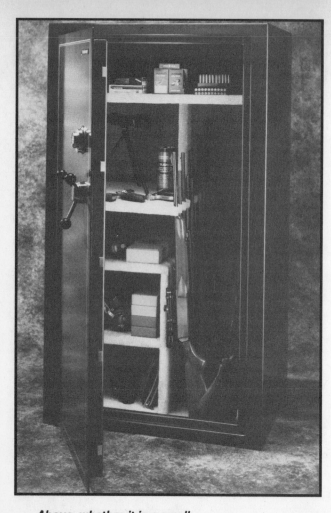

better than bad placement of a good bullet. Yes, it is far better to hit an intruder well with a .22 rimfire than it is to hit that same intruder marginally with a .45. By the same token, hitting that intruder well with a .45 is usually quite effective.

Never discount the importance of mind-set. Yes, every single shot should count. But the only situation in which a single shot in and of itself is relevant is when only one shot is available; when the firearm itself is a single-shot, or when the firearm itself contains only one shot.

Whenever a repeater is used and it contains more than one cartridge, then the mind-set has to include the potential for multiple well placed shots. Here is where the performance of a single projectile ceases being the only concern and becomes a part of the performances of more than one. Whether the firearm is a revolver or semi-auto, the practiced and disciplined gunowner can deliver a number of hits, even if the first shot is fired at the moment the attacker first physically touches the shooter. Certainly, from across a residential room, there is time for a fairly large number of deliberate shots. The truly operative concept here is "deliberate" shots. Merely spewing lead into the air accomplishes little, if any, good.

Hence, the assumption here will be that a repeater is a better home-defense firearm than is a single-shot in most situations. Likewise, if a handgun is a more convenient home-defense firearm than is a long gun, then a repeating handgun is a logical choice. And, this repeating handgun should shoot ammunition which will not cause the shooter to be intimidated. This translates generally into a small or medium-size revolver or semi-auto.

Firearms have been used for home-defense long enough that empirical data establishes this pretext to be valid. So, what has tradition established, and where, if at all, does the 9mm fit into the picture? To a degree, it depends upon where in time one wants to focus. For example, the .22 rimfire short was

Above, whether it is a small box or a full vault like this model from Treadlok, it's vital to think safety when firearms are kept in a home. Right, some 9mm guns, like the S&W Model 3913LS (LadySmith) are designed for people with small hands.

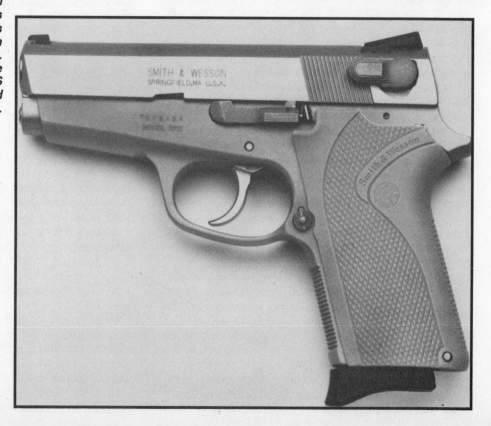

The unique safety system of the Glock 17 makes it ideal for home-defense. The auto can be kept with a round in the chamber, ready to go.

developed initially as a self-defense cartridge. It was introduced more than a century ago in the diminutive Smith & Wesson No. 1 single-action revolver. Such handguns were kept in dresser drawers or carried in vest pockets or purses. The thought at the time was that a defensive firearm would be used at arm's length or closer, and that by literally thrusting the handgun into the attacker's face and pulling the trigger, the job would be done. There is some validity to such a concept, obviously.

As cartridge firearms evolved and centerfire cartridges became viable, the concept of home- or self-defense gunnery changed. The now-infamous $3 pistol (actually a revolver) was one result. These were inexpensive revolvers which fired relatively sedate cartridges like the .32 or .38 short, or even the longer versions of either. Such firearms were the rule rather than the exception throughout the first half of this century. Although they probably provided more of a *sense* of security than *actual* security for their owners, they served their purposes well.

One must consider that those also were the times when many law enforcement agencies still were using .32-caliber revolvers, and most of the rest were using .38s with round-nose bullets. That was long before the likelihood that an attacker might be "high" on some drug. Even the bad guys then would normally turn and run at the sight or sound of a defensive firearm, to say nothing of being hit by a projectile from one. But that was then, and now is now.

Yet, all of those traditional defense firearms were small enough to be handy, and not so powerful as to intimidate their owners.

Semi-auto handguns for home-defense have been a factor for virtually all of this century. They range from the diminutive .25 autos through the .32s and into the 9mm/.38-caliber categories.

By the latter years of this century, overall top choices for home defense handguns involved revolvers chambered for .38/.357 magnum cartridges or smaller, and semi-autos involved pistols chambered for 9mmP or smaller cartridges. Recently, there has been expanded interest in revolvers chambered for the 9mmP cartridge, but more about that later.

Since the most logical of the home-defense handguns have relatively short barrels, because they must be stored in relatively small containers, it is valid to consider cartridge performance characteristics in relatively short barrels. Such a consideration precludes the .357 magnum from serious thought. Through a short barrel, there are many .38 Special loads which perform at least as well as any of the .357 magnum recipes. This means that the only difference is that the .357 magnum will likely be louder and produce a much brighter muzzle flash, while delivering exactly the same punch with precisely the same bullet as the .38 Special.

So, in the arena of the traditional revolver cartridges, the .38 Special is among the better choices available. However, in a short-barreled revolver, the 9mmP is an outstandingly good option. A .38 Special bore is .357-inch in diameter. A 9mmP is .355-inch in diameter. That is so close that there are handguns around which are chambered for one cartridge, but which actually have bores of the other. That is so close that the same bullet can be fired through either. Yet, the efficiency of the 9mmP is such that it produces high performance almost instantly and does not need a particularly long barrel to achieve credible ballistics.

What this means is that the shorter 9mmP cartridge, fired in a short-barreled revolver, actually achieves the same level of performance as do some of the Plus-P .38 Special loads in standard length barrels. So the 9mmP is as credible as any other cartridge of its diameter or smaller in short-barreled revolvers. And, since revolvers which handle substantially larger diameter cartridges are often too large for some of the hands which are likely to have to use the firearm in a home-defense situation, the 9mmP is as credible as anything out there when it comes to home-defense application via a short-barreled revolver.

Yet, it was not in the revolver that the 9mmP was born, nor where it established its preeminent position in the world. Far from it. The 9mmP is primarily a semi-auto cartridge. And since 1935, when John M. Browning's P-35 (Hi-Power) pistol was introduced, the 9mmP has been synonymous with the

If a smaller gun is required, the 9mm Glock 19 Compact model is an excellent choice.

concept of high-capacity magazines. It is common for even the scaled-down 9mmP semi-auto handguns to have magazine capacities of 12 rounds or more.

If the direction of this discussion was not evident before, the validity in home-defense situations for the 9mmP should begin to become obvious.

The 9mmP is chambered routinely in small to medium-size handguns which can be stored safely and conveniently. The cartridge itself offers performance which is on par with all but the largest of the handgun rounds. And, even in small or medium size handguns, the 9mmP is physically small enough to afford high-capacity magazines. That means lots of shots. Yet, the 9mmP does not recoil stiffly enough to intimidate any adult shooter.

But the discussion does not end here. There are other critical matters of consideration when it comes to the logical home-defense firearm.

Such firearms should not fire projectiles which will penetrate through a lot of walls, or even through an attacker and still through a wall. There are a number of reasons for this consideration, including the fact that most residences are close to other residences, and there likely could be a situation where an attacker might be shot at in one room, while other family members are in an adjoining room in the same residence. Again, this is serious stuff.

It is in this regard that one of the largest of the detracting factors involving the 9mmP as a defensive cartridge can be discounted. Traditionally, the 9mmP has been questioned as a "stopper." Detractors have argued that attackers have been hit, sometimes repeatedly, with the 9mmP, yet kept on coming and causing injury or death to others. The root of such stories is based more on the projectiles being launched than the cartridge itself.

Initially, as a military cartridge, the 9mmP sported a full-metal jacket bullet. This "solid" round-nose configuration had about as much stopping performance as did the now-maligned .38 Special round-nose lead bullet of law enforcement's past. The problem was simple. The .35-caliber bullet simply slid

through the attacker, creating a hole its diameter. Whether lethality was quick was determined solely upon exactly where the bullet went into and through the attacker.

Bear in mind that in the European military ethic of the time when the 9mmP was introduced and expanded initially, the object was merely to wound the opponent. If the wound was fatal instantly, fine. If not, so long as the opponent was essentially put out of service, the object of the exercise had been achieved.

To a similar degree, the politics of policing have dictated in many instances that law enforcement officers use "humane" ammunition — whatever that might be. Hence, even when law enforcement agencies switched to 9mmP for their handgunnery, the projectiles they threw into the air were less than the most effective for that size bullet. When establishing a home-defense rig, such concerns are moot.

Interestingly, the same projectiles which preclude extended penetration through walls also tend to perform most radically inside a target — such as an attacker!

The reason is simple. A bullet which expands rapidly following impact will not penetrate through walls as well as one which does not. And, one which expands quickly after impact will impart more tissue damage in an attacker than one that does not. But there is no free lunch, either.

A projectile which expands too quickly might cause nothing more than a surface wound in the attacker — especially when one considers that the bullet will, in many cases, have to penetrate several layers of clothing on the way. Here is where some of the more recent "wonder" handgun bullets come into play.

They expand quickly and do not over-penetrate, yet will go into a target deeply enough to do major damage. Among these bullet types are the Eldorado Starfire, Federal Hydra-Shok, Remington Golden Saber and Winchester Black Talon.

If there was a major problem with 9mmP performance in defensive situations before, these kinds of bullets have afforded a viable solution. For example, this kind of 9mmP projectile causes the same level of tissue damage as did the

The 9mmP lends itself to high performance in handguns with short barrels like the Smith & Wesson Model 940.

more traditional soft-nose designs in the full-house .357 magnum loadings when fired through long-barreled revolvers.

So what does all of this mean? Where does the 9mmP fit into the home-defense arena? Depending upon a shooter's perception, it may not be the "ultimate" answer to the question. But for most people, it represents one of the best options available.

Still, bear in mind that no firearm and no cartridge will do anything by itself. The gun and ammo are only as effective as the person at the controls. The point here is, however, that for most people at the controls, the 9mmP represents a valid choice for home- or self-defense, and for very many of them, the 9mmP is the best choice.

Having viewed the situation from a number of perspectives, it should come as no surprise that such a conclusion might be reached. As was mentioned earlier, empirical data would indicate the same thing: There are more 9mmP handguns and ammunition used in the world than any other centerfire type. Such an overwhelming endorsement must be viewed as having merit.

And, when logic dictates similar conclusions, it is safe to state bluntly that the 9mmP is among the better bets for home- or self-defense. Yes, it is in this defense arena that the 9mmP shines best of all. It is in that context that all of the advantages of the cartridge and guns which shoot it can be realized, while any of the negatives can be precluded or minimized.

The real question then, is which 9mmP cartridge and

firearm are best? The answer is very personal. It is: Whatever combination works best for the person likely to be pulling the trigger.

But what are some of these combinations, and why might some be better for some people than others? Consideration here must focus upon the likely circumstances under which the chosen firearm might be used. In home-defense scenarios, these times are both scary and tense, to say the least.

Home-defense firearms, if used in that role at all, are going to be used when the owner is literally under attack. The owner's home actually is being invaded. His or her life is really on the line. This is enough to make anyone tense, at least, and most likely extremely nervous and anxious.

Hence, some consideration must be given to the firearm configuration which will serve best under such compelling situations. The mechanics of the firearm must not serve as a hindrance to its operation. Put another way, the owner must be able to grab the gun and use it without wasting time, effort or thought upon the mechanical workings of the gun itself.

In this respect, a double-action revolver is a highly logical choice, because the owner need merely pick it up, point it and pull the trigger. The revolver does the rest. For those considering a double-action revolver, however, it is essential that everyone who might be using the firearm is able to work the double-action mechanism with relative ease. That means the gun must fit well enough that the index finger is able to pull the trigger authoritatively and through its entire length of pull. This is something which can be determined in the gun shop,

The S&W Model 940 is a double-action revolver with an internal hammer. It will not snag when drawn, yet can go into action simply by pulling on the trigger.

even before a particular model is chosen.

If the revolver chosen happens to be a 9mmP, it will generally be small enough not to be a negative factor, even for relatively small hands, and likely will have a cylinder which will hold either five or six rounds. Barrel length probably will be two or three inches.

Such revolvers are available from several companies, including Ruger and Smith & Wesson. Also, they are available in blued steel or stainless. In addition to the cosmetics involved, there are other factors which dictate which type of metal is best. Stainless handguns are less vulnerable to the ravages of humidity and climate than are blued steel ones. And since a home-defense firearm is likely to spend extended lengths of time in storage and out of sight, it is often best to opt for the stainless variety.

Assuming that everyone who might use the home-defense handgun is mechanically astute enough to operate a semi-auto effectively in a highly charged situation, there are several factors to consider when choosing a particular type of handgun.

In the realm of semi-auto handguns, the concept of "cocked-and-locked" pops up from time to time. This is a phenomenon encountered primarily with single-action semi-autos. Single-action means the handgun must be cocked physically before it can be fired the first time. Subsequently, the reciprocating action of the pistol automatically cocks itself for following shots.

Before the advent of double-action semi-autos, it was common practice for shooters carrying single-action semi-autos to carry them cocked-and-locked, which meant the handgun had a cartridge in the chamber, was cocked, then the safety was engaged (locking the mechanism and rendering the gun somewhat safe).

Although this may have evolved as standard carry practice, such a system is somewhat questionable when it comes to a home-defense handgun. Since the firearm likely will spend such long periods of time in inert storage, keeping it cocked would contribute to the creation of a negative "set" in the hammer spring. This means weakening its ability to spring. Similarly, whenever semi-autos are kept for home-defense, it

is a good idea to unload magazines periodically to allow the magazine springs to relax and preclude premature negative sets.

So, if the home defense semi-auto is to be a single-action design, then everyone who likely will use it must be mechanically astute enough to be able to pick up the pistol, cycle the slide and chamber a round, making the gun ready to shoot. This is both easy and fast for anyone really familiar with firearms, but can present an awkward challenge to others. This is especially true if one or more of the people who might use the firearm for home-defense has any physical problems at all in manually cycling the action. This is something which should be determined before opting for a particular style of firearm, and it can be determined easily and quickly in a gun shop or on the range.

Double-action means the firearm can be cocked and fired simply by pulling on the trigger. And, there are semi-auto 9mmP handguns on the market which offer a double-action feature for the first shot, with single-action firing for subsequent rounds when the gun itself cocks the action. Also, there are double-action-only handguns available. These semi-autos offer the same double-action-type trigger pull for every shot, from first to last.

With modern double-action semi-autos, a built-in decocking feature also involves a hammer-blocking device and/or a firing pin-blocking device which preclude the primer on the cartridge from being struck by the firing pin unless the trigger itself is pulled. This means it is relatively safe to keep a round in the chamber and have the action uncocked. Certainly, this type of feature has many benefits when it comes to home-defense handguns. It means the handgun can be stored loaded and ready to fire, yet be relatively safe and not present a problem for the critical springs. It is about the best of all worlds.

However, some of these firearms are configured in such a way as to be comparatively unwieldy for some people. In such instances, it is better to opt for a handgun design which handles quickly and smoothly, whatever it might happen to be.

A quick trip to any well stocked gun shop can help a person

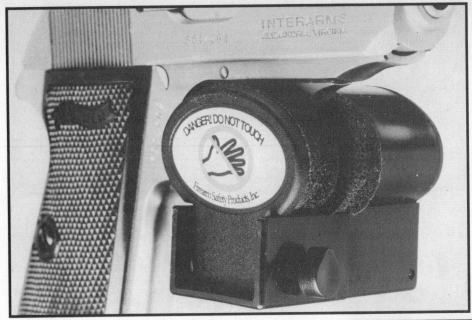

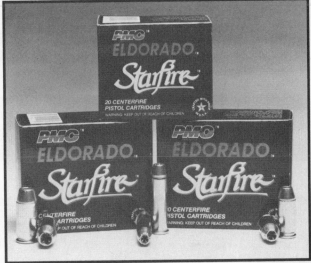

Left, attached to the trigger, the TriggerAlarm from Firearm Safety Products, Inc., is one of many devices available to keep a home-defense firearm at hand, yet safe from curious fingers. Below, the Starfire from PMC/Eldorado has become favorite for those using a 9mm gun for home-defense.

decide which type of firearm will *not* work well. It may or may not indicate which type of firearm is best. Unfortunately, it isn't until an individual actually shoots a particular kind and size of firearm that this person knows whether it is totally right.

For such determinations, there are a number of options available. In many of the urban and suburban areas around the country, there are indoor shooting ranges where handguns can be fired. These same ranges routinely offer rental handguns in about every configuration imaginable. That means a person can go there and actually try out different kinds of guns before having to decide which is the best to acquire.

These same ranges also routinely offer instruction in the safe and proper use and handling of firearms. Someone who doesn't know an avid shooter, or has no background in shooting at all, can go to one of these indoor ranges to receive the initial safety and handling training, then go to the firing line and learn to shoot.

If there are no such ranges in the area, there is likely some kind of local shooting range. And, with even a little persistence, a person usually can go to such a range and check out a number of different kinds of firearms. Some of the guns may be range equipment, but there always will be guns brought by other shooters. For such locations, check with any local gun shop. If the shop does not have some program of its own, people there usually can provide information about where a person can go to shoot or learn to shoot.

Once a particular firearm has been chosen for home- or self-defense, it is not enough simply to buy some ammo and have it ready. At least a minimal amount of practice and familiarization are a must. For this, there will need to be a trip or trips to the local range or to some other legal shooting spot.

During these sessions, it is a good idea to pay close attention to how the firearm works, and to become as familiar as possible with the way it works, the way it shoots and where it shoots. After all, a home-defense firearm needs to shoot where the shooter is looking. This might require some form of sight adjustment and, to accomplish that, check the manufacturer's instructions.

However, as a defensive firearm, it need not deliver target-level accuracy, and the sights, if any, need not be precise. Consider the home in which the firearm might be used. What is the longest available shot? What is the longest likely shot? There is no need for such a firearm to be able to hit anything at distances beyond those.

In fact, if the target can be hit at distances no farther than two or three paces, it is likely at least credible. Hence, the operation of the gun and the shooter's familiarity with it are of the most concern.

Although any practice is better than none, it is a good idea to practice with the same ammunition that will be used in the firearm when it is pressed into service in a defensive situation. It is important that the shooter become as familiar with the characteristics of the actual defense ammunition loads as it is to be familiar with the gun itself.

The whole concept of maintaining a firearm for home-defense is serious business. It should not be entered into lightly or frivolously. However, if such a decision is made, it is valid to say that the 9mmP is a logical choice and worth consideration.

CHAPTER Four

FOUR LIVES OF THE 9mm PARABELLUM

Nearly A Century Old, This Cartridge Has Seen Historic Military Use!

The Mauser broomhandle M1916 9mm Parabellum was the only 9mmP pistol, besides the Luger, made in quantity until about 1935. The M1916 had a large "9" carved in the grips. Except for that feature, it looked like these .30 calibers.

Pat Cascio fires the Korean Daewoo D/A 9mm large capacity pistol. Many countries have produced a D/A 9mm.

THE 9mm PARABELLUM cartridge, also known as the 9mm Luger and by other names, is used so universally today as a military cartridge that most people do not realize it took many decades for it to gain such a level of acceptance.

Today, the 9mmP is the military handgun and submachine gun cartridge of nearly every country in the world, except most of the present and former members of the Communist Bloc and some of the Third World countries they have supplied with arms. For the latter, the standard military handgun cartridges are either the 9mm Makarov or the 7.62x25mm Tokarev pistol cartridge.

West Point graduate Chuck Karwan has made a study of military use of the 9mmP cartridge. Here are his findings:

"Among the former members of the Communist Bloc, both Yugoslavia and Czechoslovakia are switching to the 9mm Parabellum, as has the former East Germany since it reunified with West Germany. It also would not be a surprise to see countries like Poland, Hungary, Lithuania, Latvia and others do the same in the near future. Similarly, with the decline of influence of the former Soviet Union, the same thing is happening in the Third World where the movement is almost universally toward the 9mm Parabellum for handgun use."

About the only other military holdouts from the 9mm are such countries as Greece and South Korea that still use the .45 ACP for their handgun cartridge, because their handguns are M1911A1 pistols supplied them through U.S. foreign military assistance. Since the U.S. adoption of the 9mm Parabellum, many of those countries also are dropping the .45 ACP for more modern pistols chambered for the 9mmP cartridge.

Since the 9mm Parabellum is the primary military handgun cartridge of over 90 percent of the countries of the world, and the numbers are climbing, few realize that this almost univer-

sal acceptance came with extreme slowness. Actually, acceptance in the military world has come in four distinct phases stretching over a period of 90 years. It is hard to believe, but in less than 10 years the 9mm Parabellum cartridge will be a century old and more popular and widely used than ever!

During phase one of the military acceptance of the 9mm Parabellum, the cartridge's growth was tied almost completely to the Luger pistol. In the late 1800s, while working for the German arms firm DWM, a talented German gun designer named Georg Luger redesigned an awkward and ugly toggle-locked pistol originally designed by Hugo Borchardt, a naturalized American citizen. The result was the sleek and handsome handgun we now know as the Luger. It was available for military adoption in about 1900.

Following in the footsteps of Borchardt and Mauser, the new pistol was chambered for a bottlenecked .30 caliber high-velocity cartridge called the 7.65 Luger (.30 Luger). However, Luger's native Germany indicated displeasure with that cartridge and expressed interest in the Luger if it could be chambered for a cartridge that fired a larger diameter, heavier bullet.

By 1902, Luger had developed just such a cartridge. Basically, all he did was remove the bottleneck in his 7.65mm Luger cartridge case, shorten it slightly and load it with a 9mm bullet so as to have about the same overall length as the 7.65mm Luger cartridge. The result was the 9mm Luger cartridge, also known as the 9mm Parabellum, 9x19mm, 9mm NATO, 9mm P'08 — and by other names.

By taking this route, the only modification to the Luger pistol needed to adapt it to the 9mm cartridge was a new barrel.

The first military adoption of a 9mm Parabellum-chambered handgun was the M1904 Marine Model Luger adopted by the German Navy. Commonly called the Navy Luger, it

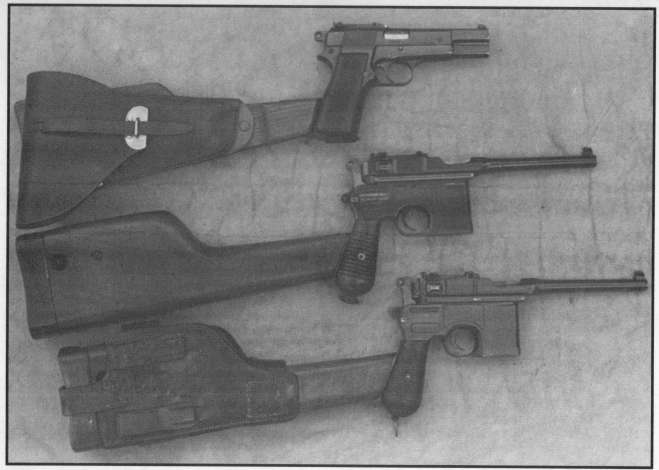

In the early days of semiautomatic pistols, it was popular to have them produced so that they would accept a shoulder stock that also doubled as a holster. Here, a Browning Hi-Power 9mm (top) accompanies two Mauser Broomhandles.

featured a six-inch barrel, an adjustable rear sight, a lug to take a shoulder stock and a grip safety. Later models of the Navy Luger did away with the grip safety, but were otherwise pretty much the same in specifications. The Navy Luger is considered the handsomest of the large Luger family.

A few years later, a Luger variation in 9mm was adopted by the German Army as the Pistole '08 and the 9mm Parabellum cartridge was adopted as the Pistolenpatronen (pistol cartridge) '08. The P-08, as the Army model Luger became known, differs from the graceful Navy model by having a shorter, stubbier barrel of about four inches, no grip safety and a simple fixed notch rear sight. The P-08 is by far the most common of all the Lugers.

About 1914, the German Army adopted yet another version of the Luger, commonly called by collectors the "Artillery Model." It featured an eight-inch barrel with a rifle-type tangent sight mounted on the barrel calibrated to an extremely optimistic 800 meters. It also had an interesting accessory that consisted of a 32-round drum magazine that used the normal Luger magazine well. When the Artillery Luger was combined with a shoulder stock and its drum magazine, the results were roughly equivalent to a submachine gun that can only shoot semi-automatically. In those pre-submachine gun and pre-assault rifle days, it was an excellent close range defense gun for artillery and other crew served-weapon crews.

The Luger was purchased widely by the military forces of many countries, usually in 9mm, though the Swiss and Finns went with the 7.65mm Luger cartridge. Germany was by far the major user of the 9mm Luger cartridge and gun, but others were Portugal, Netherlands, Bulgaria, Persia and Latvia.

Until 1935, no 9mm Parabellum pistol other than the Luger was adopted by any military with one exception. That one exception occurred during WWI. The German military was so short of Lugers that they contracted Mauser to make their M1896/M1912 broomhandle in 9mm Parabellum. Adopted as limited standard, these 9mm pistols were designated the Model 1916. To distinguish them from the otherwise indentical 7.63mm-chambered guns that had also been pressed into service, these Mausers have a large *9* carved into their grips which usually is accented with red paint. Thus, these pistols are called "Red Nines" by collectors. Approximately 150,000 9mm Parabellum-chambered Mauser broomhandle pistols had been produced by the end of WWI.

The year 1935 started phase two in the military history of the 9mmP cartridge. World War II was hovering on the horizon. Many countries were starting to re-arm and their handguns were largely holdovers from WWI. The only handgun of WWI which was not obsolete by then was the U.S. M1911. It was clear that all the others, including the Luger, were not nearly state of the art.

In Poland, 1935 saw the adoption of an excellent 9mm Parabellum pistol called the VIS or Radom. It was based on the Colt M1911 but had a number of improvements including changing the Colt's swinging link to a solid ramp-type locking

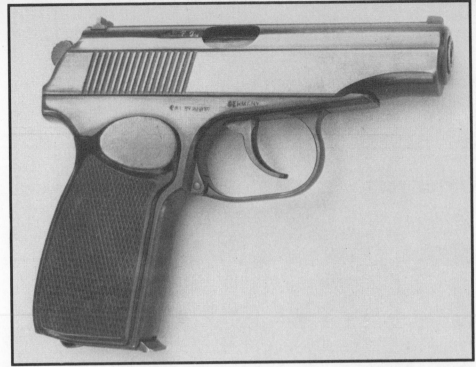

Except in current Communist countries, the 9mmP is the world's most popular military handgun cartridge. This gun is chambered for the 9mm Makarov.

mechanism. It also had no manual safety, as we know it, but instead depended on a slide-mounted decocking lever to safely lower the pistol's hammer on a loaded chamber for carry with the hammer down. Naturally, putting the pistol into action required manual cocking of the hammer before it could be fired.

The 9mm Polish Radom, as built prior to WWII, is one of the best-made military handguns ever produced. As a military pistol, it is far superior to the Luger in reliability, durability, simplicity, safety and other factors. When the Germans overran Poland in 1939, this fact was not lost on them. They continued the production of the Radom throughout their entire occupation of Poland and issued them widely to their own forces. As the war progressed, the quality of manufacture of the Radom pistol became progressively worse to the point that the last ones were quite crude. Even these normally will function well, though their accuracy is not great due to the loose fit of parts and loose bore dimensions.

In 1935, Finland introduced a new 9mm Parabellum pistol called the L35 Lahti, named after Aimo Lahti, the native Finn designer of the gun. Finland had been using the Luger pistol in 7.65mm Luger for many years with mixed results. In one

After WW II, countries in the Soviet sphere adopted Soviet firearms. That's why the Chinese Type 54 (top) is virtually identical to the Soviet TT33. The bottom auto is a Hungarian T58. It features a thumb safety not found on a regular TT33

At the end of WW II, these handguns were the best military pistols. The P38 9mm (top) had a double-action trigger. The Browning Hi-Power 9mm (middle) had a large capacity magazine. The M1911AI .45 ACP had stopping power.

swoop, they were able to go to a more effective chambering and a superior pistol design with adoption of the Lahti.

The L35 Lahti is an interesting pistol, though unnecessarily heavy and complicated. It uses a vertically moving block to lock the bolt to the barrel extension in much the same way as the Mauser broomhandle. Unique among pistols, it uses a bolt accelerator, as found on a number or machine guns, to ensure reliable functioning even under difficult sub-zero conditions. In addition, the gun is well sealed against the introduction of dirt to the pistol's mechanism. All parts are robust to the extreme and made from high-grade steels. As a result, the Lahti has an excellent reputation for reliability and durability in adverse conditions.

The Lahti pistol also has a number of shortcomings. It is styled after the Luger and shares that pistol's excessive muzzle lightness and tendency to point high when held at shoulder height. It also has an awkward safety and magazine catch. Field-stripping is easy, but detail-stripping is extremely difficult and is best left to a trained armorer with special tools. This gun is also unnecessarily heavy for the cartridge.

Sweden adopted a minor variation of the L35 Lahti in 1940, calling it the M40. Both the L35 and M40 are still in service to this day in reserve units in their respective countries, though they are obsolete by any reasonable standard.

There was one more 9mm Parabellum pistol introduced in 1935 — and it was by far the most important of them all. This,

the FN 9mm Browning Hi-Power, was one of the last designs worked on by John Browning before he died in 1926. However, much of the pistol's excellence also must be attributed to D.J. Saive, FN's master gun designer, who has many other successful designs to his credit like the FAL and MAG 58.

The "Hi-Power" name has confused many folks, since the auto is no more powerful than any other pistol chambered for the 9mm Parabellum cartridge. The name comes about from the fact that the gun was preceded by Browning-designed pistols chambered for the less powerful 9mm Browning Short (.380ACP) and 9mm Browning Long cartridges. Thus, this was the high-powered Browning.

The Browning Hi-Power (HP) is light and handy and has one of the most comfortable grips of any handgun ever made. Its major claim to fame is that it was the first powerful pistol to have a large-capacity, staggered-column magazine in its grip frame. The standard HP magazine holds 13 rounds, but some variations comfortably hold 14 cartridges. There are also a number of extension magazines available that hold 20 or more rounds, but they stick out the end of the pistol's butt.

The Browning HP was a major factor in putting the 9mm Parabellum cartridge on the international map. Prior to WWII, the gun was adopted by Belgium, China and several other countries. When WWII broke out and Germany invaded Belgium, they took over production of the HP just as they had with the Radom; they continued production until they with-

Variations of the Beretta Model 92FS 9mm (top) are used extensively by military forces throughout the world. Originally, the Glock 17 (bottom) was developed for use by the Austrian military.

The Browning Hi-Power in 9mm (top) was a favorite during WW II along with the M1911A1 .45 ACP.

drew from Belgium later in the war. The HPs were widely issued to Germany's forces and were well thought of and sought after. Fit and finish declined as the war progressed, but even the last ones made in that era were good pistols. Later issues had plastic grips instead of wood and the magazine safety was deleted to simplify production.

Some of the FN technicians had been able to escape from Belgium before the country fell to the Nazi onslaught. Through their help, production of the Browning HP began about 1943 in Canada by the John Inglis company. These guns were supplied to the Chinese as well as Canadian, British and other Commonwealth Forces. As a result, the Browning HP was the only handgun made and used by both sides in WWII.

One other extremely significant 9mm Parabellum military handgun was developed in the pre-WWII period. It was the 9mm Walther P38. This was the handgun the Germans chose to replace their venerable Luger. It was far superior to the Luger in most ways and far easier to manufacture, as well. Its claim to fame was that the P38 was the first successful high-powered combat handgun to have a double-action trigger. That is, the trigger both cocks the hammer and drops it for the first shot, then the cycling of the pistol's slide cocks the hammer for subsequent shots.

For the first time, a pistol could be carried fully loaded with a round in the chamber and the hammer down, yet still be instantly able to be shot with just a pull of the trigger. The P38 also had a slide-mounted, hammer-dropping safety which, to this day, still is probably the most popular safety system in use

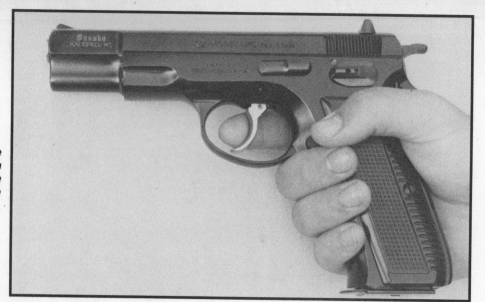

The Czech CZ-75 was one of the first military 9mm pistols to combine a large capacity staggered magazine with a double-action trigger.

The SIG-Sauer P226 was co-winner of the U.S. pistol trials that sought a large capacity double-action auto. The Beretta M92F prevailed during competitive bidding.

for double-action autoloaders, though it is losing ground to other systems. The P38 was produced in relatively huge quantities beginning in 1940, while production of the Luger ended rather early in the war.

When the Nazis absorbed Austria in 1938, that country's standard military handgun was the Steyr-Hahn (hammer Steyr) M1912 chambered for the 9mm Steyr cartridge. Rather than rearming the Austrian army with Luger pistols to keep commonality of ammunition, a decision was made to rebarrel the Steyr pistols on hand to 9mm Parabellum. The Austrians got the better of the deal since the M1912 is considerably simpler, more robust and more reliable than the Luger. However its fixed magazine, which is loaded with a stripper clip from the top, is certainly less convenient than the detachable magazine of the Luger.

It was WWII that really caused expanded use of the 9mm Parabellum cartridge on a huge, international scale. The seemingly insatiable demand for 9mm Parabellum-cham-

bered pistols by Germany and her allies caused the Spanish handgun manufacturers of Astra and Star to modify their standard offerings to take the 9mmP cartridge. Astra modified their 9mm Bergmann-Bayard M400 into the M600 in 9mmP. Star made a slight modification of their Model A in 9mm Bergmann-Bayard to make the Model B in 9mm Parabellum. Both of these fine pistols were delivered in quantity to the Germans, until France was liberated and delivery from Spain was cut off.

On the Allied side, the British Commonwealth Forces and the Chinese got a tremendous amount of favorable combat performance from the Browning Hi-Power in 9mmP, not to mention their use of the same cartridge in the Sten, Owen, Lanchester and Austen submachine guns.

On the Axis side, there was tremendous use of the 9mm Parabellum cartridge in the Luger, the P38, Browning HP, Radom, Astra 600, Star Model B, Steyr M1912 P-08 and even red Nine Mauser broomhandles left over from WWI. There

The SIG-Sauer P228 9mm was adopted by the U.S. military as its compact 9mm service auto, called the M11.

was also a tremendous amount of use of the cartridge in various submachine guns with the major player being the German MP40.

The net result of the WWII experience was that most of the world, except for the U.S., the Soviet Union and Japan, had made extensive use of the 9mm Parabellum cartridge by the end of the war. Also, the rise in the use of submachine guns — most chambered for the 9mm Parabellum cartridge — also caused expansion of interest in the cartridge.

With the end of WWII came the end of phase two and the beginning of phase three in the history of the 9mm Parabellum as a military handgun cartridge.

The post-WWII period saw a great number of realignments, reorganizations and consolidations. Many countries ended up with substantial supplies of captured or abandoned German arms. It was only natural to employ them with their own forces. Thus, such countries as France and Norway ended up using former German 9mm Parabellum P38 pistols even though they had not used the 9mmP cartridge before the war. The French went on to develop their own 9mmP handgun, the MAC M1950. It was an enlarged version of the pre-WWII MAC M1935S that shot the pipsqueak 7.65mm Long cartridge. It is of basic Browning design along the lines of the M1911.

During WWII, Italy had used the 9mm Parabellum in the excellent Beretta submachine guns, but used the 9mm Corto (.380 ACP) in the standard military handgun, the Beretta M1934. After WWII, it was only natural to adopt a 9mm Parabellum handgun to go with the similarly chambered submachine guns. Italy adopted the Beretta M1951 in 9mm Parabellum, an excellent pistol that also was adopted by Israel and Egypt and still is being made in Egypt today.

Switzerland also decided to retire its old 7.65mm Lugers. SIG developed a nice 9mm called the P210 that combined some features of the Browning, the MAC M1935A and a bit of the Tokarev TT33. It was adopted as the Model 49. Denmark also purchased quantities of this pistol.

Austria, Portugal and Pakistan adopted the 9mm P38, while the entire British Commonwealth adopted the Browning HP, as did a huge number of other countries all over the world. Licensed production of the Browning HP was undertaken in Argentina, Venezuela, Nigeria, besides Belgium and Canada in WWII. Unlicensed production has taken place in Indonesia, Hungary and India. The number of countries that use the Browning HP reads like a roster of the United Nations.

The third phase of the military history of the 9mm cartridge continued into the mid-1970s with more and more countries adopting 9mm Parabellum handguns. However, virtually all of the handguns adopted were pre-WWII designs like the Browning HP, the P38 and the Star Model B, or one of the post-WWII designs that were technologically equivalent like the MAC M1950, SIG P210 and Beretta M1951.

In 1971, S&W introduced the 9mm Model 59, the world's first large-capacity, double-action 9mm pistol. It was quickly followed by the Beretta M92 and the Czech CZ-75. This was the beginning of phase four in the 9mm Parabellum's history as a military handgun cartridge, and this phase continues today. One country after another is replacing military handguns with high-capacity, double-action 9mm handguns. Italy has adopted the Beretta M92, as have many other countries, including Brazil, Chile, France, South Africa, USA, Indonesia, Iran and others.

Austria has adopted the Glock 17, as has Norway, the Netherlands and other countries. Spain has the Llama M-82, while Czechoslovakia has adopted their superb CZ-75 which is also sold widely to Third World countries. And so it goes. Practically every country that does not have a high-capacity, double-action 9mm Parabellum probably will adopt one eventually. However, many older 9mm pistol designs, particularly the Browning Hi-Power, are likely to hang on for decades to come.

The 9mm Parabellum has taken 90-plus years to be totally accepted in military handguns, and its growth has not yet ended. Indeed, it is clear that the 9mm Parabellum will be the world's primary military handgun cartridge well into the next century.

CHAPTER *Five*

OF GADGETS AND GEAR

Accessories For 9mm Handguns Meet Virtually Any Need — Or Want!

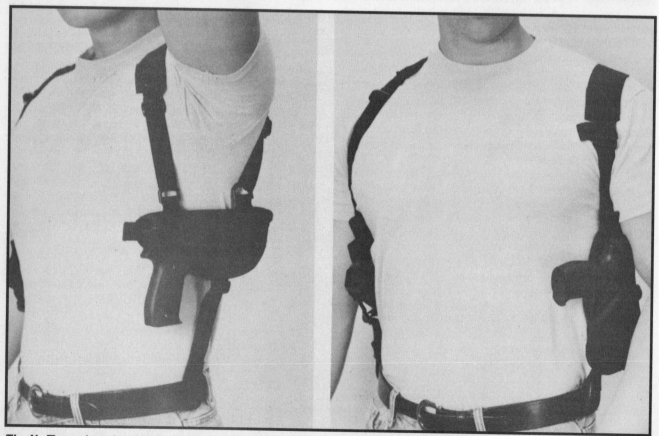

The Ny/Tex nylon shoulder holsters from RanShar have the ability to carry a sidearm either vertically or horizontally.

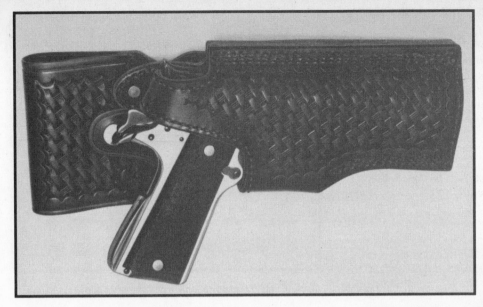

Tex Shoemaker & Son offers the US Swivel holster (left) which has an adjustable riveted swivel top, and the Quick Front holster (below) that allows for a speedy draw.

ANY SERIOUS discussion of the ethics of the 9mmP eventually comes to an undeniable conclusion: It is a study in economy. Everything about the 9mmP is efficient. This reality too often is overlooked when shooters think or talk about the cartridge, the firearms and the gear related to them

What this means to shooters is that there is no burning need to have more than the gun and ammo for the 9mmP to be credible. Yet, when it comes to personalizing the gun and gear to go with it, there are virtually no bounds. It is as wide open as the imagination of the shooter.

The most basic of accessory gear for the 9mmP is the holster. Although it is possible to go through life with a 9mmP and never have a holster or other specialized carrying device, most shooters find that some sort of holster is, at the very least, handy. Yet, it is common for shooters to opt for the first budget priced holster they encounter at the store, then learn to live with it.

Serious action shooters and other competitors, of course, are the opposite: They spend a lot of money for rigs which they perceive as possibly giving them even the slightest of added edges. Actually, the better bet usually lies somewhere between those two extremes.

There is a logical way to approach the question: What is the best holster design for me? Keep in mind that selection of a carrying device for a handgun is an extremely personal matter. What works or is best for one shooter may not be a good bet for another. Ultimately, the situation goes beyond just a holster. Consideration should include serious thought about the entire holster rig which usually includes the holster, a belt and probably some form of magazine pouch.

It also should be noted there are essentially two major classifications of shooters involved in the world of the 9mm, and they can have decisively different needs, or the gear which works best for one of the groups also may be credible for the other. The two groups are shooters in uniform — military or police — and civilians.

To a greater or lesser degree, the rigs used by uniformed 9mm users are dictated by the agencies with which they are affiliated. For example, military organizations usually allow

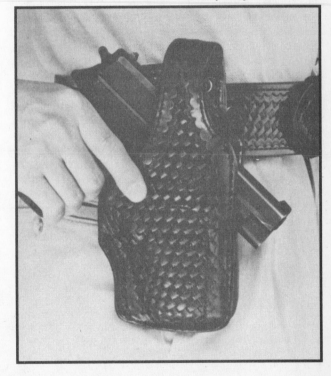

the use of only the rigs which are issued. The same is true of many law enforcement agencies. In such situations, there is little to consider. Whatever the organization issues and/or requires is what is used. That simplifies life.

Yet, within most of such organizations, there are special units or special job assignments which allow the use of non-standard or generally non-issue rigs. For example, when I was in the U.S. Army, the 1911-type .45 auto was the standard sidearm, and the classic leather flap holster which fit onto the web pistol belt was the norm. However, there were times when specific assignments dictated I use the standard shoulder holster rig instead. So, there are some options, even though minor.

Law enforcement agencies run the gamut. Some require

total uniformity when it comes to duty rigs, while others allow some degree of personalization or, in rarer instances, total personalization. Certainly in the law enforcement arena, off-duty rigs become non-standard and extremely personal.

Of all the 9mm shooters, civilians have the widest options, because each is his or her own boss when it comes to such matters. Regardless of which category — or categories — a particular shooter happens to be in at a given time, there is a logical series of considerations which can help in the myriad choices available. Oddly, it does not begin with the high-tech tactical features a particular rig may or may not offer. Instead, it begins with where and how the pistol will be stored when not in use.

STORAGE

The fact is that most 9mmP handguns spend much more time in storage than they do in use. So, the initial "gadget" to consider is something in which to store the firearm. Interestingly, this can be a tough decision.

For example, when not in use, will the pistol be maintained in a "ready" mode or will it simply be stored? If one or even the major role for a particular 9mmP handgun is home-defense, then quick and easy access to the pistol is important. Hence, a "holding" device could be as basic as a gun rug or a small, lockable box. It is always important to think a lot about where and how a "ready" firearm is stored.

A recent rash of laws in states around the country have added severe criminal penalties to the existing civil liabilities incurred should some unauthorized person, like a child, get hold of a firearm and hurt someone with it. So it is important to store a ready gun in such a way that will make it accessible when needed, but not a problem should unauthorized hands get near it.

The safety device arena has become an entire sub-market

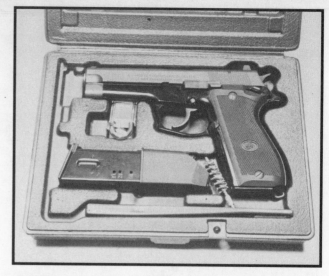

Many 9mm handguns come in lockable storage boxes.

in the gun world. There are trigger locks, action locks, mini-vaults with locking systems which can be opened by the owner quickly and by touch so they work in the dark. It is worth a trip to the gun shop just to inspect the many variations. Then consider the individual situation and opt for whatever type of device or devices are most valid.

Things are simplified a lot if the pistol is to be stored in what might be termed an "inert" condition. This means it is stored totally unloaded, and probably locked away in a closet, vault or some other secure area.

If the storage is in a locked area like a vault, it may be best to place the handgun on a padded shelf, then close and lock the door. The most sophisticated piece of gear needed in such

The MiniVault has a slotted combination system for quickly unlocking the small safe, even in the dark. It is made by GunVault, Inc., of Albuquerque, New Mexico.

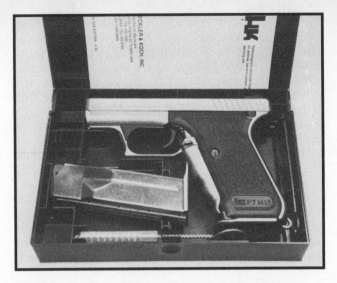

The H&K P7 M13 storage box also has cleaning gear.

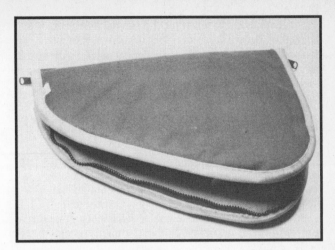

A gun rug is an inexpensive way to protect a firearm.

This H&K is kept clean and safe in a low-cost gun rug.

situations is a basic gun rug, which serves more to prevent the handgun from being bumped or scratched than anything else.

Storing a handgun in a holster may be common, but it is not always the greatest of ideas. Under some circumstances, like in humid areas, this can result in damage to the finish of the gun, or may even cause rusting which can attack the metal of the gun itself. In the worst cases surface pitting can result. It is usually a good idea to make certain any firearm being stored is able to "breathe." This means that, unless it is in some sort of oiled and sealed environment, air should be allowed to circulate around it. Keeping it zipped tightly in some of the padded cases or rugs can cause moisture to be trapped in the padding, and the moisture eventually will attack the surfaces of the gun.

Interestingly, some of the better storage containers available also happen to be the boxes in which some 9mmP handguns come when they are new. There is nothing wrong with storing a pistol in the original box. After all, the manufacturer used the box to protect the firearm from the time it left the factory until it was purchased by its ultimate owner — a process which routinely includes a lot of shipping, stacking and moving.

Although a basic cardboard box or one made of some form of foam will do the trick well, manufacturers in recent years have been offering an added perk for consumers. It is common now for many of the makes of pistols to come in moulded plastic boxes which also serve as reusable storage and carrying containers. Most of them have holes aligned so a small padlock can be attached to lock the box, while others actually come with a small lock.

There may be fancier gadgets available, but the original boxes — and especially the moulded, reusable kind — are among the most effective devices available. As mentioned earlier, the 9mmP is a study in economy.

TRANSPORT

A great many 9mmP handguns have rather uneventful lives. They are stored at home most of the time. Only infre-

quently are they taken to the range or some other shooting area by the owner where they are shot recreationally or for updated familiarization. Then they go right back home, and resume their storage existence.

For such use, the original box will suffice nicely, and the moulded, reusable boxes are totally credible. In fact, shooters who do no more with their pistols than store them and occasionally take them to a shooting area for informal practice need consider nothing more. Unless the handgun is to be carried as part of its activities, there really is no need for a holster at all.

Should the original box be absent, a simple gun rug is all that is needed for transport, assuming that local laws do not also require some other form of container. If a lockable container is required, there is a wide variety available on the market. Although those kinds of devices are what might be termed "gun specific," there are other options available for those who want to save a few bucks. For example, if the shooter already has a lockable attache case for his job, it can serve nicely as a transport container. To avert damage to the handgun, however, it is a good idea to pad it in some way so it won't bounce around inside the case.

For that kind of application, the gun rug again comes into the picture. But for those who want to keep saving money, one or a pair of old socks works well, depending upon the size of the gun. Or, wrap it in a small terry cloth towel. It doesn't take a lot of inventiveness to come up with something that will work well.

CARRY DEVICES

The list of options literally explodes when it comes to carry devices for 9mmP handguns. Here is where holsters and such come to the fore. Again, a series of considerations can answer the question about which sort of rig will serve best.

First, the shooter must determine what mode or modes of carry will come into play. It is important to note here that rarely will one kind of rig serve well for different modes of carry. Generally, each mode requires its own specific form of rig.

The easiest form of carry to discuss is that of informal, open carry. Interestingly, this is also the most common form, so it is a legitimate concern for most shooters.

As mentioned earlier, the basic open carry rig generally includes a holster, a belt and perhaps a magazine pouch. There is no need for bullet loops on belts for 9mmP users for two reasons. First, most 9mmP handguns use magazines, and second, any such loops would have to be closed on the bottom, because the 9mmP is a rimless cartridge. Closed-bottom

looping is quite expensive, and there is not enough room on most belts for enough loops when it comes to the 9mm and its high-capacity reality.

Breaking things down to basics, a simple holster attached to the same belt which holds up the trousers would suffice for some open carry purposes. Generally, however, this calls for a number of compromises which are often not desirable.

For example, if a trouser belt is used for the holster, the shooter has relatively few options when it comes to positioning the holster around the trunk of the body. Belt loops on the trousers pretty well dictate one or two logical locations for the holster, and that is about it.

More importantly, however, is the fact that such an arrangement allows for only one vertical placement of the holster — exactly at the waist. For many shooters, that is not the best location for easy access. Often, the better location is slightly above or slightly below the trouser belt line. Here is where a regular pistol belt comes into the picture.

Assembling the handiest holster/belt combo can be more complex than it first appears to be. When in doubt, it is not a bad idea to acquire matching components from a single manufacturer. After all, makers of holsters and belts have made extensive studies of what combinations work and what ones don't. Yet, not all combinations work in all instances, so there are still decisions to be made.

For example, does it matter whether the holster is able to slide up or down the belt, or should it be affixed to a specific

Perfect Partner holsters include hand-moulded leather models and those made of Propex, a water resistant synthetic.

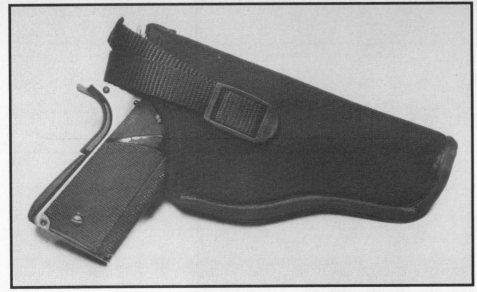

This Colt, with Pachmayr grips, is housed in a holster from Michaels of Oregon.

Leather goods from Gould & Goodrich are considered to be some of the finest.

spot on the belt via some sort of horizontal "loop?" This question is really important for shooters of single-action revolvers, and generally is of less import for shooters of semi-autos. However, it is something to think about.

How wide should the belt be? The subject here is the comfort zone. Generally speaking, the longer the periods of carry are to be, the wider the belt should be. Again, it is not a bad idea to start out with a heavy, wide belt. It will serve well for extended carry periods, and also will be totally comfortable for shorter term outings.

Another factor which enters the equation here is whether there will be anything else attached to the belt. The more weight the belt has to support, the wider and heavier duty it should be. For example, if it is to carry a full-size 9mmP and one or more magazine pouches, a medium belt would probably work. However, if other things like a knife or a flashlight are to be part of the ensemble, then definitely bigger is better.

For example, the author's favorite widths range from two to 2-1/4 inches for most uses. These widths are enough to carry a considerable load as comfortably as possible, yet are handy enough for shorter term, informal carry. For extended carry,

civilians have a number of handy options. For example, the basic, full-size Sam Browne rig, complete with shoulder strap, is totally functional.

Law enforcement folks may have abandoned this style, because the shoulder strap for them is nothing more or less than another big handle for combatant criminals to grab. But for informal civilian carry, the distribution of weight from such a rig is very nice.

What style of holster is best? Again, it depends upon likely uses and personal preferences. For example, a holster with a full flap will protect a handgun from bumps and scratches better than one with an open top. But full-flap holsters preclude any form of really fast draw. Should the bottom of the holster be open or closed? If the handgun is to be carried in the woods where it likely will be exposed to all manner of debris and wetness when brushed against foliage, a closed holster is not a bad idea. However, if the bottom is closed, then the top should have a full flap. Otherwise, debris or water can fall into the top and be trapped inside.

For general open carry, a holster with some sort of strap to secure the pistol is a good idea. Granted, for some law

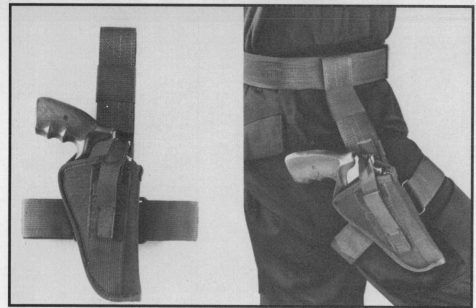

From Michaels of Oregon, the Sidekick Professional tactical holster system is built for SWAT and other emergency response teams.

enforcement and military purposes, a clamping design which allows the pistol to be drawn quickly and smoothly can be handy. But for general carry, a snap strap accomplishes everything nicely.

Hence, style means a lot in a holster — and not just for aesthetic reasons. Consider the likely situations that will be faced, and select the holster accordingly. When in doubt, consider the acquisition of more than one holster if the applications likely will be extremely diverse.

Almost as important as the design of the holster and width of the belt in a rig is the material from which it is made. Certainly, the classic holster rigs were made of leather. Leather, of course, is a credible option for many circumstances. How-

ever, it is not the end-all material for holster rigs.

Leather is by far the most romantic of holster rig materials. It feels nice and even smells delicious. And when maintained properly, such a rig can last a lifetime — or more. But the "M" word is a factor — maintenance. Leather requires more maintenance than some of the other materials.

In addition to maintenance, leather is less than the best bet if the rig is likely to get wet often. Granted, leather can be treated and coated to minimize the negative effects of moisture, but eventually wetness will cause problems for leather rigs.

High-tech rigs now are made from a number of synthetic materials, with some form of nylon or a close cousin to that

This lady's handbag has a compartment to hold a gun. The bags are handmade by En Garde of Dallas, Texas.

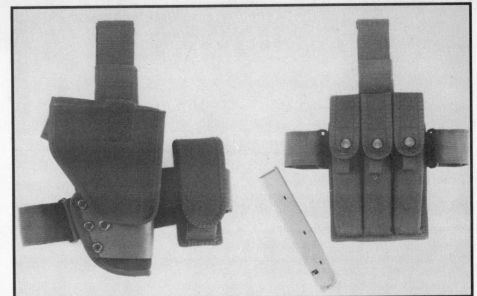

Right, the tactical holsters from Michaels of Oregon are of Sidekick laminate, featuring a Cordura nylon exterior, waterproof foam padding and smooth nylon lining. The company also makes tactical submachine gun triple magazine cases. Below, also from Michaels is a high ride hip holster.

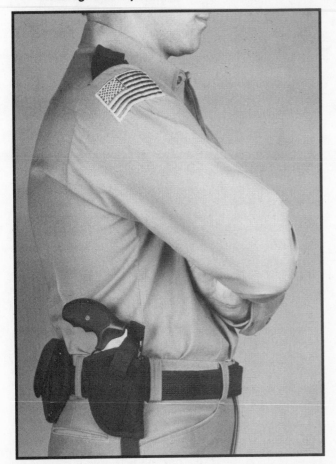

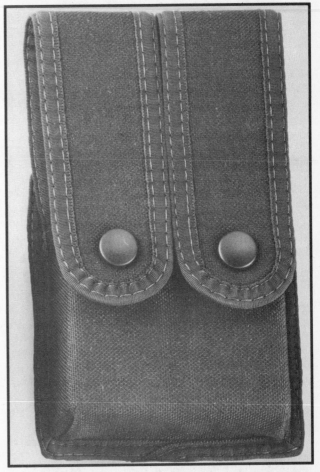

Michaels of Oregon makes this 20-round magazine case for magazines of the Sig, Beretta and Smith & Wesson.

synthetic being the basic fabric. And, where leather rigs feature snaps or hooks, synthetic rigs often have hook-and-loop fastening surfaces.

For the most part, synthetic rigs are impervious to inclement conditions. If they get wet, merely allow them to air dry and they are back in action. If they get dirty, scrub them with water, rinse them off and let them dry.

And when it comes to synthetic holster rigs, even the least expensive of the lot generally hold up well. So, durability and

practicality are the two main factors offered by the synthetic rigs.

For 9mmP shooters, there is a type of rig which should be considered, even if the shooter plans only to carry the pistol informally. That is a shoulder holster rig. Such rigs are among

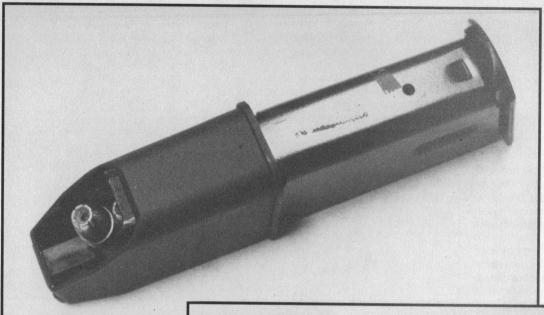

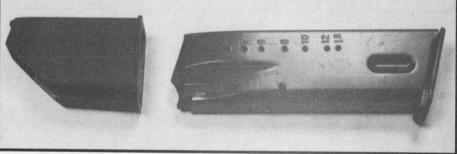

An inexpensive magazine loader can help reduce the abuse of a shooter's thumb.

the most versatile of all. They afford concealed carry yet serve well when used in any of the open carry modes. For hunters who carry a 9mmP as part of their battery, a shoulder rig often is the handiest of all designs.

EXTRA MAGAZINES OR CLIPS

Even though many current production 9mmP handguns come with two magazines, shooters find they may want to acquire either more magazines, or ones with different capacities than whatever came standard with the pistol.

It is always prudent to have at least one spare magazine. Magazines are notorious for two things: They are either lost or they are damaged. Either way, they are useless.

Because they are designed to be removed from the handgun, they are subject to being lost, left behind or disappear in some other way. Hence, a backup spare is in order.

Magazines also suffer all kinds of abuse, and can be damaged enough to inhibit or preclude proper function. They find themselves being dropped, kicked, stepped on and even run over by motor vehicles! Once bent, a magazine likely is no longer serviceable and should be replaced.

One of the most common areas to suffer damage is around the magazine lips which hold the top cartridge in place and ready to feed. When the lips become bent, function suffers. For example, if they are bent outward, they may not hold the cartridges in place. If bent inward, they may not allow loading, or they may prevent the top cartridge from feeding into the

chamber. Either way, function suffers.

If left compressed long enough, a magazine spring can lose power and cause the pistol to malfunction by not keeping the top cartridge properly in place. The remedy in such cases is to replace the spring. However, in most magazine malfunction scenarios, it is best to replace the whole thing.

Even though some magazines can be bent back into shape, it is common for the entire magazine to have been sprung enough that attempts to put it back in shape will result in inconsistent performance. That can be the most frustrating and potentially dangerous. It simply is not worth the hassle to deal with a bad magazine. It is simply best to replace it.

Replacement magazines come in many forms. There are factory replacements which are identical to those supplied with the pistol when it was new. And, there are clones of the standard magazines. Some are as good as the originals, some are better and some are not as good. Buyer beware!

Some shooters like to acquire spare magazines made of stainless steel, even if the original magazine was made of blued steel. Ease of maintenance is generally the moving force in such cases.

Or a shooter may want to acquire a spare magazine which has more capacity than the standard one provided with the pistol. Check local laws before acquiring really high-capacity magazines. Anti-gun forces of late have been pushing heavily to limit legal magazine capacities.

For those who shoot 9mmP revolvers, any of the many kinds of clips might be handy, if not required for functioning and quick reloading. These clips are usually flat stampings of spring steel which hold cartridges in place when they are put into the cylinder. The most common types are third-moon, half-moon and full-moon clips. Third-moon clips hold two cartridges, half-moon clips hold three rounds, and full-moon clips hold an entire cylinderful of ammo — either five or six rounds, depending upon the handgun in question.

In addition to aiding in the quick extraction of empties, these clips also serve as a form of speed loader. In the case of full-moon clips, an entire cylinder can be charged in a single movement by dropping the loaded clip into the cylinder, or the cylinder can be unloaded by a single push on the ejector rod.

Shooters who use 9mmP revolvers should consider a good supply of clips to be mandatory. Since these clips are small, thin and light, they can be misplaced or easily lost. They are inexpensive, and it is advisable for anyone who uses them to lay in a good supply.

GRIPS

The handles — or grips — which come standard on 9mmP handguns generally work fine for most shooters. In fact, of all the pistol sizes, the 9mmP family seems to fit more sizes and shapes of hands than any other. Grips generally are neither too large nor too small. Yet, there are a number of reasons why a shooter might want to install different grips.

Most important among those is handling quality. Grips which are configured in such a way that they enhance the handling qualities of the pistol are definitionally valid. By changing grips, a shooter can slim the handle area, fatten it up or add stabilizing features like finger grooves or a thumb shelf.

In addition to a wide variety of aftermarket configurations, there are custom-made grips which are crafted specifically to an individual shooter's hand. These vary in price and degree of work. Thus, they can be relatively inexpensive, or they can cost a lot. Needs of the individual shooter dictate what is best.

In addition to handle design, the material from which the grips are made can be an important consideration. For example, are alternative grips being installed purely for functional purposes, or is there a decorative aspect, as well?

Handgun grips have been made from about every kind of material imaginable. Standard factory grips generally are limited to wood, hard or soft rubber or plastic.

Replacement grips might be any of those materials or something more exotic. It is probably safe to suggest that if a type of material could be used for a handgun grip, it probably has been. Among the more common materials are metals, animal antler or horn, ivory, or some exotic variant of them.

Add to all of those above the growing number of high-tech synthetic materials which look like any of the natural materials, and what the grips are made of is limited more by the imagination of the maker than anything else.

SIGHTS

Generally in the industry, current production 9mmP handguns come equipped with a basic set of sights which sometimes feature the three dot system. There is one dot (usually white) on the left side and one dot on the right side of the rear sight, and a third dot on the rear of the front sight. The idea is that the shooter need only align the three dots in a horizontal line and the pistol is on target. Such a system allegedly works well in low light conditions. Some shooters like them, others don't. If the dots are a distraction, a couple of daubs with a felt marker can eliminate the problem.

Most sighting systems which come standard on production 9mmP handguns feature drift-adjustable rear sights to adjust the left-to-right bullet placement. Few are equipped to adjust for elevation. With such systems, changing the elevation of the bullet placement is intended to be accomplished by using a higher or lower front sight — most of which are drift-removable in some sort of dovetail slot in the slide.

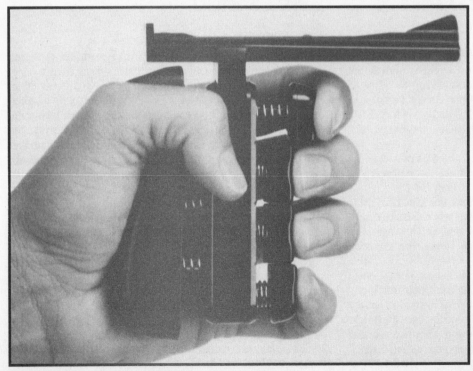

The Grip-Master develops a shooter's strength while enhancing firearm control.

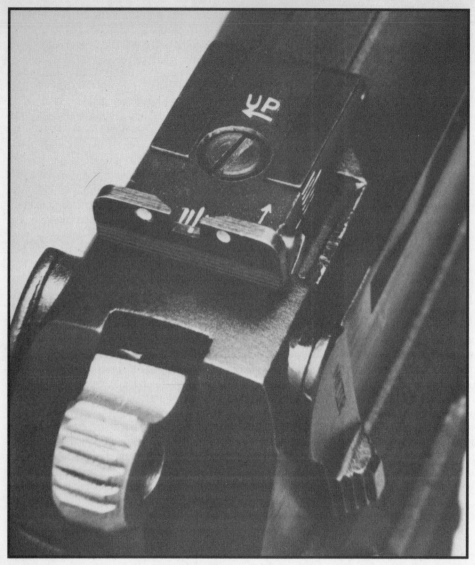

The Ruger P-85 sights from Pachmayr have windage and elevation screws that are micro-click-adjustable.

If the shooter wants to fine-tune the sight picture to the bullet placement, or if he intends to use a variety of different loads, sighting systems which are designed to be adjusted might be in order. There are many different designs available, at a wide range of prices, depending upon whether basic adjustment is desired, or whether repeatable target-level adjustment is needed.

Some shooters want to have sights which work well in the dark. Most of these shooters happen to be law enforcement officers, but there could be some civilian interest in such sighting systems. Most common among this kind of sight is the variety which uses tritium — a slightly radioactive substance which glows in the dark. Such sights, however, are relatively expensive and are valid only if there is a real need for them.

Another form of sighting system is the red dot "scope." Some red dot systems are also slightly telescopic, but many are merely a form of optical sight which shows a glowing red dot in the middle of the glass as the shooter looks at the target. These units normally are battery powered and feature dial adjustments much like those encountered on traditional telescopic sights. In use, the shooter needs only to put the dot on the target and squeeze the trigger. Such systems are preferred by some of the rapid-fire competitive shooting crowd.

There is also a growing number of laser sights available. These sights transmit a beam of light (laser) which, when adjusted properly, shows a red dot on the target where the bullet will hit. Such sights are handy for nighttime work, but they require a power source such as a battery, and are subject to the many things which affect electronics. Such sights are without doubt going to be a major factor in the future, but as of this writing, remain less than totally acceptable for the widest ranges of applications.

Finally, there are standard telescopic sights being used on some 9mmP handguns. As they do when used on long guns, telescopic sights on 9mmP handguns can offer an added level of tactical accuracy. Bullet placement can be much more precise. However, some shooters find it takes a considerable amount of practice for them to become totally credible with such sights.

Whenever any of the "scope" sights are used, shooters are well advised to pay total attention to the mounting system. Such sights are no better nor any stronger than the mechanism which holds them to the firearm. When installed, it is critical

These Master Red Dot Scopes from Simmons are lightweight and can be finely adjusted to the needs of the shooter.

that the entire rig be assembled properly, and that it be tightened and secured well enough that it won't work loose. When such systems become loose, they are worse than having no sights at all.

ASSORTED ACCESSORIES

Oddly, there are relatively few other accessories for 9mm use. Perhaps the most prevalent of such accessories is the magazine loading device.

Charging 9mmP high capacity magazines can be a real chore. And, it can be tough on fingers and thumbs as the shooter repetitiously fights the spring tension to slide cartridges into place.

Most common among the magazine charging tools are the small, boxy-looking fixtures which slide over the top of the magazine and make it easier for the shooter to depress the spring and follower, and rounds on top of them, enough to slip added rounds into place, one at a time.

Another magazine-related accessory is the aftermarket base plate or shoe. There are a number of different types of accessory bases, depending upon what the shooter wants them to accomplish.

For example, there are bases which also serve as magazine extensions. Most of these afford one or two more rounds to be held by the magazine. They are simply add-on bottoms for the magazine. Commonly, shooters who use one of the shorter-gripped compact 9mmP handguns might want to extend the magazine a bit to put total capacity at a higher level. However, there are trade-offs, and one of them is that, with the extension, the handle area of the pistol will be larger — which may or may not negate the advantages of using a compact handgun in the first place.

Another popular add-on is a magazine base extension which also provides a finger rest for the pinky finger. These usually are encountered on small-handled pistols carried by large-handed shooters.

Some kinds of competitive shooting call for quick changes of magazines. Shooters in such sports want the empty magazine to pop out, or at least fall out freely when the release button is pushed. For them, time is important, and they don't want to have to fumble around, removing an empty magazine. Also, when their portion of the event is over, they need to go back and retrieve the magazines they have strewn all over the ground.

As a result, it is common for such shooters to attach a colorful base to their magazines which also add enough weight to assure that the magazine exits the pistol cleanly and quickly every time.

Cleaning and other maintenance tools also are necessary. Fortunately, most 9mmP handguns come from the factory with at least a cleaning rod. Many also are furnished with a bore brush. Target model handguns often are provided with specialized sight adjustment tools, which can be anything from a basic screwdriver to some form of exotic tool which fits a specific sighting system. Add to such tools the necessary solvents and lubricants, and the gun care front is covered well. These items need not be expensive, but they should be obtained.

So, it is easy to see that even though there is no need for any accessories to own and use a 9mmP handgun, some or many of them can make the whole process easier or more enjoyable.

When it comes to accessories, it is sound advice to suggest that the basics be addressed first. There will be plenty of time to add a gadget here, a goodie there. When in doubt, shoot more and become more proficient with the handgun itself.

The Laser Is Not A Cure-All For 9mm Inadequacies, But Is A Definitive Aid To The Handgun's Accuracy

This BA-2, five megawatt sight from Laser Devices, Inc., is designed to conform to the shape of the Walther P88.

Mention the term "laser" among the general population, and images of Star Wars characters dueling with laser swords pop into the minds of some. Others will perceive the subject as some high powered light beam being used for everything from intricate surgery to the Strategic Defense Initiative that some think might involve the zapping of military targets on earth from devices in satellites orbiting earth.

In a practical sense, lasers in the world of the 9mmP these days are limited to sighting devices. Briefly, the laser in such applications is little more than a red beam of light which shines onto a target and shows the shooter where the bullet will go if the trigger is pulled.

From a scientific perspective, this may constitute a rather limited, fringe use of the laser. Perhaps so, and perhaps in

years to come the laser itself may become the "projectile," replacing the bullets it sights for now. But that is in today's terms nothing more than a form of dream — a fiction which may be fascinating to imagine, but impossible to realize.

Even laser sights as they currently are constituted are not cure-alls and end-alls for shooters. Hardly. They are not even useful in a way so universal as the traditional sighting methods. However, laser sighting devices have demonstrated that in a number of situations, they do have merit and, in a smaller arena, they are the preferred type of sighting system.

In the late 1970s, when laser sighting systems first began appearing on the shooting front, they were viewed primarily as curiosities. Some shooters saw them as little more than interesting "toys" which could not be taken seriously. To a degree, that viewpoint had merit, because the initial devices

The sight from Laser Devices fits snugly on the P88. It attaches easily to the auto without the need of a gunsmith.

were bulky, had wires hanging around to snag on anything and everything, and were heavy enough to change the handling characteristics of whatever firearm they found themselves mounted upon.

Like most things in the electronics, miniaturization has happened to the laser aiming element of the firearms industry. These days, the laser sighting systems available are small enough and light enough, including power sources, that they no longer turn a fast-handling firearm into a boat anchor. They are small enough, in fact, that some are now being built into the firearm itself. Without question, laser sighting systems will become integral in a number of firearm models on the market over the next few years. It is beginning to happen on a limited basis as this writing is being completed.

There will be no effort here to attempt to create any form of "laundry list" of laser sighting systems available on the market. After all, that segment of the industry is evolving quickly enough that any list compiled as of this writing would no doubt be obsolete by the time the book is published. Or, certainly, it would be out of date by the time many readers pour over the pages of this tome.

Much of the meaningful development among laser sighting devices has hinged around a change from the use of a tube to the use of diodes. It was a move into solid state hardware, and that afforded entirely new possibilities in the arenas of weight reduction, size reduction and tactical usage.

Regardless what the exact design and make, laser sighting devices as a classification are uncommonly simple. This revelation should come as no great surprise. Any meaningful sighting device throughout history necessarily has been simple. Consider the fact that with the development of the various laser and red dot sighting systems over the past couple of decades has come more real change in sights than had happened in the entire history of hand-held firearms.

Simply put, there are three basic types of sighting systems extant in Gundom. There are the "iron" sights which require the alignment of two sighting fixtures with the target, optical sights which require the alignment of some form of reticle with the target and electronic sights. The electronic sights are, for practical purposes, quite recent on the scene. The other two types of sighting systems have been around for more than 100 years, in the case of optical sights, and since firearms began in the case of iron sights.

Laser sights as they are now constituted emit a focused beam of light. When mounted on a firearm and adjusted so the dot of light which appears on the target is at the same spot where a bullet will go when fired, these sighting systems offer an expansion of possibilities for shooters — especially since most companies offer units that do not preclude the use of the more traditional sighting systems. That means that in situations when traditional sights work best, the shooter can use them, or when the laser beam is a better bet, it also is available.

As much as most shooters have been aware of the presence of laser sighting systems since their inception, relatively few have availed themselves of opportunities to use them. Cost prohibits flippant trials by the masses, because the devices

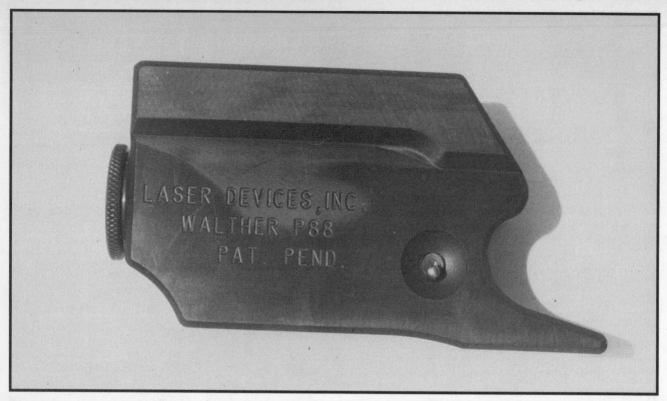

The major portion of the BA-2 is the form-fitting mount that is built for a specific gun. The laser slides inside the case.

typically cost more than $100 and very often can cause the outlay of several hundred dollars, by the time everything is factored into the equation.

But there is another factor which has retarded universal acceptance of this new form of technology among the rank-and-file shooters. It is called "tradition." Face it, tradition guides the lives and activities of most shooters. We are, as a group, traditionalists in the purest sense of the term. Change, when it does happen, comes reluctantly. Anything "new" must prove itself over and over again before it can take its rightful place in the overall order of things. So it has been with the laser sighting systems.

One could hardly fault many shooters for taking any step toward change with less than total deliberance. Shooting, after all, is a most serious business. In all but the most informal of target and plinking disciplines, shooting is at the least a serious matter, and quickly becomes a question of life and death in other manifestations.

With all of this in mind, the author, a newcomer to the actual use of laser aiming devices, headed to the range for a test drive. What is it really like to shoot a laser-sighted firearm? The answer is an unqualified "different."

There were several techniques and tricks which had to be learned. Equally large were the number of habits which had to be "unlearned" before the laser sighting systems began to show what they really could do. Perhaps that is among the major stumbling blocks for manufacturers of laser sighting systems. They are useful immediately to anyone who is not familiar with traditional sighting systems, yet require some degree of re-learning and re-thinking for those who have developed a level of proficiency with the more traditional systems.

For newcomers and re-educated firearms veterans, using the laser sighting systems is as simple as pointing at the target and squeezing the trigger when the red dot shows up where the bullet should go. For shooters who refuse to open their minds to the changes in technique needed to maximize the potential of the laser systems, they represent a form of frustration which might be considered unacceptable.

For the laser sighting system test drive at the range, the author opted to focus on some of the products from Laser Devices, Inc., one of the original companies in this segment of the industry. That company's BA-2 series of sighting devices was used, one mounted on a Walther P-88, the other mounted on a Glock 17 — both well known 9mmP handguns.

By far, the most difficult procedure involved the sighting-in of the units. They were not more difficult to adjust and put on-target than are many of the optical sights (scopes), but as any experienced shooter realizes, fine tuning the adjustments for optical sights can cause a noticeable degree of effort and is not always without frustration.

Once sighted-in, the actual use of the laser sights demonstrated to the author that one needs to re-think how one shoots if the advantages inherent in laser sighting are to be realized fully. It simply takes practice.

The first challenge involves holding the pistol steady. Even if laser sighting devices were never used in any tactical situation, they would have intrinsic value as practice tools. With optical or open sights, the shooter is not nearly as aware of just how much the muzzle is jiggling when the red dot dances around on a target downrange.

Laser sighting systems help extend the only acceptable form of gun control there is — control of the gun in your hand. The bouncing light beam on the target literally forces the

Because of the way the BA-2 is mounted to this Walther P88, it doesn't prevent the use of the auto's regular sights.

shooter to concentrate on basics like hold. Yes, it takes a while to get to the point where the dot on the target is standing still enough to attempt a shot.

It is in the act of shooting, though, that beginners have an edge over experienced shooters when it comes to acclamation with the laser system. A new shooter, whose mind is not clouded with habits and techniques developed through the years, simply puts the light beam on the target, keeps it there and fires the shot. The experienced shooter, armed with ingrained reactions to sight pictures, usually compounds any problem with such reactions.

For example, when aligning open sights with the target, there actually are inverse relationships created among the three points of focus. With the laser beam, there is only a direct relationship. What this means in practice is that experienced shooters at first can find themselves walking the beam right off the target when they try to move it from the side to the center. A few minutes of concentrated effort can overcome this tendency.

The single most difficult task for the author was in the trigger control department. Keeping the red dot of light on the target while pulling the trigger truly was a challenge. It felt different, looked different and was just plain weird. Again, however, following a brief period of practice, these problems disappeared and the system became effective — even in the author's hands.

Another old habit experienced shooters must learn to overcome is that of automatically trying to align the iron sights

and then look for the red dot on the target. Frankly, the quickest way to learn to use laser sights is to hold the pistol in some unorthodox way which precludes looking across the iron sights. Hold the pistol at hip level or, if shooting off the bench, purposely hold the head so high that there is no way to look down the slide or along the top of the barrel.

This altered relationship of the eyes and the firearm force the shooter to focus on the light dot on the target, moving it to the desired spot solely by using instinctive hand-eye coordination. Once this practice is undertaken, the laser system becomes quicker to use and contributes to more accurate bullet placement.

It took the author a 50-round box of ammo to adjust to some of the basic procedures. Before the expenditure of more than 100 rounds, there was a noticeable degree of proficiency beginning to develop. It became clear that with regular practice and added familiarization the use of laser sighting systems could become as "second nature," as have the usage of the other more traditional sighting systems.

By the end of a single range session, the author was hitting as quickly and accurately with the laser sighting system as with any other. And, at the longer ranges (like 30 to 40 yards), the groups were actually better with the laser than with the regular sights.

Keep in mind, however, that all of this was in broad daylight. This is the worst scenario for laser sight usage. Simply put, the darker things get, the better the laser systems look. In lighting as subdued as normal indoor environments,

Author tests the accuracy of the BA-2 sight from Laser Devices on a Glock 17. He fired the auto without using the standard factory sights.

laser sights are totally workable. When things begin to get dark, the lasers really come into their own — into an arena where they take the lead.

In the shooting industry, several types of groups normally serve as catalysts for change and serve as guiding forces when it comes to equipment. These include the military, law enforcement and serious target shooters.

Certainly, the pioneering forces in the use of laser sighting devices have come from the military and law enforcement communities. There are logical reasons for this. Laser sighting systems are most useful in some of the kinds of situations faced by military and law enforcement personnel.

Specialized units first put some of the laser sighting systems to the test in specific situations. Experiences dictated that the big, bulky and heavy systems which were offered initially had to change if they were to be valid. Changes continue to be made, and with each advancement in design, the useful potential of the system is expanded.

Currently, laser sighting systems offer effective ranges of several hundred yards (under the right lighting conditions). Yet, the really meaningful applications for laser sights involve across-the-room distances.

Obviously, law enforcement officers who must operate in the dark, or in darkened indoor areas, can make use of sighting systems which work best in such an environment. But the real future for laser sighting systems necessarily has to be in the hands of civilian gun owners and shooters. That is where the largest numbers exist.

For self or home defense, laser sighting systems make a lot of sense. Civilians, after all, have more options than do uniformed officers or soldiers. Civilians can custom-tailor their gear to their own specific needs and preferences. Also, civilians generally don't have to carry their gear on a duty belt, along with all kinds of other equipment for an entire working shift.

What this means is that civilian shooters can opt for a setup which allows them to use the standard sights on their 9mmP handguns, as well as the laser system. Bingo! What a concept! This suddenly expands from a question of whether one should have traditional or laser sighting systems in a situation that allows the optional use of either — or both. Things become more interesting all the time.

For example, if a person had a 9mmP handgun equipped with a laser sighting system for home defense, there would be no disadvantage, compared to the same handgun sans the electronic option. If worst came to worst, the pistol would still function the same way. This means that even if the owner, under stress, failed to turn on the laser system, or had been negligent and allowed the battery to drain, the firearm would remain at least as useful as it ever would have been without the laser system.

However, assuming the owner had maintained the power supply properly and remembered to turn on the laser system, the laser sights would afford an added tool at the moment of truth which could help make the difference between a hit and a miss. Is that not really what this discussion is all about?

Speaking of panic moments, there is an added advantage to the laser sights. They can be used effectively by people who do not know how to use standard sights. There is no effort here to suggest that people who are unfamiliar with firearms should be using them under normal circumstances.

But facts are facts, and some people simply refuse to take the time and effort to acquaint themselves with firearms. Yet, these same people are more likely to find themselves in life-threatening situations than are the firearms-fluent folks. To a degree, the subject here often involves the spouses of gun owners and shooters.

When such people are awakened in the middle of the night by a criminal intruder, it is a little late to think about practicing at the range. Instantly, it is do it or die time. Since laser sighting systems now are available routinely with switches which work when the pistol is grasped, there need not be a deliberate "turning on" of the switch.

What does this mean to an inexperienced shooter? In a

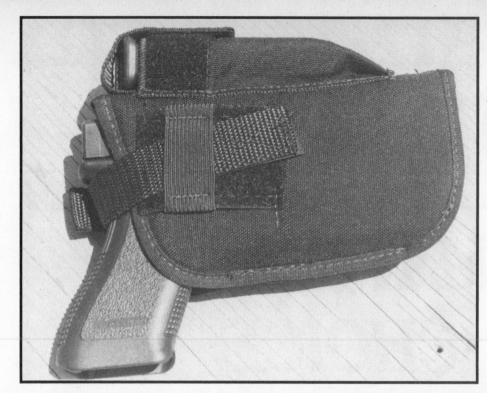

Laser Devices also makes holsters to accommodate guns with their sight systems attached. This holster holds a Glock 17, extra magazine.

The BA-2 laser teamed with a Walther P88 to produce this five-shot group at 25 yards. The special target from Laser Devices allows the shooter to see the laser's dot even in bright daylight.

moment of terror, all that the person needs to do is grab the gun, point it at the attacker and pull the trigger when the red dot is on the attacker. Certainly, such a scenario is not meant that one should preclude familiarity with firearms and range practice. However, in an imperfect world, laser sighting systems do offer advantages to those who refuse to prepare for problems.

Indeed, laser sighting systems are likely to develop in the future. Without question, they are a reality whose time has come. And, it is in the 9mmP arena that the laser sighting systems really make sense. These sights lend themselves to the kinds of situations in which 9mmP handguns routinely find themselves.

In a way, it is a form of high-tech marriage. Just as the 9mmP has redefined how many shooters operate, the laser sighting systems are in the process of redefining how sights are viewed.

Still, for the crusty old shooters who find anything with batteries to be foreign to the firearms ethic, there is bound to be some resistance. So it shall be. Laser sights, after all, are not the best bet in all circumstances, nor are they the best answer for everyone.

However, laser sighting systems are becoming more valid for more shooters all the time. They are indeed the sights of the future—at least until laser beams themselves replace the need for projectiles like bullets. Hmmmm.

CHAPTER Six

A MATTER OF CHOICE

Auto Or Revolver? Smith & Wesson Has Both For The 9mmP

Rick Kennerknecht uses a Smith & Wesson Model 3913 pistol in 9mmP. It's a highly accurate, compact package.

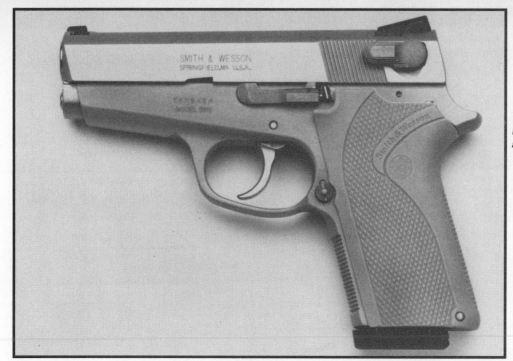

The S&W Model 3913LS has a satin stainless finish and a 3 1/2-inch barrel.

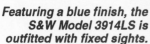

Featuring a blue finish, the S&W Model 3914LS is outfitted with fixed sights.

WHEN SMITH & Wesson introduced what it calls the "third generation" of semi-auto handguns, many shooters responded with a measurable level of sarcasm. "Yeah, right!" was heard frequently around the gun world. Other shooters, however, were excited, and justifiably so.

In my opinion, these new S&W 9mmP handguns are not just better than anything that company ever produced before, but are winners in every respect. Maybe it took a stroll all the way back to Square One to get all of the ducks in line.

Whatever it was, S&W struck pay dirt.

During the same period, S&W also did a lot of model house cleaning. That meant the company dropped a whole slew of models, which was another good thing. Frankly, over the years, there had evolved so many different models that it seemed like just about every handgun coming off the line had a different model designation.

For 9mmP shooters, S&W's new model numbering system makes total sense, and is easy understand. For example, there is the 3900 series of compacts, the 5900 series of

Roger Combs handles the S&W Model 5946 in 9mmP. This DA-only pistol is one of the best bets in the S&W lineups.

The S&W Model 6906 has checkered panels on the front of the trigger guard and grip for a solid grasp. It also has a coned barrel which enhances accuracy.

standard-size pistols with stagger-box, high-capacity magazines, and the 6900 series of compacts. Throw in the generic, budget-priced entry level Model 915, and you have the entire S&W offering of 9mmP semi-autos. Granted, there are several variations within most of the series groupings, but the differences encompass features like the finish of the pistol, or the kind of sights it has, rather than anything radically substantial.

All pistols in the third generation from S&W offer double-action on the first shot at least. By series, the models are:

3900 Series

The Model 3913 has a satin stainless finish, the Model 3914 is blue, Model 3953 is double-action-only stainless, and Model 3954 is double-action-only blue. Completing the 3900 series is the Model 3913 LadySmith.

5900 Series

The Model 5903 is satin stainless with fixed sights, the Model 5904 is blue with fixed sights, while the Model 5906 is satin stainless with fixed sights. There also is the 5906 option with the tritium night sight. Rounding out the 5900 series is the Model 5926 with a frame-mounted decocking lever, and the Model 5946 double-action-only.

The S&W Model 5946 in 9mmP has a flat profile. It carries and draws nicely.

6900 Series

S&W's Model 6904 has a blue finish, the Model 6906 has a clear anodized satin stainless finish and the 6906FNS has a fixed tritium night sight.

A detailed look at one example from each of the third generation series provides some insight into what sorts of roles each can play. By model, they are:

Model 3913

This is a compact handgun with a 3 1/2-inch barrel and eight-round magazine capacity. It is 6 7/8 inches long overall and weighs 25 ounces empty. Sights are fixed (drift-adjustable for windage), with post front sight and square slot rear sight. The three-dot system is incorporated for those who prefer to follow the dots.

The first shot is double-action, with successive shots in the single-action mode. This gun's hammer is bobbed flush with the rear of the slide when it is carried de-cocked.

Metal checkering is located on the front of the grip and on the front of the trigger guard, with checkering moulded into the sides and rear of the wrap-around black synthetic grips. Ambidextrous slide-mounted safety levers also serve as decocking levers, and the slide release lever is located on the left side of the frame just above the trigger area in the traditional place for such controls. Also in the traditional location just aft of the trigger area is the slide release button.

Two magazines are provided with the pistol. One has an extended shoe on the bottom for added finger control on the compact grip, and the other features a trim, flat base. Both hold eight rounds each.

Disassembly of this model, as well as the other models in the third generation, is simple and straight forward. After assuring that the pistol is unloaded, remove the magazine and allow the slide to return to battery.

Next, move the slide to the rear until the slide stop notch in the left side of the slide is aligned with the forward, rounded portion of the slide stop. Then merely press inward on the slide stop pin from the opposite side of the frame and remove the slide stop.

Now move the slide forward and off the frame. Once the slide is off, remove the recoil spring assembly by depressing the spring slightly and releasing it carefully from the small radial undercut in the barrel lug. Be careful here to avoid letting the spring and guide launch themselves across the room, or into your face. It really isn't a problem, but could be if it is not done carefully.

The barrel then can be pulled out of the slide. The barrel bushing on third generation pistols is built-in, so there is no concern there when it comes to field stripping. Reassembly is the reverse.

One note here, however. When replacing the slide, it is necessary to depress the ejector and firing pin safety levers so the slide will clear them when it is reinstalled.

The Model 3913 has an extremely thin profile. The frame is a scant .729-inch wide and the slide is not much thicker at .819-inch. Grip width is 1.050 inches and the widest part of the pistol is the distance across the ambidextrous safety/decocker levers. It measures 1.315 inches.

Shooting the 3913 is a lot of fun. The pistol holds and points well, and is easy to keep on target in either the single- or double-action mode. Trigger pull on the test pistol was a robust 14 pounds on double-action, and a legally "correct" nine-pounds on single-action. These numbers, however, are somewhat deceiving by themselves.

The trigger pull in either single- or double-action was extremely smooth and positive. Despite the seemingly heavy pull in either mode, working the trigger did not cause the pistol to stray off-target during the range workout. There is a secret to shooting any of the third generation S&W pistols well with the factory trigger systems, however. Simply use an authoritative, smooth squeeze and don't prolong the operation (don't rush, either). This procedure made all third generation pistols perform surprisingly well in tactical kinds of shooting situations — those for which these guns really were designed.

Because of its extremely thin grip area, the 3913 was the

The S&W Model 6906 is given a workout by Roger Combs. It's a higher capacity version of the compact Model 3913.

The S&W Model 915 in 9mmP is a high performance, high capacity handgun. It carries a 15-round magazine.

most difficult of the third generation pistols to hold steady, but that is far from a criticism. It held on target extremely well, and I had no difficulty hitting four-inch targets at random dis-

tances ranging from seven to 10 yards. Those targets, at varying heights and distances, were shot as quickly as the gun could be positioned, with no time for careful aiming.

When it was time for more serious work, the 3913 proved to be an effective handgun even at the 25-yard line where the same four-inch targets were hit repeatedly, both when the gun was hand-held and when the base of the slide was rested on a bench.

The pistol performed flawlessly with a wide variety of ammunition, including both factory and handloads, jacketed bullets and cast ones.

For a compact 9mmP, this pistol has a lot going for it. The 3913 could easily be categorized as a "can't go wrong" proposition for someone who needs a compact pistol, or for someone with small hands.

Model 5946

Of all the 9mmP pistols in the third generation line-up, the Model 5946 in double-action-only configuration is a top choice for all-around winner. The test model with fixed sights and DAO operation doesn't claim to be a paper-punching target gun, yet it shoots very well. What it does claim to be is one supremely serious handgun.

Because it is DAO, the only controls are the slide release lever and the trigger. This translates into about as goof-proof as a pistol can be.

The trigger pull is one of the smoothest, slickest 12 1/2 pounds I've ever felt on a production pistol. Coupled with the

Author tries his hand with the S&W Model 940 revolver in 9mmP. He found it fun to shoot and extremely effective.

full-bodied size of the grips, this is a natural pointing, easy-to-hit-with proposition.

Furnished with the pistol are two 15-round stagger magazines. It's just a lot of pistol in a pretty package. Finish on the 5946 is satin stainless, and the front edge of the trigger guard is checkered. Vertical striations on the front of the grip help keep a firm hold, and the wrap-around synthetic handle is checkered on the sides and back. For general carry and tactical kinds of shooting, the 5946 could easily be considered the best bet among the entire third generation lineup.

The same four-inch targets were hit at random distances from seven to 25 yards, and hitting them was so predictable that the rate of fire was increased so that the sights weren't even used. Rather, the target was spotted, the gun was pointed and fired in one fluid movement. Hits were both routine and predictable.

Model 6906

For lack of a more succinct way of putting it, the Model 6906 is essentially the fat brother of the 3913. Both are compacts, and the only real difference is the thickness of the grip and the number of rounds held in the magazine. The 3913 holds eight rounds, and the 6906 holds 12.

Because the Model 6906 has a larger grip area, it held steadier for my large hands. However, that steadiness was not a factor, because both pistols performed equally as well in the tactical shooting sessions. I had no problem hitting four-inch targets every time at distances of seven to 25 yards, whether

the gun was hand-held and shot quickly, or rested informally on a bench.

Trigger pull was 14 pounds in double-action, and nine pounds in single-action. Again, however, the pull was extremely smooth and slick, making the handgun perform admirably, even with the legally correct amount of pull.

Model 915

The Model 915 is without question the best buy in the S&W auto 9mmP line-up. It is a full-size pistol with 15-shot magazine. What it does not have is much fancy or many whistles and bells. It's a basic, nice gun.

Controls are located on the left side only. There is the combination safety/decocking lever at the rear of the slide, and the slide release lever just above the trigger on the frame. The magazine release button is located just aft of the trigger housing.

The flat black finish on the gun is actually rather appealing. It has fixed sights and an exposed hammer. Trigger pull was 12 pounds in double-action, and 7 1/2 pounds single-action. Again, the trigger system was smooth and slick.

For a basic 9mmP, it is totally credible and would make a fine all-around pistol for everything from serious tactical work to plinking fun.

Smith & Wesson created this model as an entry-level offering, but don't let that designation limit expectations. Granted, it is economically an entry-level proposition, because it is competitively priced. However, it is also a real

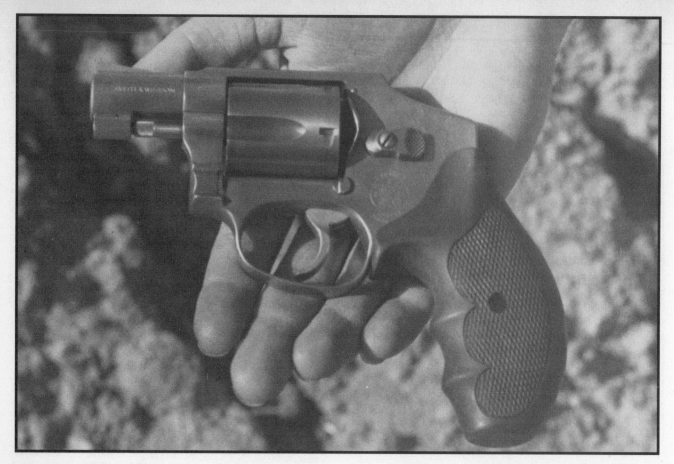

The two-inch barrel version of the S&W Model 940 weighs 23 ounces with the three-inch model hitting 25 ounces.

pistol, and is ready to offer years and years of service. In fact, during the range workout, it performed as well or better than any of the other S&W pistols during the tactical sessions.

S&W 9mmP Revolvers

Smith & Wesson also offers three revolvers chambered for the 9mmP cartridge. They are called Centennials, and one is the Model 642 Centennial Airweight. The other two are the Model 640 Airweight and the Model 940 Centennial.

The primary difference in models is that the Airweights have a lighter aluminum alloy frame. All three revolvers feature a serrated ramp front sight and a square notch fixed rear sight.

Barrel length on the Model 642 is two inches, while the barrel length on the Model 640 is three inches. Barrel lengths available for the Model 940 are two and three inches. Weight of the Model 642 is 15.8 ounces. The Model 640 weighs approximately 17.8 ounces, and the Model 940 weighs 23 ounces with a two-inch barrel, and 25 ounces with a three-inch barrel. All three models feature fully concealed hammers.

For this writing, a Model 940 with two-inch barrel was put through the paces on the range. Results were intriguing, and the snub-nose five-shot revolver performed well, considering what such a handgun is designed to do.

Such a handgun is not a target proposition. Rather, it is intended for recreational applications like plinking, or for more serious uses like self-defense. For either kind of activity, it is a good bet.

Depending upon where one wants to begin, the fact that it is made of stainless steel is a plus. Most guns of this configuration find themselves fired relatively seldom in a lifetime, but carried and/or stored for years. This means the best idea is to have the handgun made of materials that require little, if any, maintenance.

Whether it is to be carried or kept in a drawer, the outer configuration of the 940 works well. It has a concealed hammer, which means there is nothing to snag when it is pulled out and put into service.

The double-action-only feature of such a revolver is also quite handy. What it means is that operation is a no-brainer proposition. Just point and pull the trigger. When such a gun is used in defense modes, the stress factor is usually at its peak. Hence, the simpler the better.

The more the 940 was shot at random distances in plinking/combat modes, the more fun it became. It would be safe to stress that when it comes to snubby revolvers, the 9mmP cartridge is a superb alternative to any .38 Special ever made.

There is no effort here to suggest the stubby 9mmP cartridge has the potential to be more potent than the more voluminous .38 Special. However, in terms of snub-nose revolvers, the 9mmP cartridge offers higher tactical and actual performance — and that is from standard 9mmP loads, not some form of Plus-P proposition.

Like most cartridges, the 9mmP is aided by longer barrels, but, unlike some other cartridges, it reaches credible operating ballistics very, very quickly, which means that even when shot through a very short barrel, the bullet is cooking well.

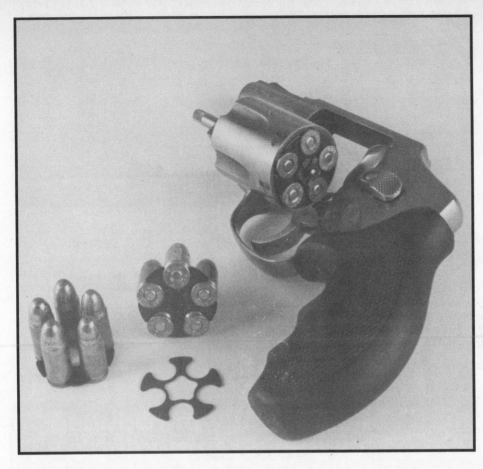

Full moon clips are supplied with the S&W Model 940. They make the lightweight handgun even easier to use.

To put this into perspective, the 940, using factory ammo, churned up velocities of 1000 feet per second with 124-grain loadings, and 1100 feet per second for 115-grain loadings, as measured over the Oehler 35P chronograph.

The Model 940 handled well in tactical testing. Its sights are basic, and that is totally proper. The low front ramp sight and square notch cut in the top of the frame for a rear sight are what is best for such a gun.

At random distances of two feet to seven yards, point and shoot tactics saw bullets hit within a couple of inches of each other for most shots. Because of the trigger pull, there was an occasional bullet pulled "off" target, but that distance was always less than half a foot, which means this is an effective handgun right out of the box.

Personal preferences, however, would cause me to have the trigger slicked-up by a competent gunsmith. Such a trigger job could eliminate the pulled fliers instantly. There is no need to reduce the weight of the pull, which on the test revolver was a constant 11 1/2 pounds and is proper.

Because of the likely uses of such a handgun, one would not want the revolver to go off inadvertently. The only thing that might be improved would be to smooth out the long, double-action pull. That could be done quite easily by any credible gunsmith.

The rubber grips with finger grooves provided on the 940 are both comfortable and useful. There is even a hint of a thumb groove at the top of the grip on each side, which means this design is equally credible for right- or left-handed shooters.

The revolver is supplied with four five-shot full-moon clips to hold the rimless 9mmP cartridges. There are advantages to the five-shot clips. The first is that they aid in extracting casings and/or unfired rounds from the cylinder, but there is another handiness to the clips. They serve as abbreviated speed loaders, as well. During tactical testing, the revolver was shot with and without the clips.

Small parts like these clips are lost easily. I wondered whether the handgun would work credibly without a clip—by simply loading 9mmP cartridges singly into the cylinder.

The 940 worked superbly in such a mode. Fired cases popped out easily when pushed one-at-a-time with a ball-point pen (anything, including a drinking soda straw, also would work well).

For a snubby, the 940 is a great bet. And, the more I test short-barreled handguns, the better the 9mmP looks as a viable cartridge. In the future, though, some maker could have a significant effect on the market by designing a 9mmP snubby which is totally a 9mmP proposition.

For example, the Model 940 is obviously a .38 Special design which has been chambered for the short 9mmP cartridge. The cylinder is long enough to accommodate a cartridge like the .38 Special, which is much longer than the 9mmP.

In other words, as a thoroughbred 9mmP revolver, the snubby could have a significantly shorter cylinder, and thus be significantly shorter and lighter overall.

Until that happens, the Model 940 S&W and its snubby siblings are certainly worth a serious look. They are outstanding designs for anyone who wants a small handgun which is totally easy and simple to use.

CHAPTER *Seven*

BROWNING &
THE NINES

Like The 9mmP, The Recently Introduced BDM Will Be A Mainstay In Browning's Inventory Far Into The Future!

Author fires the Browning BDM 9mmP semi-auto. He found it a substantial handgun in a smooth, slick package.

Browning's BDM (Browning Double Mode) 9mmP pistol is slim, trim and loaded with high performance features.

Browning's BDM (Browning Double Mode) 9mmP semi-auto is a design which will be valid far into the 21st Century, and it is a fitting sibling to the only other lasting 9mmP to wear that company's name. The BDM is the first design by the firm since the master himself defined what a high capacity autoloader should be like.

The inventiveness of John Moses Browning remains unquestioned in the firearms world, and his last pistol design is no exception. That handgun has been called variously the Model 1935 or Browning Hi-Power, and it continues in that company's line today.

Perhaps the best way to understand this particular pistol is to consider it an "improved" version of Browning's own 1911 design. It uses the same general lock-up design, but does not incorporate the sometimes troublesome barrel bushing of the 1911, nor the at times awkward pivoting barrel link.

Although the basic features of this short-recoil-operated, locked-breech semi-auto pistol would be enough to make it a desirable handgun, it was the magazine capacity which really set this model apart from everything else for decades. The Model 1935 features a magazine which holds 13 rounds of 9mmP. Add another cartridge in the chamber, and this is a 14-shot proposition.

The high-capacity magazine incorporates the staggered, double-column concept, and the Model 1935 had been around for several decades before other designs became generally available which used the high-capacity approach. That single feature not only set this model apart, but it guaranteed a validity which could not have been realized in any other way.

Yet, John M. Browning himself never lived to see this handgun reach production. Its patent was applied for in 1923, and was not granted until Feb. 22, 1927 — three months after the designer's death. Fabrique Nationale in Belgium began production of the pistol in 1935, hence the Model 1935 designation.

This pistol is 7 3/4 inches long with a 4 5/8-inch barrel. It weighs two pounds, three ounces. Through the years, in both military and civilian format, the pistol has been supplied with blade front and fixed rear sights, or with a variety of adjustable rear sights ranging from a folding leaf type on some military models to fully adjustable target sights on some civilian variations.

The Belgian army adopted it as its sidearm in 1935, and it also was used by other European nations, including Germany during the World War II years. Additionally, there were more than 200,000 Model 1935s produced during World War II for China in Canada, and the pistol became one of the official models of NATO countries during that international organization's long lifespan.

Although it is doubtless that the Model 1935 will become obsolete so long as there are centerfire cartridge handguns, it is a single-action proposition. To a degree, this reality has been viewed in recent times as somewhat of a drawback, given

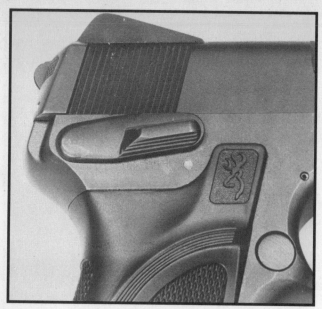

The right side of the BDM features the ambidextrous lever that serves as a safety, decocker and slide release.

The BDM disassembles into two major groups: receiver and slide. The disassembly is both simple and logical.

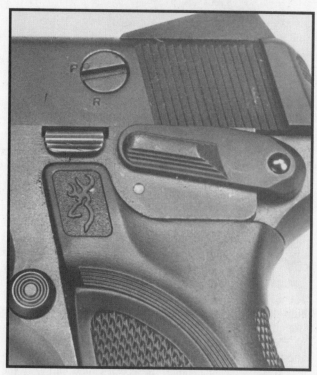

The BDM's take-down lever is just above the trigger, the magazine release to its right. The slide hold-open latch is between the Buckmark logo and mode selector.

the proliferation of double-action semi-auto handguns.

There have been some modifications of the design which feature a double-action capability, but the Browning offering continues to be single-action only. Through the years, there have been numerous knock-offs of the Model 1935, and many of them are in production today. This is just another testimonial to the validity of John Browning's last pistol design. Yet, it wasn't his only 9mmP handgun model. In 1923, Browning, while working with the French government, designed a 9mmP pistol with a large capacity magazine, only it was a blowback-operated model. This handgun, however, never was patented nor commercially manufactured. Later in the same year, Browning developed what was to become the Model 1935, and the rest is history.

Although the fact that the 9mmP cartridge itself, and the Model 1935, as well, are prime candidates for high capacity application, that single marriage of cartridge and pistol is not solely responsible for the model's long life and widespread acceptance.

The Model 1935 also happens to fit a wide spread of human hand sizes, and is noted for its inherent accuracy. Couple that with the high level of functional reliability, and the model is one of this century's true winners.

In fact, the Model 1935/Hi-Power was so valid that it wasn't until 1977 that Browning offered any other type of 9mmP handgun. Pressed by demands for a double-action handgun, Browning marketed the BDA (Browning Double-Action) pistol in 1977. This model was available for a short time in 9mmP, .45 ACP and .38 Super.

Frankly, this pistol might have been designated the "Brownauer," or the "Signing," because it was essentially the SIG Sauer Model P220 with a Browning name on it. This model was in the line for only that one year, and there were only about 1,000 of these handguns ever delivered.

For the next decade and a half, Browning's only 9mmP

offering continued to be the Hi-Power, despite recurring rumors through those years that some form of double-action handgun was in the offing. The company was not happy with the various conversion efforts to turn the Hi-Power into a double-action model, and it wasn't until 1992 that Browning actually produced its own handgun design with double-action capability.

It may have taken Browning a number of years to get fully involved in the double-action pistol market, but when it did make the move, the company again redefined the genre. It came in the form of the BDM (Browning Double Mode) semi-auto handgun.

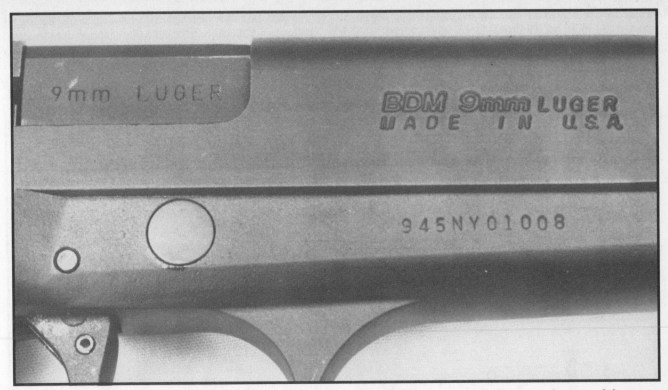

The BDM has a large ejection port. When a round is chambered, the brass is seen in the cut near the rear of the port.

Perhaps the best way to describe this new model is to explain that it features virtually all of the "whistles and bells" one might imagine for a single handgun model. After all, it is not just a double-action pistol.

Early generations of double-action autos had what many shooters considered to be a design fault which appeared to be a necessary evil for years. Pistols so designed operated as double-action handguns for the first shot, then as single-actions for the successive rounds.

This meant a gross disparity in both weight and length of trigger pulls from the first shot through the remainder of the shots. Lacking a viable alternative, many shooters accepted this phenomenon as the preferred trade-off, reasoning that the convenience of the double-action first shot outweighed the awkwardness of two distinctively different types of trigger pulls.

During this period of prolific handgun design development, some companies addressed the problem of differing trigger pulls in another way. They offered double-action-only models which incorporated the same weight and length of pull for every shot.

Although this type of system was applauded by many folks in the gun world, it is necessary to understand the frames of reference extant during that transitional period.

A large percentage of those who carried and used handguns on a daily basis had cut their teeth on double-action revolvers. Typically, those revolvers could be fired in double-action mode simply by pulling the trigger for each shot, or they could be fired in single-action mode by cocking the hammer before firing. The only major drawbacks of the double-action revolver involved relatively small ammo capacity (generally

Because of its simple design and ease of operation, shooters don't hesitate to perform routine maintenance on the BDM. This has kept the guns in operation.

five or six rounds) and comparatively slow reloading capability — even with any of the speed-loading devices.

Enter the Browning BDM semi-auto pistol. This Made-in-USA handgun is unique in that it can act like a double-action revolver, a double-action semi-auto or even a single-action gun, depending upon the whims of the shooter. This switch in operation can be accomplished by rotating a round, slotted mode selector on the left side of the slide just above the grip.

By rotating the selector to "P," the handgun is in the pistol mode. Rotate the selector to "R," and it is in the revolver mode. The selector can be moved by a screwdriver, a thin coin, or even with the "screwdriver blade" nub on the rear base of the magazine.

When in the pistol mode, the handgun operates like traditional double-action semi-auto pistols. The first shot is double-action, and successive shots are single-action with shorter and lighter trigger pulls.

However, a combination decocking lever/safety/slide release lever on both sides of the slide offers the shooter still another option. This lever works similarly to the decocking levers on many other handgun models, but once the BDM is "decocked," the double-action trigger pull is both shorter and lighter than it is on an initial double-action shot from the full hammer-down position, yet somewhat longer and heavier than it is in full single-action form.

When the gun is switched to the revolver mode, the trigger and hammer mechanism behave like that of a double-action revolver, with a consistent double-action trigger pull for each shot. No other handgun offers this much variety in operational modes.

The list of up-to-date features seems endless on the BDM.

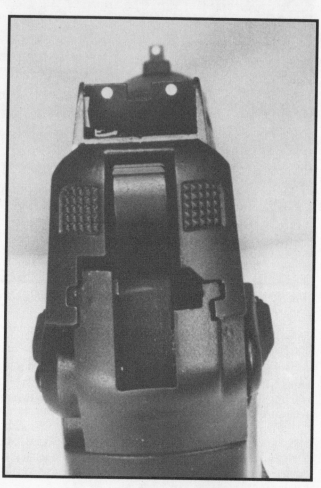

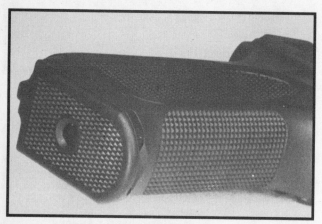

Checkering is where it's needed. There's checkering on the front of the grip and bottom of the magazine.

Above, the BDM features a three-dot sight system. Left, this Browning Hi-Power has factory optional fully adjustable target sights.

Charles Conyers fires the Browning Hi-Power. The handgun has a well-deserved reputation for being highly accurate.

It has a removable front blade sight; loaded chamber indicator; two redundant, passive, internal safety systems (hammer block safety and a firing pin safety which disengage when the trigger is almost fully rearward); snag-proof hammer; black, moulded, wrap-around grips which are checkered on all sides; bevelled magazine well; all steel frame and slide; reversible magazine release; checkered front strap; extended lip at the bottom of the magazine which holds 15 rounds; gripping extensions on each side of the slide to complement the grooves for easier slide cocking; and checkered thumb surfaces on either side of the hammer to help assure that the slide remains in battery when holstering the handgun.

That's a large list of features, but it is not all. The grip is designed into the frame, affording the BDM an uncommonly narrow compactness. And, the rear sight is Allen wrench adjustable for windage.

In function, the BDM is a recoil-operated semi-auto with no dramatic surprises. Rather than focus on some totally new or distinctively different general operations design, the company opted to use established and proven technologies, but offer them all in a single handgun. And it works.

Disassembly is simple and straight-forward, beginning by rotating the take-down lever on the left side of the frame just above the trigger, after pulling and locking the slide rearward (always make certain the handgun is fully unloaded before beginning the disassembly procedure).

Simply move the slide slightly more rearward after rotating the take-down lever clockwise a bit more than 90 degrees, and the entire slide group can be removed by sliding it forward.

Once the slide is removed from the frame, it is simply a matter of disengaging the head of the recoil spring guide from the barrel lug to remove the recoil spring, recoil spring guide and barrel. This procedure is virtually identical to that of the

The business-like Browning BDM, available for only one year, looks a lot like the popular SIG Sauer P220.

traditional Hi-Power, even though the parts are somewhat different.

Full disassembly sees the slide, recoil spring and guide, barrel, frame assembly and magazine as component parts. Reassembly is the reverse.

Hence, even though the list of Browning 9mmP models is exceedingly short, considering that John M. Browning's first design was done in 1923, Browning has been a formidable name in the 9mm business for most of the life of the cartridge.

And, the new BDM promises to keep Browning in this segment of the industry for a long time to come.

CHAPTER
Eight

BERETTA'S MODEL 92 SERIES

This 9mm Is Available In Numerous Variations

The 92S is one of Beretta's basic double-action 9mm autos.

IF IT IS a Beretta 9mmP handgun, it's one of many in the long line of pistols in the 92 series from the world's oldest industrial enterprise. No other industrial enterprise in the world has been in business longer.

The Beretta story, of course, began in Italy. That was the year 1526, to be exact, and a time contemporary with Leonardo da Vinci. Through the years, the company expanded a number of times and remains a major force in the firearms industry.

The firearms industry around the world tends to have among its ranks some of the long-term operations. For example, Beretta may be the oldest industrial enterprise in the world. In a similar situation, Remington is the oldest company in the United States which is still engaged in its original manufacturing activity — making firearms. So much for that part of history.

Backbone of the Beretta 9mmP lineup is the full-size Model 92FS — a high-capacity, short-recoil semi-auto pistol that features an aluminum alloy frame.

Of all the 9mmP pistol designs in the world, the Berettas — and their clones — are among the easiest to identify at a distance, because they incorporate an open-slide design. That means most of the top of the slide is open. By comparison, other designs incorporate a solid slide with an ejection port. Because the Beretta design has an open slide, any problems with jams essentially are precluded — there is nothing there to catch.

Incidentally, this design also allows easy loading of one

There's not much size difference between Beretta's full-size Model 92SB (top) and the compact 92SB.

round at a time directly into the chamber, should the shooter opt for single-shot operation. And, when it comes to instructional sessions, this feature is handy, indeed.

During the earlier decades of this century, the Beretta look in handguns was not associated generally with the 9mmP. Rather, it was the flood of this company's pistols in smaller calibers, like .22 rimfire and .32 ACP that dominated a large part of the pocket pistol market.

However, by the late 1980s, it was the 92 series in 9mmP that would capture the handgun press headlines. The reason? The United States opted to retire the Model 1911A1 single-action .45 ACP in favor of the Beretta 92. The move literally sent shock waves through the domestic firearms industry in the United States. Although there was a fair degree of politics involved in the decision, politics always have played heavily in the adoption of any firearm design for the military. It was an historic move, however, from the standpoint that it was the first time since the American revolution that a foreign maker would be producing the official military pistols at the exclusion of a domestic-based operation.

Certainly, there were provisions that soon after adoption there would be facilities in the United States to produce the pistols, and that came to pass without incident. But in the process, that move alone served as a brutal wake-up call to some of the domestic operations who apparently thought they might have had a lock on the decision.

In overall military terms, the size of any contract for handguns falls somewhere in the lower reaches of the "pocket change" category. However, the message was delivered loudly and clearly. First, the U.S. military would adopt the standard NATO (North Atlantic Treaty Organization) handgun cartridge and abandon the .45 ACP which had been in service for about three-quarters of a century and through two world wars as well as a gaggle of smaller fights.

There had been a rather steady and somewhat strong emergence of the 9mmP on the American scene but, frankly, it was the Beretta breakthrough with the U.S. military that sent the 9mmP soaring in sales all around the United States.

The military adoption of the pistol and cartridge raised the consciousness nationally to a point that the 9mmP instantly took on an air of credibility it never could have achieved in any other way. And, as quickly as the credibility shot upward in some circles, it came under renewed fire from others. To this day, there is a measurable cadre of American shooters who consider anything associated with the 9mmP to be somehow un-American. Yet, what would anyone expect? A "foreign" cartridge chambered in a "foreign" pistol gave the KO punch to the single most successful and longest-running All-American military handgun/cartridge combination in history — the John M. Browning-designed Model 1911 Colt and the .45 ACP.

The phenomenon of the military switch, however, also triggered another onslaught. That metamorphosis occurred within the law enforcement community. Looking back on the era with the clarity of hindsight, one might conclude that it simply was the Time of the Nine. In fact, it was more than that. It was that brief point in American history when the entire concept of handgunnery changed — and changed dramatically. It not only changed how handguns were viewed, but rewrote tactics to be used both militarily and by police.

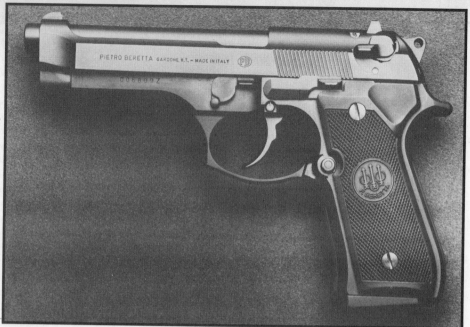

In the 1980s, the U.S. military selected the Beretta 92SB-F 9mm as its standard service auto, replacing the .45 auto.

Although the military had been using a semi-auto for decades, the standard police sidearms in most departments were revolvers. Most of them were .38 Specials or .357 Magnums, with a lot of departments adopting .357 Magnums through which their officers were forced to shoot the more sedate .38 Special loadings.

The dust had not yet settled in the military arena when the law enforcement community jumped enthusiastically onto the 9mmP, and Beretta was Johnny-on-the-spot with a high capacity 9mmP handgun that had just received one of the most formidable endorsements possible — Uncle Sam.

Regardless how one views the situation, the fact is that Beretta literally cracked the market in the United States wide open when it came to 9mmP handguns. Much of the resultant successes of other 9mmP designs in this country can credit the theater of opportunity to Beretta and its Model 92 series.

So what is this pivotal pistol all about? Actually, it is a rather simple, straight-forward design. And, although there are many model variations, all of the Beretta 9mmP handguns are extremely similar, differing primarily in length, height and magazine capacity or in features like double-action only as opposed to being double-action for the first shot, then single-action for the remainder of the shots.

In all, there are a dozen Model 92 variants. A table of specifications is provided nearby to detail comparative sizes and features. Additionally, there are a number of factors which are common among some of the variants, unique to others.

For example, all pistols in the 92 series feature a short recoil, falling block system. Also, most 92 handguns have

Blaine Huling bench tests a Beretta 92FS. Its magazine is a 15-round stagger-box.

exposed hammers — except the Models DS and D, which are without a hammer spur. (There is a hammer there, but since those models are double-action only, the hammer cannot be hand-cocked, so it has been bobbed to be flush with the rear of the slide).

There are two variations from the norm in action operation among the various Beretta pistols. Most are double-action and single-action, with the double-action feature designed for the initial shot. However, the Combat model is a single-action proposition, and the DS and D models are double-action only.

Rifling pitch among all of the Beretta 9mmP pistols is right-hand, six grooves with a twist of one turn in 9.8 inches. Incidentally, this means the barrels tend to stabilize the heavier 147-grain bullets well.

The front sight on most models is a blade integral to the slide. However, on the Competition Conversion Kit models there is a high front sight which is dovetailed to the counterweight. The rear sight on most models is a notched design which is dovetailed into the top of the slide. The rear sight on the Competition Conversion Kit, Target and Combat models is fully adjustable.

Safety mechanisms on semi-auto pistols have become major items of concern among shooters and among the administrators of departments who decide what handguns their troops will carry. Hence, it is not uncommon for modern pistols to have a number of interrelated safety mechanisms, all intended to help make the pistol goof-proof. Beretta pistols are no exceptions. The company describes it thusly:

All models: automatic firing pin safety; when the trigger is not pulled completely back, a blocking device secures the firing pin and prevents it from moving forward. Manual safety which separates the firing pin from the hammer, lowers the hammer, when cocked, and interrupts the connection between the trigger and sear. Models G: when the manual safety lever is released after having been activated to lower the hammer, it automatically returns to the ready-to-fire position. Models DS: the manual safety separates the firing pin from the hammer and interrupts the connection between trigger and sear. Models D: without safety. Models Combat: the manual safety interrupts the connection between trigger and sear and locks slide in its closed position.

The frames on the various Model 92 pistols are made of light alloy, sandblasted and anodized black. On the De Luxe models, the frames are anodized, then plated with either silver or gold, and on the Inox models, the frames are anodized gray.

Slides and barrels on the Model 92 handguns are made of steel, "phosphatized and Bruniton coated." The inside of the barrel is chrome-plated. In addition to the blue versions, the Inox models feature stainless steel slides and barrels with the frame anodized to match. All models come with one extra magazine. Grips are checkered and sandblasted plastic on most models, with rubber or wood grips available on request.

MODEL 92FS

The basic Model 92FS features a 15-round stagger-box magazine and has an ambidextrous manual safety which also functions as a decocking lever.

"With the safety on, the firing pin striker is rotated away from the hammer, physically disconnecting the front part of the firing pin from the hammer," Beretta explains. "Consequently, a falling hammer can never break safety. In addition,

Author test fires the Beretta 92FS-P Compact Type M. This model's grips are narrower to fit smaller hands.

This Beretta 92FS is dressed with wood grips. All 92FS guns have a hammer block safety.

when the safety is on it activates the trigger bar disconnect mechanism and severs the connection of the trigger with the sear mechanism. Finally, the firing pin blocking device, always engaged, prevents accidental discharges caused by internal movement of the firing pin if the weapon is dropped or strikes the ground muzzle down. When the trigger is pulled all the way back, it deactivates the firing pin block."

Also, all of the 92FS pistols incorporate a slide block, described by Beretta:

"This device, a modification of the hammer hinge pin, engages the slide groove and prevents rearward travel of the slide beyond normal function limits."

There is a reversible magazine release button on the 92FS pistols and the squared combat-style trigger guard is designed to aid in two-handed shooting.

The Model 92FS Compact Type M allows a straight pull on a double-action trigger for enhanced accuracy.

MODEL 92FS COMPACT

The Compact version retains the same basic features of the full-size 92FS pistols, including a large magazine capacity (13 rounds). Dimensions, however, are reduced on the Compact. Overall length is 7.8 inches, compared to 8.5 inches for the standard 92FS. Barrel length on the Compact is 4.3 inches (4.9 inches on standard), overall width is 1.5 inches (same as standard), overall height is 5.3 inches (5.4 inches standard), weight unloaded is 32 ounces (34.4 ounces standard) and sight radius is 5.8 inches (6.1 inches standard).

MODEL 92FS CENTURION

This variant retains the same frame and magazine as the basic 92FS, but has the reduced length of the compact version (7.8 inches overall with 4.3-inch barrel).

Above, the controls on the Beretta 92 Series include the magazine release button, trigger, slide release lever and the takedown lever. Right, the Model 92FS-P Compact Type M easily fit into the author's hand.

The Model 92FS-P Compact Type M can only handle a single-column, eight-round magazine. Its slender grips provide a flatter profile.

MODEL 92FS COMPACT TYPE M

This variant is identical to the 92FS Compact except that the "M" version has a narrower grip with a single-column, eight-round magazine. This sub-model is designed for those with smaller hands, or who want a flatter handgun profile through the grip area for carry purposes. The magazine release button on this sub-model is not ambidextrous.

MODEL 92G

This variation was designed to satisfy some requirements of the French. It differs from the 92FS in the safety.

"The hammer drop does not function as a traditional safety: when the lever is released after having been activated to lower the hammer, it automatically returns to the ready-to-fire position," Beretta explains. "The automatic firing pin block always stays on."

The Beretta 92G Police Special is a full-bodied service pistol. It is a no-frills, basic gun, ready for everyday use.

Above, author noted that the test 92G Police Special pointed extremely well, an important feature in a police handgun. Left, author puts the 92G Police Special to the test, using a variety of 9mm factory ammunition.

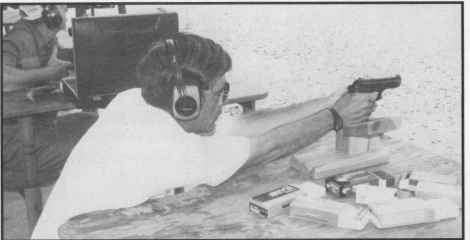

Blaine Huling put the Model. 92G Police Special through a series of rapid fire tests.

MODEL 92DS

This is the double-action only version of the standard Model 92FS.

"Every time the trigger is pulled, the hammer is armed and released," Beretta explains. "Without the half-cock position, the hammer returns to the disarmed position after every cycle of the slide. The hammer spur has been removed in order to provide a smooth flush effect at the back of the slide. The double-action has been softened to improve shooting precision. The manual safety is the same as that of the 92FS."

MODEL 92D

This sub-model is the same as the 92FS, except it is without a manual safety. Even the lever has been eliminated. It is a double-action only version, and also features the same bobbed hammer design as the 92DS. Overall, this is one of the smoothest outward appearing of the Beretta 9mmP handguns, and echoes a movement within the industry to eliminate the number of hand controls on the DAO (double-action only) sub-models.

MODEL 92FS INOX

This is the stainless steel version of the basic Model 92FS.

"The barrel, slide, trigger, extractor, safety and other components are made of stainless steel," Beretta reports. "The frame is manufactured in lightweight aluminum alloy anodized to perfectly match the other parts."

Grips are checkered black rubber, and the rear sight is Bruniton coated.

MODEL 92FS DE LUXE

These are the fancy entries in the Beretta lineup. There is an engraved blued version, as well as ones plated in gold or silver. Grips are highly figured, smooth-finish walnut, and each pistol comes in a cowhide-covered presentation case with extra magazine and cleaning brush.

MODEL 92FS TARGET

This variant is a full-on competition pistol which meets the UITS (International) standards for large caliber pistols. It has

The Beretta 92D is built for double-action only operation.

The Model 92D (left and below) is a double-action only auto. The hammer is bobbed to avert snagging and there's no manual safety.

a 5.9-inch barrel with an aluminum counterweight sleeve, fully adjustable sights and contoured grips made of walnut.

MODEL 92FS COMPETITION CONVERSION KIT

This kit allows conversion of a standard Model 92FS into a competition handgun. It includes a 7.3-inch barrel with counterweight and elevated front sight. The rear sight is fully adjustable, and the walnut grips are contoured.

MODEL 92FS COMBAT

These new handguns are being designed for the combat-style shooting disciplines. Operation is single-action only, and magazine capacity is 17 rounds. Some specifications still were being changed as this sub-model was being developed at the time of this writing.

This may be a long list of model variations, but the truth of the matter is that all share the same basic mechanical design. And why not? It seems to work well, all things considered.

As mentioned earlier, Beretta was in a position to capitalize on the new-found fondness of the 9mmP high-capacity semi-autos among members of the law enforcement community.

Factors which played major roles in Beretta taking such a large, early lead was the fact that Beretta was able to deliver a lot of handguns relatively quickly when the movement from revolvers to semi-autos took place.

Also, Beretta had a fairly highly developed system of factory representatives. That, coupled with an effective distribution network, didn't hurt. In short, Beretta took an aggressive approach to the U.S. market, and is still one of the biggest players. However, in the meantime, other companies have established major presences, but Beretta continues to be a force for still another reason — perhaps one of the more important ones when it comes to acceptance by budget-conscious administrators in public agencies. It's called price. And, the Beretta 9mmP handguns remain competitively priced in that arena.

If there is one thing the Beretta pistols are, it is easy to disassemble and reassemble. This is no mistake. They are designed in such a way that even a shooter who is fatigued or operating under hostile conditions can perform the tasks.

Disassembly is as simple as making certain the pistol is not loaded, removing the magazine and, with the slide forward and hammer decocked, pressing inward on the disassembly release button on the right side of the frame just in front of the top of the trigger guard, then rotating the disassembly latch (lever) which is located on the left side of the frame just above the front of the trigger guard. Then, in a single movement, slip the slide forward and off the frame.

The recoil spring and guide can be lifted up and out of the slide when the slide is held upside down in one hand. Some

Author found the Beretta 92 Series autos to be credible service handguns. Out of the box, they're ready for duty.

degree of care needs to be taken to avoid allowing the spring to "fire" out of position, sending itself and the guide across the table, across the room or into the face.

Next, the barrel can be taken out of the slide by pulling upward on the pivoting barrel lug, moving the locking block upward. The barrel then lifts up and out of the slide. This is about as far as the pistol needs to be disassembled for routine cleaning and field maintenance. Reassembly is the reverse process, and it is really just that simple.

Shooting the several variants for data for this chapter revealed that all were easy to understand, simple to operate and delivered good levels of accuracy, given the fact that they were not target models, and in some instances, were full-on combat versions.

The full size of the 92FS makes it totally controllable in the hand, and the accuracy achieved on all but one sub-model (92FS-P Compact "M" with Trijicon sights) was equal, whether the pistol was being shot from the bench, from a two-hand hold, or one-handed.

What this meant was that three to four-inch groups were the largest normally encountered, and it didn't matter under what conditions the shooting was done. From a target shooting standpoint, this may be less than exciting. However, from a tactical perspective, those are quite impressive groups, considering that all were essentially concentric. That meant that under any of the shooting conditions, the pistols delivered groups no larger than three or four inches in diameter at 25 yards. That is quite sufficient for most tactical applications.

Somewhat better groups were obtained with the 92FS-P Compact "M" with the Trijicon sights. The author felt this was due more to the fact that the sights were crisper and outlined themselves against the target better than the standard sights.

For the sub-models used for this writing, some of the author's impressions were:

MODEL 92G 3-DOT POLICE SPECIAL

This is what might be considered the basic Beretta offering for American law enforcement agencies. Essentially, it is the plain Jane version of the basic 92FS, full size and with fixed sights.

The pistol felt good in the hand, and the double-action trigger pull was long, but smooth and the let-off was consistent. That meant it shot well in the double-action mode. Trigger pull in double-action was approximately 12 pounds, with the pull in single-action mode being an even five pounds.

Single-action pull was virtually without travel; crisp and clean. In fact, the single-action pull on this pistol was exceedingly nice for an out-of-the-box police handgun.

During the shooting sessions, this particular pistol did not produce the smallest group of the Beretta line — nor did it shoot the largest group. Instead, it seemed to handle all loads at least okay for the kind of pistol it is, and it shot a couple of them surprisingly well for what is a no-trills, basic tactical handgun.

For example, 2-1/4-inch groups were produced by three different loadings: CCI Blazer 147-grain TMJ, American Eagle 124-grain metal jacket and Sure Fire 115-grain jacketed hollow-point. This performance is notable, because it shows that the pistol shot equally well with loadings that include the three major bullet weight classes ever used in tactical situations. Few 9mmP handguns will do that.

Groups measuring three inches were recorded for two loads: USA 115-grain ball and Remington 115-grain metal case.

The pistol seemed not to like the PMC 115-grain jacketed hollow-point loading too well, delivering only a four-inch group with that ammo. Consider, however, that this pistol's worst group was four inches at 25 yards off the bench. That's not bad — and the consistency was there, as the pistol performed similarly, regardless how many groupings were attempted.

Interestingly, the best group fired came from the author's cast bullet handloads. That loading is a 125-grain hardcast bullet over five grains of Hercules Unique powder, CCI primer and Winchester case. The groups measured an even two inches for the most part, expanding once to 2-1/8 inches.

Most impressive about this pistol was the consistency with which it handled any of the loadings shot. Such performance contributes significantly to the shooter confidence factor.

MODEL 92D POLICE SPECIAL

The general size and shape of this model is the same as the 92G. However, since this one is double-action only, there is no manual safety lever, and the hammer is bobbed. The author felt that the double-action trigger pull was better on this pistol than on the standard police model. It is a quick, effective handgun for daily use.

For some unknown reason, this particular pistol loved the author's cast bullet handloads. That loading features a 125-grain hardcast bullet over five grains of Hercules Unique powder, CCI primer and Winchester case. The best group of five shots from the bench at 25 yards measured an even one inch. Other groups fired to confirm that it had not been a fluke measured one inch for the most part, and expanded to 1-1/8 inches in one instance.

This particular pistol did not particularly like the USA 115-

grain ball loads. Five-shot groups were four inches at 25 yards from the bench. However, it must be noted that they were a consistent four inches, with nothing noticeably smaller, nor anything noticeably larger.

The story was pleasurably different with CCI Blazer 147-grain TMJ loads. The best group was 1-1/2 inches at 25 yards off the bench, and the largest group was 1-3/4 inches. Again, consistency was typical of the performance.

PMC's 115-grain jacketed hollow-point loads seemed to confuse the pistol. Its groups were both large and inconsistent. Typically, they were in the six-inch category, and the distribution of the bullets within the group seemed to be in a random placement.

The American Eagle 124-grain metal jacket loads produced a most uninspired four-inch group. Although this grouping at 25 yards off the bench was four inches in diameter, it was concentric. Subsequent groups fired repeated the performance, and were the targets to have been overlaid, the aggregate group for 50 rounds on the target would have been no larger than five to six inches.

MODEL 92FS WITH 3-DOT SIGHTS AND WOOD GRIP

The only thing that distinguishes this sub-model from the standard 92FS is the grip material — wood instead of plastic. For tactical work, the standard plastic grips on Beretta pistols work well.

However, for those who want a little dressier handgun for personal use, the wood grips are nice. In fact, they are some of the better looking of the factory wood grips on the market.

On the test pistol, the wood was dark, straight-grained walnut with nicely checkered panels on both sides of the grip frame. Medallions adorn the wood panels — a "PB" on the left and the Beretta arrow logo on the right.

MODEL 92FS-D CENTURION DOUBLE-ACTION ONLY

This was a fast-handling handgun that captured the author's affections. Outwardly, it was smooth — no manual safety and the hammer spur was bobbed off.

It was one of those guns that all the shooter needed to do was pick it up, point it and pull the trigger. How handy! And, it shot as well in double-action only as some handguns do in single-action. Trigger pull was about 10 pounds, but when the trigger approaches the point of let-off there is a positive feel which allows for quick and accurate shots.

Of all the sub-models used, this one was among the author's favorites as an all-around 9mmP performer.

Considering that this pistol is double-action only, the performance from the bench at 25 yards was surprisingly good and consistent. In fact, it did not matter whether it was fired from the bench, from the two-hand hold, or one-handed. Similar groups were produced under all conditions. Very impressive.

The best 25-yard group was produced by CCI Blazer 147-grain TMJ ammo. It was an even two inches. Sure Fire 115-grain jacketed hollow-points registered the next best group at 2-1/4 inches.

Groups of 2-1/2 inches were produced by USA 115-grain ball loads and PMC 115-grain jacketed hollow-points. The largest group, 3-1/2 inches, was recorded by American Eagle 124-grain metal case ammo.

Imagine that, a double-action only pistol which shoots random loadings into groups that do not exceed 3-1/2 inches at 25 yards. That's good tactical performance.

MODEL 92FS-P COMPACT "M" WITH TRIJICON SIGHTS

Normally, compact 9mmP handguns present problems when it comes to anything that approaches accuracy at distances of 25 yards or more. However, this Beretta offering is a notable exception.

It felt much different in the hand than did any of its other Beretta stablemates, and the feel was good. Much of that good feeling came from the relative size and weight of the slide/barrel group compared to the grip area. If the barrel and slide were much shorter, the feel would be entirely different and probably harder to control.

However, in this configuration it's is a real shooter. Overall, the trigger pull — double-action or single-action — was as good as any of the Berettas used, and better than some.

The grip/handle of the Compact is noticeably slimmer than the full-size 92 models. Yet, this slimness does not inhibit accurate shooting. The slim dimensions of the grip are possible, because this model has an in-line, single-column magazine that holds eight rounds.

It didn't seem to matter what ammo was fed into this little gem. It shot them all well, and one of them superbly. Consider that this is not a target handgun. It is a full-on tactical pistol with fixed sights. Yet, it behaved much like a target pistol.

For example, when it was fed the USA 115-grain ball loads, the first five-shot group at 25 yards from the bench measured one inch. Three more groups followed and they were virtually identical. That's good performance for just about any 9mmP handgun, to say nothing of a compact tactical model.

The story was good with other loads, as well. For example, with American Eagle 124-grain metal jacket loads, the pistol fired consistent groups of two inches, and the same size groups were produced when the pistol blasted away with Sure Fire 115-grain jacketed hollow-point loadings.

Remington's 115-grain jacketed round-nose loads also came in with groups in the two to 2-1/4-inch category — the same size groups produced by the author's handloads whether they were made with 125-grain hardcast bullets and five grains of Hercules Unique powder, CCI primer and Winchester cases, or whether they were made with the same components behind a 115-grain jacketed hollow-point bullet from Winchester.

CCI's 147-grain TMJ Blazer loads also registered groups in the two to 2-1/4-inch category. Winchester's subsonic 147-grain hollow-point loading put holes in the target in the same size area, and at the same point of impact, meaning this little gun seemed to like anything it was fed.

Whether all such compacts from Beretta will shoot this well is not known, but it is certain that this one particular pistol performed superbly. The author felt that the sights on the handgun contributed significantly to the consistency, because they presented a crisper, more well defined image than did the standard Beretta sights.

Overall, the entire Beretta line performed well — with one particularly memorable entry. There were no malfunctions of any kind with any of the pistols, regardless what loads were fed through the pistols.

Hence, it is easy to understand why Beretta continues to maintain a notable presence in the marketplace.

CHAPTER
Nine

THE 9mmP HANDGUNS OF COLT

This Cartridge Never Has Been a Big Item In Hartford, But...

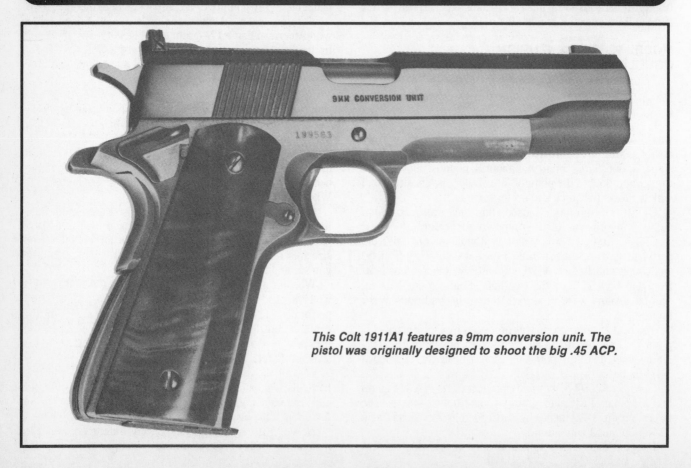

This Colt 1911A1 features a 9mm conversion unit. The pistol was originally designed to shoot the big .45 ACP.

Colt offers the Government Model in 9mm as part of its extensive Series 80 line-up.

WHENEVER ANYONE sits down to write anything about Colt handguns, the first key to be struck on the typewriter or computer should be the asterisk (*), because there are extremely few totally straightforward statements that can be made about those firearms. Usually, some form of footnote or other expanded explanation needs to be inserted, just to keep the record straight.

And so it is when it comes to Colt handguns in 9mmP. It is safe to suggest, that the 9mmP cartridge has been less than a big item with Colt. In a general sense, this world famous company has done little more than dabble in "nineness" through the years. Of course, what could one expect from a revolver maker that ignored the .44 Magnum until 1990?

One of the reasons it is so incredibly difficult to make definitive statements about Colt firearms is that the company has been in business so long and has made so many guns. With such a lengthy history, punctuated by the intermittent presence of its own custom shop operation, there are bound to be many non-standard guns actually leave the factory.

On the 9mmP front, the less frequently encountered type of handgun bearing the name of Colt is the Single Action Army. Yes, there were SAA revolvers made in 9mmP — intended for the European market. This is not at all uncommon. In fact, it is the rule rather than the exception for U.S. manufacturers to offer different chamberings for specialized foreign markets. And that's the way it was for the Colt SAA revolvers chambered for the 9mmP.

Although Colt may not have been in the 9mmP business in a big way ever, the company was involved with the cartridge for a relatively long time. Some of the very first of the Commander prototypes made in 1940 were chambered for 9mmP.

And, Commanders have been available in 9mmP all along. It took a number of years, but eventually Colt began to offer its time-proven, full-size 1911 Government model in 9mmP, as well as the double-action Double Eagle MKII/Series 90 pistol.

It was as though Colt was being led to the trough, kicking and screaming, when it came to the 9mmP, however. Yes, the company had offered that chambering for years in both of the Commander sub-variants, but it wasn't until the Series 80 pistols that the 9mmP was offered in the full-size Government Model. And, the 9mmP was added to the chamberings for the Double Eagle in 1991 — the same year Colt decided to take a major plunge into the world of the 9mm.

In 1991, Colt introduced the All American Model 2000 double-action, high-capacity auto. It was Colt's first high-capacity 9mmP handgun — exactly 89 years after the cartridge was introduced.

There is no effort here to grind upon Colt for its manufacturing and marketing decisions. It is just that when discussing the 9mmP, one cannot help but wonder openly why it took so long for the firm to read the writing on the walls.

To comprehend the change in attitude, one must view the circumstances under which the Model 2000 (and Colt's entry into the high capacity 9mmP market) emerged. Financial times were far from good nationally, and they had been bad for Colt for years. The company had been strapped by a number of problems, including everything from labor problems to corporate buy-outs. By the time 1991 rolled around, Colt needed something to give it a financial jolt — something to kick-start the empire and get it going again.

"This is the beginning of a new era at Colt, a time for new thinking, new products, and new dialogue with you, our customer," stated Colt's Manufacturing Company President Ronald E. Stilwell at the time. "It is a time of rebirth for an American legend."

Stilwell noted that the company planned to tie its long tradition (Colt started in 1836) with innovation — innovation which was to include the radically different Model 2000.

"To create these products, we have united the best of the past and the present: state-of-the-art technologies and leading edge manufacturing methods, such as computer-aided design (CAD) and computer numerical control (CNC) manufacturing techniques, with the time-honored care and craftsmanship you expect from Colt."

With that prologue, Colt unveiled the Model 2000 — billed

Colt All American Model 2000 is strictly a 9mm auto.

as "a radical departure from ordinary double action design." It was stated: "The new Colt Model 2000 is a locked breech, recoil-operated, double-action-only 9mm semiautomatic that sets new standards."

So much for the send-off. There were delivery delays and initial function problems that, at times, put its entire future in question. But the company was determined to make a go of it — after all, it had put an incredible amount of its eggs in the 2000 basket. But what is this gun?

Essentially, it is a high-capacity semi-auto that, due to its double-action-only trigger pull, offers the simple operation of a revolver. But it is much different from other double-action-only 9mmP handguns on the market. The action of this pistol is truly different.

"The All American is a radical departure from any other handgun you've owned," Colt reported when introducing the new model. "First of all, it shares important technology with the famous Colt M16 military rifle. The locked breech, recoil operated action features locking lugs integral to the barrel like those on an M16 rifle.

"Barrel and slide lock together and work as a unit, with the shot-after-shot consistency of performance needed for top accuracy," the company continued. "This precise rotary action reduces felt recoil by slowing down the unlocking cycle."

Because of the action design, the Model 2000 is easy and simple to use. For example, there is no external safety or decocking lever, and the roller bearing mounted trigger is smooth. Magazine release is reversible for right- or left-handed shooting.

Even some of the materials used in the pistol are space age. For example, the 2000 is offered with either a polymer (plastic) receiver or an aluminum receiver. Specifications are:

Barrel length .... 4 -1/2 inches.
Overall length .... 7-1/2 inches.
Weight (empty) .... 29 ounces with polymer frame, 33 ounces with aluminum frame.

Rifling .... Six grooves, right-hand twist, one turn in 10 inches.
Magazine capacity .... 15 in magazine, one in chamber.
Front sight .... Ramped blade, glare proof, fixed.
Rear sight .... Square notch, glare proof.
Sight radius .... 6-3/8 inches.
Safety system .... Internal striker block.

For development of data for this chapter, I used a Model 2000 with a polymer receiver. Repeated trips to the range resulted in a number of conflicting impressions and results.

For example, the pistol is a full-size service model handgun. Yet, the grip size and weight distribution make it feel much lighter than it actually is. That's nice.

However, for my hand size, relationship of the grip to the trigger, coupled with the longish trigger pull, took a while for any familiarity to develop.

The handgun was most at home during quick point-shooting at random targets located at random distances. It was common for hits to be made at distances of five feet to 10 yards.

But when the distance stretched to 25 yards and shooting was done off the bench, a number of things happened. With the author holding the pistol on a rest, 25-yard groups were frustrating. There would be two or three shots in close proximity to one another, then there would one or two "fliers." And the fliers, at times, were six inches away from the other shots.

I do not claim to be the world's greatest pistol shooter, so the initial feeling was that the problem resulted from some mysterious form of pilot error. Okay, that accepted, it was decided to have the pistol judged by an impartial entity — the Ransom Rest.

For those who never have experienced one of these marvels of modern times, the Ransom Rest is a totally adjustable machine rest which locks the pistol in place and allows it to be put precisely back into battery for repeated shots. When used correctly, the Ransom Rest allows a pistol to demonstrate its full accuracy potential — without the human error problems

COLT® All American™

Model 2000 • All Double Action
Semiautomatic Pistol
Caliber: 9x19mm

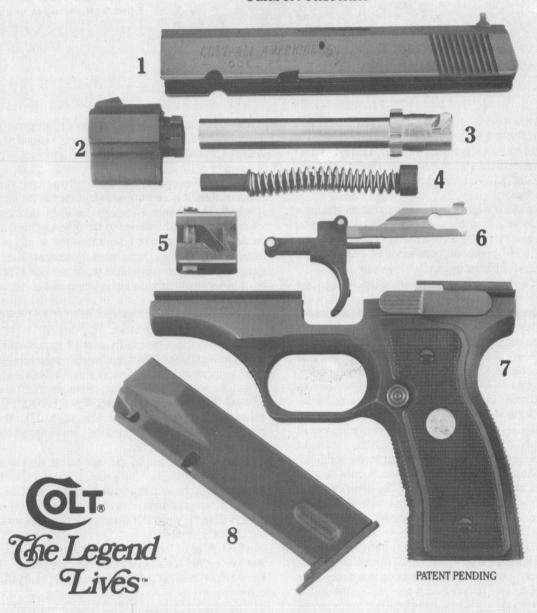

COLT®
The Legend Lives™

PATENT PENDING

The Colt All American's unique design is featured in this photo of the pistol field stripped to its eight major parts. Takedown is simple and easy to perform and takes only seconds. Sub-assemblies include the (1) carbon steel slide, (2) barrel bushing, (3) barrel with integral locking lugs, (4) recoil spring and guide, (5) cam block, (6) sear, trigger assembly, (7) light weight polymer receiver and (8) magazine with 15-round capacity. Note the locking lugs on the barrel assembly are similar to those found on the Colt M16 military rifle.

This Colt 9mm was made especially for long-time gun scribe Dean A. Grennell. He authored the first edition of this 9mm handgun book.

often faced when a person is pulling the trigger.

In fact, the Ransom Rest was used frequently during the development of data for this book. Usually, it was pressed into service when a particular handgun demonstrated either extremely irregular behavior, or when a pistol seemed to be shooting terrifically well.

The Ransom Rest was used to help rule out human error and establish the accuracy potential of the pesky guns, and it also was used to see just how accurate an otherwise apparently accurate pistol really was. In both kinds of instances, the Ransom Rest proved to be uncommonly helpful.

However, the Ransom Rest was designed before any of the handguns on the market were made of plastic. And, when using a Ransom Rest with a plastic pistol, the operator needs to take a number of carefully deliberate steps to assure the rig is adjusted properly. In fact, it takes a bit of shooting to establish a real working familiarity with the rest for any kind of gun, but once established, the rest can be a great help.

So it was when the Model 2000 was clamped into the rest. More than 100 rounds went downrange, and the barrel was defouled twice before I was certain it was absolutely in correct adjustment. The problem was that the groups coming out of the pistol in the rest looked strikingly familiar — almost identical to the ones shot from a bench rest by the author.

Of all the 9mmP handguns fired while collecting data for this book, the Colt 2000 was the most finicky when it came to ammunition it would accept and ammunition it would shoot well. All groups were five shots at 25 yards.

Best group by far was with Winchester's 147-grain JHP subsonic loading. That group was exactly one-inch in diameter and concentric. Next best group came from Winchester's 147-grain Black Talon ammo. It was exactly two inches wide and rather concentric. If pressed for an opinion, the author would suggest that the particular pistol used in the tests should be fed these two loads and these two loads only. Such a combination could make the shooter very happy.

The CCI Blazer 124-grain JSP loading left a horizontal string 3-3/4 inches wide, and the CCI Blazer 147-grain TMJ loading resulted in a "pattern" which was 5-1/4 inches from corner to corner. PMC's 115-grain FMJ loading produced a group that was so scattered that one of the rounds never was accounted for properly. It was estimated the group was about seven inches across.

My own handloads — consisting of a 115-grain Winchester hollow-point bullet over 6.0 grains of Unique powder and using CCI small pistol primers and Hansen cases — produced a group of 4-1/4 inches.

When one considers that those groups were shot from a Ransom Rest, it is easy to understand the author's confusion. The two Winchester 147-grain loadings performed well enough, but what happened to the others? Groupings were inconsistent enough that I quit recording results as I tried a number of other loads from other companies. They were no better — and no worse — than those mentioned above.

It is rumored in the handgun world that it can take some time to shoot-in a new pistol. In other words, a pistol has to be shot a lot before it really shows its stuff. Perhaps that is the case with the particular Model 2000 I used.

However, other pistols from other manufacturers were shot no more and they performed more consistently. Strangely, though, there was no problem in free-hand hitting of targets in quick shooting sessions at distances to 10 yards. So, without question, the test pistol was a good service-grade pistol out to 10 yards with any ammo, and to 25 yards with the two Winchester loads. Beyond that, any comment would be more speculation than fact.

Ironically, the "tale of the tape" shed little meaningful light on the situation. The printout from the Oehler 35P chronograph showed little relationship between velocity consistency and group size. With the triple sky screens placed 15 feet from the muzzle, readings for five-shot groups from the Oehler 35P were:

CCI Blazer 147-grain TMJ loads registered a high of 999 and low of 993 for a median 997 feet per second. Extreme spread was 6 and standard deviation was 2. That is incredibly consistent.

The PMC 115-grain FMJ loading registered a high of 1180 and low of 1101 for a median of 1134 feet per second. Extreme spread was 79 and standard deviation was 30.

The author's handload consisting of 115-grain Winchester JHP over 6.0 grains of Unique powder registered a high of 1377 and low of 1301 for a median of 1327 feet per second. Extreme spread was 76 and standard deviation was 29.

Meanwhile, Colt All American Model 2000 pistols have hit the market full-bore, and sales continue. The pistol is priced somewhat lower than the Colt Model 1911 variants.

CHAPTER
Ten

RUGER'S 9MM HANDGUNS

Models Are Limited, But Meet Most Needs

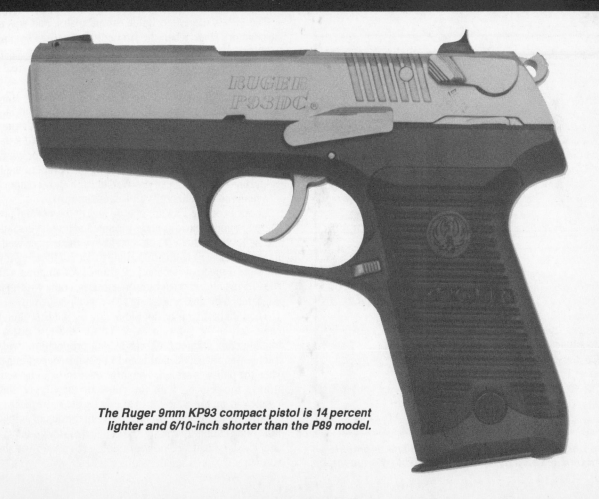

The Ruger 9mm KP93 compact pistol is 14 percent lighter and 6/10-inch shorter than the P89 model.

ONE THOUGHT of the nation's major manufacturers of handguns, Sturm, Ruger & Company has a relatively short list of pistols and revolvers chambered for the 9mmP cartridge. Currently there are two basic pistol models and two revolver models in 9mmP available from Ruger.

Ruger's original 9mmP pistol was the P85, which was introduced in the mid-1980s, but didn't actually hit the market until the latter '80s. It had been on the market a short time when it was superseded by the P85 Mk II, which incorporated a number of changes, including a new slide, firing pin, firing pin safety and other subtle internal changes.

By the end of the decade of the '80s, Ruger had introduced the P89, which became available early in the 1990s. The P89 series replaced the P85 models totally for the domestic market. There are still some P85s being manufactured for some remote foreign markets, but, domestically, the P85 took its place in history when the P89s were introduced. For 1993, Ruger introduced the P-series compact, called the P93DAO and P93DC (the letter suffixes denote double-action only and decock-only). More on them later.

Ruger 9mmP pistols, then, are the P85, the P89 and the P93. A P94 is on the drawing boards. Within those model designations are several sub-models. For example, there is one sub-model in blue and another in stainless for both the P85 and the P85 Mk II, and there are blue and stainless variations in P89 series.

In a way, it would be safe to say Ruger got into the 9mmP pistol business via a somewhat rocky road. Certain design changes were deemed necessary extremely soon after the P85 first appeared, making way for the P85 Mk II. As is common among things Ruger, the dates of introduction and the actual dates of deliveries of guns do not always coincide. And, as is common in any industry, there is always a brief period of time when model changes are made that both the old model and the new model superseding it are actually on the market at the same time. Such was the case with the Ruger 9mmP pistol progression. Suffice to say that within a matter of about five years, Ruger had gone from introducing the P85, obsoleting it and introducing the P85 Mk II, obsoleting it and introducing the P89, and then adding to the offerings by announcing a compact model — the P93.

Although the P85s and the P89s may look similar on the outside, they are actually totally different guns. There is virtually no interchangeability between them.

Ruger's two 9mmP revolvers are the SP101 and the Blackhawk. Made in stainless steel only, the 9mmP variants of the SP101 revolver feature barrel lengths of 2-1/4 or 3-1/16 inches. The Blackhawk revolver available in 9mmP is one of the several "convertible" combinations Ruger has marketed through the years. In the case of the 9mmP, it is a convertible with the .357 magnum, and is available with barrel lengths of 4-5/8 or 6-1/2 inches.

Although there are relatively few Ruger 9mmP models, the ones which are marketed cover the subject well.

P85

The author fired the entire Ruger 9mm line during his evaluation. He also used a variety of factory ammunition.

The P85 is Ruger's original 9mmP pistol, and was in its introductory stage when the first edition of *The Gun Digest Book of 9mm Handguns* was written. In typical Ruger tradition, the P85 is a full-bodied, robust handgun — a real fist-filler.

It features a 15-shot stagger box magazine, 4-1/2-inch barrel, weighs 32 ounces (two pounds) empty and is 7.84 inches long overall. Sights are of the square post front and square notch rear persuasion, complete with white dot inserts front and back. The rear sight is drift-adjustable for windage. Elevation is possible only by changing the height of the front sight. Handles are made of grooved black Xenoy composition — a material used liberally in Ruger firearms.

Controls on the P85 are classic and in the normal places. There are ambidextrous slide-mounted safety levers, a slide release lever on the left side just above the trigger well and magazine release on the grip handle just aft of the trigger well. The slide is made of steel and the frame is of aluminum alloy. The P85 pistols, whether blue or stainless, come with an extra magazine, a magazine loading tool and a plastic case.

The P85 is single- or double-action on the first shot, then single-action for subsequent shots. On the test pistol, the double-action trigger pull was a long proposition, with the sear breaking at between nine and 11 pounds, depending upon when the pull was scaled. The difference in readings seemed to have more to do with the curve of the trigger and the inability to get the scale's arm in exactly the same place twice in a row than any apparent difference in the actual amount of pull from scaling to scaling. For the sake of argument, consider it to have had a 10-pound double-action pull. The single-action pull was a legally correct 6-1/2 pounds, and was somewhat crisp.

The P85, the first Ruger 9mm automatic, also was available is stainless steel.

The P85 established the basic design for the Ruger family of 9mm automatics.

The full range of loads was fired through the P85, with rather interesting results. There were no excitingly accurate loads, and there were no "bad" loads which performed significantly differently from any of the others. Of all the 9mmP handguns fired in the research for this book, the Ruger line was the most homogeneous when it came to handling different loadings from different ammo manufacturers, or some of the various handloads.

For example, groups from the bench at 25 yards through the P85 ranged from three to five inches, with the five-inch groups generally including one or more rounds the author felt may have been "pulled," due to the trigger pull. Interestingly, group sizes were similar when the pistol was fired from a two-hand unsupported hold, or when it was fired from the rest on the bench.

What this seemed to indicate was that the pistol may not be a target proposition out of the box, but it is a consistent performer regardless what it is fed. There is something to be said for such performance in a general-purpose 9mmP handgun.

As the shooting sessions progressed, I was impressed that the P85 possesses what has come to be known as a "classic" Ruger trigger pull. Accidental discharges are difficult, if not impossible, to have happen. And, the pull is just gritty enough

to make precise shooting a real challenge. Typically on Ruger firearms, a little fine tuning by a gunsmith can put those concerns aside and the firearm probably will perform much more precisely.

However, for the purposes of this writing, there was no desire to have any retro-work done, because it is the object of the discussion to investigate the performance of the various makes of handguns as they come from the factory.

I have rather large hands with long fingers, and the 9mmP pistols from Ruger filled them fully. There is nothing small nor dainty about the P85. It is full-bodied in every respect, including width. The mechanism itself is the classic floating barrel lockup. However, some of the internal parts are uniquely Ruger. This is a pistol designed to be mass produced, and it has a reputation for working well. Certainly, the test pistol functioned flawlessly. It fed and fired all manner of loads with equal aplomb.

Field stripping the P85 for routine cleaning is simple, but slightly different from many other 9mmP pistols. After assuring that the pistol is unloaded, pull the slide all the way to the rear until it locks open. Remove the magazine, then with finger or thumb, reach into the ejector port and depress the ejector on the left side of the port until it clicks into place in the down position.

Then release the slide, allowing it to move forward. (It is a good idea to hold onto the slide and allow it to move forward slowly.) Then, pull the slide just slightly to the rear with one hand, while pushing against the end of the slide release, the lever pin on the right side of the frame. This can take a little fumbling around, but by methodically moving the slide a fraction of an inch at a time and trying to pop the pin simultaneously, the spot will be found where the pin will move, pushing the slide release lever away from the frame on the left side.

This allows the shooter to grasp the slide release lever with thumb and forefinger and pull it out until it will move no further. The slide release lever does not come all the way out, as is the situation with a number of pistols. Once the lever is pulled out as far as it will go, the slide can be pushed forward and lifted off the receiver.

Once the slide group is removed from the frame, the recoil spring and guide can be lifted up and out, a la most semi-auto 9mmP pistols. The barrel then can be lifted out of the slide, and the pistol is field-stripped as far as it needs to be for cleaning or normal maintenance. Reassembly is the reverse sequence.

Although it may appear to be a bit complicated when explained in writing, the fact is that the P85 disassembles quickly and easily in practice. And, reassembly is equally straight-forward and simple. In fact, I found that the P85 goes back together quite easily, and does not have any "secret" or "trick" movements needed to accomplish the task. Overall, cleaning of the P85 is easy and simple.

In general terms, the P85 seemed to be a viable general-purpose handgun which readily fills applications from informal target or plinking work to home or self-defense. I would not hesitate to consider it a credible choice for use in a defense mode at the normal gunfighting distances. In the out-of-the-box configuration, it is not a highly refined target handgun, and it was not evaluated with that thought in mind.

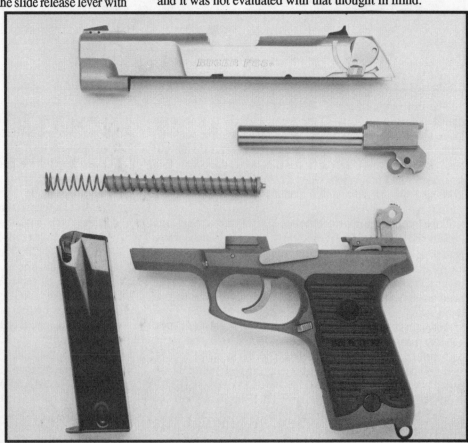

Basic field-stripping of the stainless steel P85 is done quickly without using tools.

P89 Decock-Only Model

The P89 decock-only model features ambidextrous decocking levers on the slide which lower the hammer and block the firing pin when they are pressed downward. Similarly, the P89 double-action only sub-model is much the same as the other Ruger semi-autos, except it fires double-action for every shot. Size, weight and magazine capacities are virtually the same for all of the sub-models. Actually, there are five P89 sub-models. They are the P89 safety (available in blue or stainless), P89 decock-only (available in blue or stainless) and P89 double-action-only (available only in stainless).

The P89 decocker used for this writing had a double-action trigger pull of nine pounds, and a single-action pull of six pounds. The characteristics of the pulls were similar to those on the P85, which meant that the double-action pull was long and a bit gritty, while the single-action pull was legally correct, with the sear breaking cleanly.

From a performance perspective, the P85 and the P89 decocker may as well have been twins. Group sizes from a rest on the bench or held unsupported were virtually identical, and ranged from three to five inches at 25 yards with the various loads used. The P89 digested all loadings with equal aplomb, and functioned flawlessly.

Blaine Huling evaluates accuracy of the Ruger P89DC.

The P89DC was part of the second generation of Ruger 9mm semi-auto handguns.

The first shot of the P89DC is double-action, followed by single-action operation.

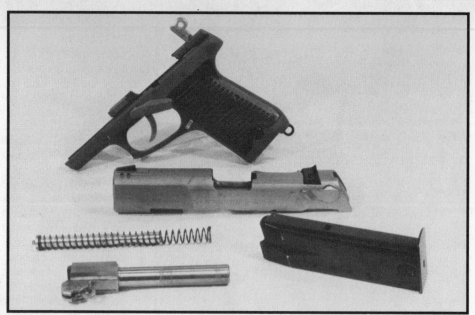

The Ruger P89DC (right and below) disassembles easily for basic maintenance.

After having test-driven the two major variants from the Ruger 9mmP pistol line, I found that the most important questions a shooter might consider if thinking about acquiring something from this company's offerings should include matters of function features more than anything else.

By that, I mean that, if a shooter is looking for a straight-forward, full-size 9mmP handgun, the P89 safety version fills the bill well. Whether it is blue or stainless is also a matter of personal, rather than performance, preference. If the shooter wants or needs a decocking feature, or wants or needs a pistol which fires only double-action, then there are specific sub-models available with those features.

Really what is being said here is that Ruger offers one generally basic 9mmP pistol, with a number of sub-model feature variations intended to address specific needs and markets.

Although it had been introduced officially in 1993, the P93 compact 9mmP pistols from Ruger were not available when this chapter was being written.

"The Ruger Compacts feature a one-piece Zytel grip frame that helps them weigh an incredibly light 31 ounces with a loaded 15-round magazine," Ruger reports. "This tough P-Series pistol is the ultimate in an easy carry compact designed for continuous use."

Specifications listed by Ruger are:

"Caliber: 9mm Luger. Mechanism: recoil-operated, double-action, autoloading. Tilting barrel, link-actuated, as in M1911A1. Magazine: Steel, staggered column, 15-shot. Weight: 24 oz. (magazine empty). Barrel length: 3-9/10". Overall length: 7-3/10". Height: 5-1/2". Width: 1-1/2". Sight radius: 5". Sights: Square notch rear, drift adjustable for windage; square post front. Front and rear sights have white dots for rapid target acquisition."

The SP101

Ruger's SP101 revolver line is one of the hot models in today's handgun market, and the SP101 chambered for the 9mmP is no exception. In addition to 9mmP, the SP101 is available in .22 long rifle, .32 H&R Magnum (six-shot), .38 Special (+P) and .357 Magnum (five-shot). The 9mmP also is a five-shot proposition.

Barrel lengths available in 9mmP are 2-1/4 and 3-1/16 inches. Weight, depending upon barrel length, is 25 or 27 ounces. Sights are fixed on the 9mmP, and the stocks are made of Ruger Santoprene (cushioned grip) with Xenoy inserts. All SP101 revolvers are made of stainless steel.

The test revolver sported a 3-1/16-inch barrel, and it was fired using both the full-moon, five-shot clips, and without clips. The revolver functioned flawlessly with or without the clips, but ejection could be performed mechanically only when the clips were used (the 9mmP being a rimless cartridge). Extraction without the clips was easy: Either use

The short-barreled SP101 is a fast-pointing gun for close-range work. Here, Blaine Huling tries the snubby.

thumbnail and fingernail to pull the empties out, or use any kind of "rod," like a cleaning rod or pencil, to pop the fired cases out one at a time.

The SP101 features a swing-out cylinder, which is unlocked via a small button-like release on the left side of the frame just aft of the cylinder. The ejector rod is protected when the cylinder is locked in place, and ejects loaded ammunition or empties with a single stroke when the cylinder is swung to the left and into the open position. The SP101 can be fired single- or double-action.

The double-action trigger pull on the test model 9mmP was noticeably l-o-n-g, with the sear break requiring a bit of added pressure when the trigger was at the rear of the pull. Double-action pull was more or less 12 pounds (it differed somewhat from one scaling to another), and the single-action pull was a nice 4-1/2 pounds.

Trigger pull seemed to contribute significantly to shooting performance. Groups at 25 yards, whether fired from a rest on the bench, or in the unsupported two-hand hold, were lateral strings of four to five inches. Because the sights were fixed and offered no degree of adjustment, bullet placement was of particular interest. Conveniently, the vertical placement was at or near the point-of-aim, with the variations depending upon the velocity of the specific loading. The vertical dispersion among all loads shot was less than three inches at 25 yards.

The SP101 is not a target handgun. It is designed to be a handy recreational shooter or a serious defense proposition. For either application, it is an interesting gun. For example, as much as the groups tend to string left-and-right for four or five inches, they never strayed farther than that in the test firings.

The Ruger SP101 is made of stainless steel. It features synthetic grips, making it a fine tactical performer.

During range testing, author put many kinds of factory ammo through the stainless steel Ruger SP101 revolver.

And, regardless of the load used, bullets printed into an area three inches deep on the targets. What this means is that, regardless what loading was used, the composite impact area on the targets at 25 yards (whether the revolver was held unsupported or fired from a rest) was in the shape of a horizontal football, measuring three-by-five inches. That's not bad for a snubby-type revolver right out of the box.

One thing should be noted here, however. When those assisting the author fired the SP101, it took a number of rounds for them to achieve that level of performance. Until they became more familiar with the revolver, they were experiencing groups of about eight inches at 25 yards. Still, this is not terribly bad for a snubby revolver, but it further demonstrates that the combination of basic sights and trigger pull can have tremendous effects on the tactical accuracy which might be achieved from the SP101. Still, as a defensive "belly gun" at normal distances, it is not a bad point-and-shoot handgun.

The size and weight of the test revolver fall into the "handy" category. It felt good in use, and pointed well. The grip handle configuration is small enough for shooters with relatively small hands, yet the rig is designed so it works well when used in larger hands, as well.

As suggested throughout this book, shooters who prefer revolvers are well advised to consider those in 9mmP as viable options. It may have been designed as an auto cartridge, but the 9mmP is an exciting performer in revolvers. In virtually any revolver barrel length (including the short-barreled snubbies), the high-intensity 9mmP performs between the hotter .38 Special and full-house .357 Magnum loadings. This means that when any of the modern high-performance bullets are used, the 9mmP is an honest-to-goodness defense cartridge when fired in a revolver. The Ruger SP101 is no exception.

THE BLACKHAWK

The basic Ruger Blackhawk convertible, single-action revolver is put through its test paces by Blaine Huling.

Ruger's single-action Blackhawk revolver is available in a host of chamberings, including a convertible option with two cylinders — one chambered for the .357 Magnum and the other for the 9mmP. This particular option is not purely a 9mmP proposition, and it was not judged as such. It is, however, an interesting way for shooters to be able to use three different cartridges in the same gun.

Even the Ruger designation for this convertible tells the story. It is the .357/9mm Convertible, and is available with 4-5/8- or 6-1/2-inch barrel. The test revolver featured the 6-1/2-inch barrel, weighed 42 ounces and measured 12-1/4 inches overall. Stocks were American walnut. Sights were one eigth-inch ramp front and micro-click adjustable rear. Trigger pull was a consistent 4-1/2 pounds.

As Ruger's own designation hints, this is really a .357 Magnum revolver with an extra cylinder chambered for the 9mmP cartridge. Its tactical performance echoed this reality, because it shot .357 Magnum loads much more accurately than it did the various 9mmP loadings. Such performance is consistent with most "convertible" revolvers, and is not uncommon among many revolver designs when auto cartridges are fired through them.

Groups at 25 yards off the bench were generally in the six-inch category, with some 9mm groups expanding to seven inches, although I would not rule out pilot error there. Hence, consider the test revolver to have fired six-inch, rather concentric, groups at 25 yards. By comparison, the same handgun produced groups less than half that size when the other cylinder was inserted and .357 Magnum loads were used.

Following more than 100 shots with the various 9mmP loadings, it appeared as though the convertible Blackhawk was not stabilizing the 9mmP bullets as well as it was the .357 Magnum loadings. This, too, is not surprising, given the fact that 9mmP bullets are slightly (one- or two-thousanths of an inch) thinner than are .357 Magnum bullets. Also, it might be appropriate to note that the test revolver also shot .38 Special loadings better than it did the 9mmP cartridges. Again, this is consistent with what one might assume.

The desirability of such a convertible revolver is more a matter of expanding the ability of a shooter to use different ammunition than anything else. In such a role, the Ruger Convertible is a good choice.

The test revolver performed well, and both loading and extraction were simple and easy. Given the general availability of totally affordable 9mmP ammunition, such a handgun is a good bet for anyone who wants to use bargain-priced ammo for general familiarization and informal shooting, yet also have a handgun which can perform very well in more serious roles with other loads.

The convertible I used shot 9mmP, .38 Special and .357 Magnum loadings to different points of impact at 25 yards, so sight adjustments to the point of impact for the most serious loading to be used might be in order.

Shooters who want to be able to fire three of the world's most popular cartridges through the same handgun might well consider the convertible Blackhawk. It is a serious handgun in its own right, yet is fun and easy to shoot.

Overall, the Ruger 9mmP lineup functioned well and

The Ruger SP101 revolver uses a full-moon clip during normal operation, however, it will shoot the rimless 9mm cartridges without a clip which doubles as speed loader.

performed within standard parameters for general purpose handguns. Their ability to handle a wide range of loads with equal effect was impressive.

The Blackhawk convertible has two cylinders. One handles the .38 Special and .357 magnum, the other the 9mmP.

CHAPTER *Eleven*

THE KOREAN CONNECTION

The Daewoo 9mmP Pistol Is Building A Reputation For Excellence!

The Korean Daewoo DP51 gets a workout by Blaine C. Huling during an extensive series of tests of 9mm firearms.

The Daewoo points nicely, offering a nice-shooting, handy semi-automatic gun.

I T WAS A COUPLE, or perhaps several, years ago when I first was introduced to the Daewoo 9mmP pistol. It was at one of the annual Shooting, Hunting and Outdoor Trades (SHOT) Shows, which are the industry conventions at which new products are introduced.

I was cruising the miles of aisles of guns and goodies, minding my own business, when I happened to stop to look up a booth number for some company which had a new product I wanted to inspect. As I stood there, leafing through the show book, a guy from an adjacent booth, noting my "press" credentials, grabbed my arm, pulled me into his booth and asked whether I'd seen his "new" product yet.

For those who are unfamiliar with such trade shows, some of the more innovative products on the market make their debuts in such places, often without initial fanfare. So it was with the Daewoo.

When he thrust one of the semi-autos into my hand, I recall wondering what was so "revolutionary?" Frankly, it looked and felt like any of the many generic 9mmP handguns available at the time. But, he had my "divided" attention, so I asked the generic question: "What's the deal? What's so new?"

I knew I had been had when the response was: "What's so new? Let me show you."

Somehow I seem to recall having experienced a similar response from at least one of the many door-to-door vacuum cleaner/encyclopaedia salesmen through the years.

"You've heard of single-action?" the guy continued. "You've heard of double-action? Well, this is a Tri-Action pistol."

It is not difficult to become somewhat cynical during the long and arduous days at the SHOT Show, and since that was Day 3, as I recall, I was in gritty form.

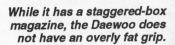

While it has a staggered-box magazine, the Daewoo does not have an overly fat grip.

Right, the Daewoo's alloy frame gives the auto fast handling characteristics. Below, the Korean pistol is imported by Firstshot Inc.

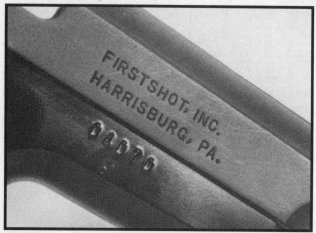

Daewoo's squared-off trigger guard permits a steady two-hand hold, increasing accuracy during rapid fire.

"Right," I retorted. "If a single-action has to be cocked manually each time, and if a double-action does it with a pull of the trigger, then this tri-action must mean the silly gun also shoots by itself, right?"

I don't want to suggest it was some sort of culture lapse, but the fellow didn't chuckle. He failed to crack a smile. I know when I've been a wise guy, and that was one of the times. After all, here was a businessman who was just trying to get someone to pay attention to a product he felt had great merit. Meanwhile, I also noticed that he and I were the only people in the booth, and that is in a setting where most booths are packed solid with buyers, peddlers and writers. It wasn't as though the world was beating a path to this guy's doorstep.

So, after committing myself to more proper behavior, I watched and listened as he gave me the industrial strength version of his sales pitch.

To explain the situation fully, it is necessary to note that the conversation happened at a time before the proliferation of decocker designs in semi-autos. At that time, semi-autos which had been cocked had to be hand decocked if they were to be decocked. For pistols with a double-action feature on the first shot, that presented some rather interesting possibilities, like fumbling which could allow the hammer to fall harder than intended.

Also, at the time, all of the double-action (on first shot only) designs featured single-action firing for shots subsequent to the initial blast. This meant drastically different trigger pulls for the first and then subsequent shots.

The Daewoo, it was shown, precluded such concerns. Certainly, it was double-action for the first shot, and certainly, it was single-action for subsequent shots. But the trigger linkage had been altered dramatically, changing several of the shooting dynamics of the pistol.

Most notable of those was the feature which gave the design its name: Tri-Action. When the hammer is cocked to the rear, it is simple to return it downward. Merely push it forward with the thumb, and it goes forward, also pushing the trigger forward — from the single-action mode to double-action.

Yet, when it is time to shoot, merely pull on the trigger and the pistol is fired just as though it had always been double-action. This simply was one of the first action alterations which allowed a cartridge to be carried in the chamber totally

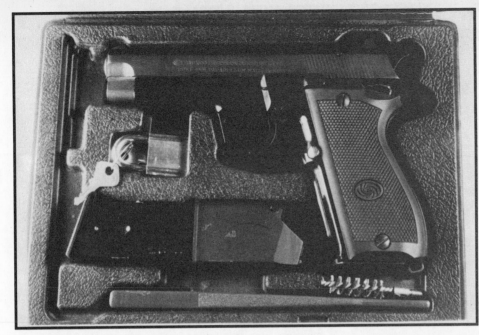

The Daewoo comes in a hard plastic carrying case that includes cleaning gear, extra magazine and loader plus a lock and two keys.

safely. The only way it could be fired would be to cycle the trigger/hammer system so the hammer could fall hard enough to set it off.

But there was more. The same built-in slip-system which allowed manual manipulation of the hammer also gave the pistol a trigger pull which, at the moment of truth, was essentially the same whether it was from the double-action or single-action starting point. That was a good idea, because it meant that consistent bullet placement from the first through the last shot would be easier.

At the time, the company was looking for an outfit in the United States to handle the pistol which is made in Korea.

Eventually, a firm called Firstshot Inc. took those honors.

Aside from the unique Tri-Action design, which works very well, the Daewoo is essentially one of the many latter-day variants of the 1911/Hi-Power concepts initiated by John Moses Browning earlier this century.

It features a stagger-column 13-round magazine, a 4.1-inch barrel and checkered composition stocks. Weight is 28.2 ounces empty, and overall length is 7.48 inches. The pistol has a blade front sight and drift-adjustable rear sight. Safety and magazine catch (located in the traditional 1911-style places) are ambidextrous. The alloy frame features a square-front trigger guard. Finish on the frame is a smooth, shiny black, and

The magazine loader and extra magazine are handy for extended range sessions.

The exposed hammer on the Daewoo can be decocked by just pushing it forward.

the steel slide is matte black/blued.

Disassembly is similar to the procedures for the 1911/Hi-Power pistols. After assuring the pistol is not loaded, remove the magazine and allow the slide to go all the way forward. With one hand, move the slide to the rear until the small cut on the bottom of the slide under the ejection port area is even with the slide release lever. It's located on the left side of the frame just above the trigger area.

The slide release lever then can be pulled out of the frame, and the slide can be removed by sliding it forward and off the frame. The recoil spring and guide then can be removed from beneath the barrel, and the barrel can be extracted. This completes the normal level of disassembly needed for routine cleaning and maintenance.

The barrel is belled near the muzzle in the fashion used to preclude the need for a separate barrel bushing as is used in the 1911 design. Lockup is similar to that of the 1911/Hi-Power pistols, and the Daewoo features the same kind of integral feed ramp as does the Hi-Power.

Assembly is the reverse procedure, and the process includes no negative surprises. It is straight-forward and simple.

Overall, the Daewoo is a well made semi-auto, with both fit and finish typical for commercial-grade (they look nice) service handguns.

In addition to being a nice looking handgun, the Daewoo is packaged well. It comes in a hard plastic case which also includes an extra magazine and loading tool, padlock with two keys and cleaning brushes.

On the range, the Daewoo proved to be a good performer. It is not meant to be a target handgun, and it did not deliver target accuracy. However, it did deliver an acceptable level of tactical accuracy for a service-grade firearm.

In all, more than a dozen different loads, both factory ammo and handloads, were fired through the test pistol. Groups ranged from 2 1/2 inches at 25 yards for Winchester's USA ball ammo to three inches for Winchester's 147-grain subsonic hollow-point loading. Three-inch groups, or groups slightly less in size, were achieved with all of the other loadings, which included various bullet weights and configurations from CCI (Blazer), Federal, Hansen, PMC, Remington

and Sure Fire. Handloads featuring hardcast 125-grain cast bullets and 115-grain Winchester hollow-points also shot within the three-inch limits.

Overall, the pistol seem to have no decided preference for one kind of load over another. Groups, however, which were all five-shot propositions, tended to string somewhat right-to-left. This characteristic was credited more to pilot error than anything to do with the pistol itself.

It is difficult to describe the feeling of the trigger pull on the Daewoo. It is different from other pistols — not particularly better or worse, just different. For example, Star pistols also have unique trigger pulls. They also are not particularly better or worse than others, just different. So it was with the Daewoo.

Because of the Tri-Action feature, the resistance to the trigger finger is most pronounced during the last fraction of an inch of pull. Even though the DP51 is a full-bodied handgun, the author's long fingers resulted in a hold that was most vulnerable to inconsistency when the trigger was in its rearmost position. This meant that at the point where the most rearward force was needed, the author had the least grip control.

This situation was a factor of the author's hand size and shape, and it was assumed that such a situation would be a moot concern if the pistol were shot more — contributing to a necessary level of personal familiarization.

Even so, all groups fired at 25 yards off the bench went inside a six-inch circle, so achieved tactical accuracy would get the job done without problems.

The overall impression left by the DP51 was that it is a very workable 9mmP handgun which would have no difficulty performing well in the service pistol kinds of applications. For example, it would be a good self or home defense handgun.

Function was flawless for all of the types of loads used. In all, nearly 500 rounds were fired through the test pistol. For those who might be interested, it really is necessary to experience the Tri-Action features personally to understand and appreciate them fully.

What it all boils down to in the end, however, is that all one needs to do when the pistol is loaded is point it, squeeze the trigger and it goes bang. What more is there?

CHAPTER *Twelve*

THE 9MM HANDGUNS OF INTERARMS

The Walther Leads The Pack For This Importer

WHENEVER THE topic turns to a discussion of the guns of Interarms, several brand names and a number of different designs come into mind. The reason is simple: Interarms markets firearms from around the world, and the models in that company's stable change from time to time.

Of all the models marketed in the United States by Interarms, Walther 9mmP handguns are among the best known — and among the more pricy names in that firm's long line of guns. Leading the Walther lineup are the two P88 variants — the P88 and P88 Compact. These are totally serious handguns.

Among the world's service pistols, the Walther P88 is one of the top performers. Its controls are ambidextrous, and it is the sort of handgun that points quickly and effectively.

Magazine capacity is 15 rounds, plus there can be another round carried in the chamber. Barrel length is four inches, making the handgun 7.3 inches long overall. Weight is 31.5 ounces. Finish, of course, is blue.

The P88 Compact is essentially a smaller version of the P88, incorporating the same general features. The compact's magazine holds 14 rounds (one can be carried in the chamber). Barrel length is 3.8 inches, making the overall length 7.1 inches. The Compact weighs 29 ounces.

The Walther P88 is one of a few top-notch, top-dollar 9mmP service handguns in the world. For the price of one of these, a shooter could buy two or more of the less expensive handguns on the market today.

What makes the P88, or any of the other top-dollar pistols for that matter, able to command such a price? Is it really at least twice as good, say, as one of the more typical 9mmP pistols? The answer to this question is located directly between the ears of the buyer. It is a matter of perception.

From an objective viewpoint, the P88 and its genre are recipients of much more detailed manufacturing and finishing than are those handguns in the normal run of the mill. Materials, of course, are tops.

Time is money, and when it takes longer to produce a product, the price goes up. Similarly, there are economies of scale, and expensive models of anything rarely sell as well as less expensive models. So, there is a bit of a double-edged economic sword swinging around.

But as much as anything else, high-priced guns bring big bucks, because of some perceived edge over the less expensive offerings. On the surface, it can be things as simple as better fit and finish of parts.

Ultimately, however, it boils down to what the purchaser wants. For example, the buyer may decide that even the slightest improvement in fit and finish is worth a lot more money. Or, there is always the status factor. Put them all together and the answer becomes clear.

It is no different with other things, like automobiles. Almost any of them will get a person from Point A to Point B. The real question, then, is how one does it, compared to the other.

For those who are interested in some of the finer of the production 9mmP handguns on the market, the Walther P88 is among them.

P38, P5 AND P5 COMPACT

This triad of Walther pistols represents the progression in model development, beginning with the design which started the double-action-on-the-first-shot phenomenon. That's right, the Walther P38 (as in adopted in 1938) was the first of the handguns to feature double-action on the first shot; subsequent shots are single-action.

The P38 was a World War II model for the German army, and features a locking block system that helped redefine some of the ways handguns were to be designed. It is a full-size service handgun with a five-inch barrel. Overall length is 8.5 inches, and the pistol weighs 28 ounces. The single-column magazine holds eight rounds.

The Walther P5 was the winning number in the West German police trials of the 1970s, and remains one of the main police handguns on the European continent. It is a full-on service pistol, and the magazine has a capacity of eight rounds. Barrel length is 3.5 inches, making the overall length seven inches. The pistol weighs 28 ounces.

Walther's P5 Compact, a variant of the P5, was designed for concealed carry. As can be seen with the dimensions, it is not a lot smaller than the full-size P5, but just enough to make it easier to carry concealed. For example, the magazine capacity is the same as the full-size P5 — eight rounds. Barrel

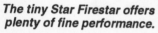
The tiny Star Firestar offers plenty of fine performance.

The Interarms Star 31P is a full-size, high-capacity, double-action auto. It's a top quality service-grade pistol.

Bill Padgett puts the Firestar through a range evaluation.

The all-steel Star Firestar sits low in the hand, making it an excellent pointing gun.

Much thought went into the design of the Firestar. The grip is proportioned well to the slide and barrel

length is 3.1 inches, making the overall length 6.6 inches. The pistol weighs 26.5 ounces.

The author has fired Walther P38 handguns frequently through the years, and has come to several conclusions about the design — conclusions which hold for the pair of P5s, as well.

Grip frames and handles on these pistols are at least full-size. There is no suggestion that the size and design is counter-productive. Rather, it is a statement of fact. This feature dictates the ways in which the pistol is shot. Lacking a better description, the very design of the pistol dictates deliberate, technical movements.

Therefore, it is the sort of design which is learned most quickly by those who have not shot other designs to a great degree previously. Mastering the effective handling of this design takes effort, but does not take a long time.

Once familiarized with the design, the shooter finds that

Gary Paprocki uses a pair of sandbags to wring out the most from the Firestar.

Field-stripped, the Firestar reveals its compact parts including the belled barrel.

personal performance levels jump upward quickly. This means that a person who shoots one of these pistols a lot can expect to become quite proficient with it. The handguns themselves are well made, which means that all it takes is a shooter who knows how to handle one properly, and accurate hits are the result.

Although there is a major trend toward stagger-box, high-capacity magazines for 9mmP handguns now, the relatively small capacities of the magazines in these pistols should be considered as no particular handicap for most applications.

As mentioned above, shooters find that once they have become familiar with these pistols, they can hit well and consistently with them. This means that, in most situations, seven or eight shots is more than enough to get the job done.

These Walthers are not inexpensive. They are really handguns for very serious shooters who not only know precisely what they want in and from a handgun, but who have need for a handgun of such configuration.

STAR PISTOLS

For Interarms, the Star line of handguns from Spain has been one of the major names on the market over the past several years. Among those sales performers, the Firestar in 9mmP stands out as one of the really hot numbers on the entire market.

There are a number of reasons the Firestar handguns have become so popular. First, they are considered officially as "ultra compacts," which means they are small and handy. The

The 9mm Helwan Brigadier receives a workout by Gary Paprocki. Despite its low cost, it's extremely accurate.

price tag also is small and handy, and this line is available in three different chamberings—9mmP, .40 S&W and .45 ACP.

Firestar pistols are single-action, and list a long line of tactical features like ambidextrous safety, reverse-taper barrel, four barrel lugs and a combat three-dot sight system. They are available in two types of finish: blued or with the weather resistant "Starvel" finish — like brushed chrome.

The Firestars have seven-round magazines in 9mmP. Barrels are 3.39 inches long, making the overall length 6.5 inches. and weight 30.35 ounces.

Firestars may be small, but they are big on the performance front. One major feature is the fact that both the slide and frame are made of steel. That's nice, and it gives the handgun just enough weight to make it easy and comfortable to shoot.

Yes, these may be small pistols, but they shoot like the larger varieties. Accuracy does not suffer (it is typical to achieve groups of three inches or less at 25 yards), and they function very well.

For home or self defense, the Starfire should be considered as a most serious contender. It is not a handgun for serious target work, although it happens to be one of the better bets for informal target blasting or just plain plinking.

The Firestar is a fun gun. Because of its size, this pistol fits all sizes of hands, and that means it is a workable choice for women who have hands which are not large enough to steady the full-size service model pistols.

Another place the Firestar comes into its own is as a carry gun. Again, its size and design are just right for this application. If there is a small, handy multi-purpose 9mmP pistol on the market, this is it.

For shooters who prefer a full-size 9mmP, Star also offers an appropriate model — the Starfire 31P and its companion

Clockwise (from right to left) are the Helwan Brigadier and the Firestars in .45 ACP, .40 S&W and 9mm Parabellum.

The Helwan Brigadier is a modern day version of the World War II Beretta.

sub-model, the 31PK. The PK designation is for the same pistol, but with an alloy rather than steel frame.

This line of double-action, high capacity 9mmP handguns began with the Model 28, which was supplanted by the Model 30. That design was followed by the Model 31P, which is offered in 9mmP, as well as .40 S&W.

Will the Starfire hold up? Well, at one California indoor shooting range, one of the Starfires went through more than 40,000 rounds without a problem. That's not bad.

The Starfire 31P is double-action/single-action (first shot can be double-action, with subsequent rounds fired single-action), and has a 15-round magazine in 9mmP. It is available in either blue or Starvel finish. Barrel length is 3.86 inches, making overall length 7.6 inches. The pistol weighs 39.4 ounces.

HELWAN BRIGADIER

Of the full-size service 9mmP handguns on the market, the Helwan Brigadier is among the more interesting for a number of reasons. Many consumers find the totally affordable price a cause for concern. It offers maximum bang for the buck.

But what are these pistols? They are a combination of one of the older designs which is being produced in Egypt. Older shooters probably would recognize the design, because it is a modern-made version of the old Beretta Brigadier.

This design incorporates the same type of locking block design as the Walther P38, but has an outward appearance which is decidedly Beretta-ish. It is single-action and of all steel construction.

The single-row magazine holds eight rounds of 9mmP. Barrel is 4.5 inches long, making overall length eight inches.

The Helwan Brigadier has an unusual magazine release. It is located on the rear of the grip, near the bottom.

Bill Padget handles the Helwan Brigadier. He found the 9mm auto easy to shoot.

The pistol weighs 28 ounces.

Several features on this handgun are different from things found normally on 9mmP pistols of the '90s. Totally apparent when one picks up the pistol is the finger rest extension on the bottom of the magazine. This contributes to a firm hold and aids in controlling the pistol when shooting.

However, when it comes to removing the magazine, the shooter realizes that he or she has taken a step backward in time. The release is a round button on the lower rear of the left grip. Compared to more modern designs, this release may seem a bit out of place, but once one gets used to it, it is actually handy.

Similarly, the safety is a round button, located in the upper rear of the left grip. It is a cross-bolt safety.

The pistol has a blue finish, and a close inspection reveals that it is not as well finished as the more expensive 9mmP handguns on the market. Milling marks are evident at various places on the frame and slide. Yet, the pistol not only functions well, it shoots well with most 9mmP loads.

Shooters who plan to run thousands and thousands of rounds through their 9mmP handguns might not be too interested in the Helwan. It is strong and works well, but is not known for holding up under constant firing — no safety problem, they just shoot loose after a number of thousands of rounds. For most consumers, this is not an important factor. And, considering the price, this handgun is a viable option for those who want to have a 9mmP around "just in case."

During a session at the range, a test Helwan Brigadier showed it could shoot with some of the better 9mmP handguns on the market. Groups of two inches (a couple of them a bit

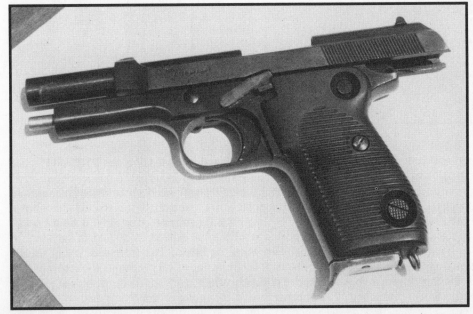

The Helwan Brigadier also has a through-bolt safety, located at the top of the grip.

The barrel lock-up system on the Helwan Brigadier is the same as the modern Berettas and Walther P-38s.

While the Helwan Brigadier is a full-size auto, it presents a slim, functional profile.

less) at 25 yards off the bench were routine and predictable. There are a lot of more expensive 9mmP handguns on the market which will not match that performance.

Overall, the author was intrigued with the Helwan. It fills a niche due to its affordability, yet offers a level of performance that puts it right up there with any of the mainline models from any maker.

What it is not is pretty, or cute. Sights are as basic as they come: notched rear, post front. Yet, the test Brigadier shot right where it looked. It digested a wide variety of loads with aplomb, exhibiting a particular preference for Winchester's generic USA 115-grain ball loading and PMC's 115-grain hollow-point loading. How about that? A budget-priced 9mmP handgun that likes budget-priced ammo! Nice combination.

Through the years, Interarms has marketed a number of other types of 9mmP handguns. Certainly, it would not be surprising to see the line expand, or change, in the future, as well. One thing is certain. The Interarms lineup usually includes at least one line of very high quality handguns, one line of popularly priced handguns that perform well, and one line which fills the needs of the totally budget conscious shooters. This marketing strategy obviously has merit.

CHAPTER
Thirteen

THE 9mm STABLE OF SIG SAUER

This Maker Has Tried To Come Up With A Line To Meet All Needs!

Author test fires the SIG Sauer P226. He found it lived-up to the SIG Sauer's reputation for superb-shooting firearms.

AS THE 20TH CENTURY comes to a close, Sigarms is evolving as one of the major players in the firearms industry, as well as one of the most prestigious names in the field of 9mmP handguns. To be specific, it is the SIG Sauer line of semi-auto handguns which is responsible for this phenomenon.

When it comes to service-grade semi-auto 9mmP handguns, the various SIG Sauer offerings are among the world leaders. Although these handguns offer a number of important features, the two things that make this line of pistols so popular are that they are reliable and accurate. In other words, when the shooter pulls the trigger, the gun goes bang, and when it goes bang, the bullet hits the target. Yes, that is simple. As importantly, it is all that really matters.

Accuracy and dependability are not accidents. They happen only because the SIG Sauer design is excellent and the manufacture is executed with precision.

In 9mmP, the SIG Sauer lineup includes the P220, P225, P226 and P228. Although the specifics of each model will be discussed in detail, it is handy to keep in mind that essentially they are all the same pistol design, but differ in some dimensions and magazine capacity.

The actions on all of the models is of the mechanically locked, recoil-operated type, and are basically double-action/single-action in function. However, there are also double-action-only options available on some models for those who prefer that system.

THE P220

It was on America's 200th birthday that the SIG Sauer P220 was introduced — the first of the now totally successful line of such pistols. Not only was the P220 the first of the double-action SIG Sauers, but it was the first commercially successful autoloading pistol to eliminate the need for external manual safeties. This is accomplished via the patented automatic firing pin locking device. It was also the pistol which showed the world what a "decocker" was all about.

Although the suggestion that a pistol might not need an external manual safety and that it has a decocking system may sound routine and mundane in the 1990s, those were totally radical concepts back in the '70s when the design debuted.

Currently, the P220 is available in three chamberings — 9mmP, .38 Super Auto and .45 ACP. The pistol has the same overall dimensions in all three chamberings. The dimensions are:

Overall Length	7.79 inches.
Overall Height	5.63 inches.
Overall Width	1.37 inches.
Barrel Length	4.41 inches.
Rifling Twist	One turn in 9.84 inches.
Number Of Rifling Grooves	Six.
Sight Radius	6.29 inches.
Weight (Without Magazine)	26.5 ounces.
Weight Of Empty Magazine	2.9 ounces.
Weight Of Pistol And Empty Magazine	29.4 ounces.
Trigger Pull Weight	12.12 pounds (double-action) 4.4 (single-action)
Magazine Capacity	Nine rounds.

Browning imported and marketed the handy SIG Sauer P220 under their name during the mid-1970s.

The SIG Sauer P225 was made for the West German police. It is Europe's most widely-issued police pistol.

For the author, one of the most impressive of the specifications is the rate of rifling twist. At one turn in 9.84 inches, the twist rate is fast enough to stabilize any weight 9mmP bullet normally encountered — and that includes the 147-grainers.

For those who have not experienced the problem, there are a number of handguns on the market which may shoot the 115-grain and 124-grain bullets well, but which fall short when the subsonic 147-grain bullets are used. Not the SIG Sauer. It devours all bullet weights with equal aplomb.

For those who think a quick look at this pistol is like deja vue all over again, fear naught. Yes, the P220 was offered in the United States as the Browning BDA in the 1970s.

THE P225

Next, and what might be considered one of the more interesting of the models when it comes to quick handling and natural pointing, is the P225. It is available only in 9mmP, and the dimensions are:

Overall Length	7.08 inches.
Overall Height	5.15 inches.
Overall Width	1.34 inches.
Barrel Length	3.86 inches.
Rifling Twist	One turn in 9.84 inches.
Number Of Rifling Grooves	Six.

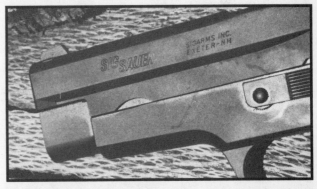

The SIG Sauer P225, because of its short barrel and slide, is known for its quick pointing characteristics.

Sight Radius	5.71 inches.
Weight *(Without Magazine)*	26.1 ounces.
Weight Of Empty Magazine	2.8 ounces.
Weight Of Pistol And Empty Magazine	28.9 ounces.
Trigger Pull Weight	12.12 pounds *(double-action)*
	4.4 pounds *(single-action)*
Magazine Capacity	Eight rounds.

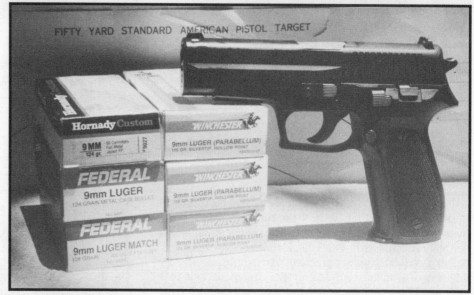

Above, of the police units using the SIG Sauer in the U.S., the P226 (left) is the most popular because of its high capacity. At right is the P225, the most popular police handgun in Europe. Right, the SIG Sauer autos will handle most any type of 9mm ammo with ease. Below, the frame of the P226 is built for service.

The P225 was designed originally for the West German police, and has become the most widely issued police pistol in Europe. It has a couple of things going for it, when compared to the other SIG Sauer models. For example, it is smaller than the standard-size P220 and the high-capacity P226, which means that it lends itself better to plainclothes carry or for undercover work.

Frankly, of all the SIG Sauer 9mmP pistols, the P225 is my own favorite. For lack of a better way to put it, this model simple "felt" better in use. However, it is important to note that this difference in "feel" is subtle at most, because they all felt good and performed well. It is just that when comparing the line against itself, the author liked the P225 the most.

Granted, it has the single-column, in-line magazine which holds "only" eight rounds. That is about half of what some 9mmP handguns hold these days. But, with such a magazine, the grip frame of the pistol is slimmer, and in this design that thinness fit the author's hand like it was made for it. What this meant when it came time to shoot was that the pistol pointed

Above, Geoff Barclay takes careful aim with a P226, testing the accuracy of the factory sights. Left, the P226, like all SIG Sauer pistols, is truly well made.

perfectly and naturally. This, in turn, resulted in quick, consistent hits.

Not only was I able to hit any part of the target at will, but the pistol made it easy to "walk" the bullet hits left, right, up or down. It was almost like drawing a picture with bullets. How enjoyable, and how such performance boosts confidence!

THE P226

The P226 is SIG Sauer's full-size, high-capacity 9mmP semi-auto offering. It might well be considered as the law enforcement workhorse of the line. It also has been picked as the preferred model by the Federal Bureau of Investigation for its hostage rescue teams and for its SWAT (Special Weapons And Tactics) units. Specific dimensions of the P226 are:

Overall Length	7.71 inches.
Overall Height	5.47 inches.
Overall Width	1.45 inches.
Barrel Length	4.41 inches.
Rifling Twist	One turn in 9.94 inches.
Number Of Rifling Grooves	Six.
Sight Radius	6.29 inches.
Weight *(Without Magazine)*	26.5 ounces.
Weight Of Empty Magazine	3.4 ounces.
Weight Of Pistol And Empty Magazine	29.9 ounces.
Trigger Pull Weight	12.12 pounds *(double-action)* 4.4 pounds *(single-action)*
Magazine Capacity	*(20-round magazine available)*.15 rounds

The slide of the SIG Sauer P226 is made of steel and configured to continue performing even during heavy use.

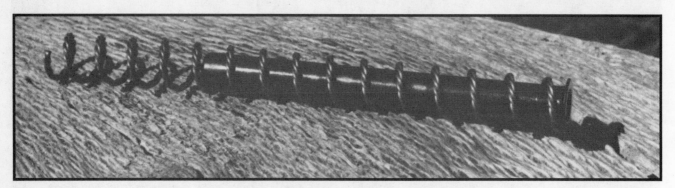

The recoil spring on SIG Sauer autos is made of double wire, making it effective even in extremly cold conditions.

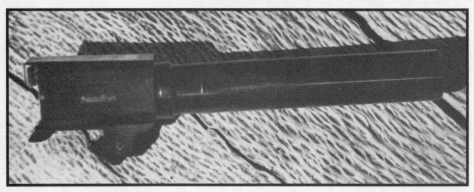

The squared breech end of the SIG Sauer barrel also serves as a locking block.

The author found the double-action-only option for this model to be intriguing. It took a few shots to become familiar with the trigger pull dynamics. They are different from even the double-action first shot in the other SIG Sauer models.

Quickly, one's trigger finger becomes educated. For example, there are no "surprises" with the trigger pull in DAO (double-action only). Yes, it is a comparatively l-o-n-g pull, but it is consistent and it always lets off in the same way and at the same spot in the finger movement.

More than anything else, the trigger pull on the DAO submodel is akin to an exaggerated two-stage military rifle trigger. There is a discernable amount of rearward movement involved in the first stage, and then a shorter, more precise second stage. So it was with the P226 in DAO.

The first few shots remained in the 8, 9 and 10 rings, but they put holes within those rings more or less at random. The next few shots saw the author able to put the holes into the 10 ring. Then, like with the other models, I was able to "walk" the hits around on the target at will.

There is little doubt that should a shooter use a P226 in DAO regularly, it could become one of the most "user-friendly" pistols in the entire lineup.

As a DAO, however, this is not what one would consider to be a target shooting proposition. It is a service pistol all the way.

THE P228

The SIG Sauer P228 might be considered as the compact version of the P225. It is slightly smaller than the full-size P225, yet remains what one would term a "high

SIG Sauer autos are noted for their natural, fast point features which makes them easy to control during rapid fire.

capacity" semi-auto pistol.

Although the major market for such a pistol is in the law enforcement arena, where it lends itself to off-duty and concealed carry, this also happens to be the model which was adopted by the U.S. Army for all of its "compact" pistol uses. The P228 used by the Army has the K-Kote finish and tritium night sights.

Essentially, the P228 is a high capacity variant of the P225. The only real differences are the magazine capacity and the grip frame contour to accommodate the larger capacity magazine. Specifications for the P228 are:

Overall Length	7.08 inches.
Overall Height	5.35 inches.
Overall Width	1.46 inches.
Barrel Length	3.86 inches.
Rifling Twist	One turn in 9.84 inches.
Number Of	
Rifling Grooves	Six.
Sight Radius	5.71 inches.
Weight *(Without Magazine)*	26.1 ounces.
Weight Of	
Empty Magazine	3.0 ounces.
Weight Of Pistol And	
Empty Magazine	29.1 ounces.
Trigger Pull Weight	12.12 pounds *(double-action)*
	4.4 pounds *(single-action)*
Magazine Capacity	13 rounds.

When a shooter grasps this model, it has a comfortable feel. It points about as naturally as any of the SIG Sauer line, and might be considered one of the better bets for self- or home-defense. It is configured in such a way that shooters with

smallish hands would have no problem handling it. Yet, it fits larger hands, like the author's, comfortably. That's quite an achievement.

Like all of the SIG Sauer pistols, the P228 is available with blue, nickel or K-Kote finish.

Another feature available on any of the pistols is the option of tritium night sights which are called SIGLITE sights. The pistols come standard with fixed sights (drift adjustable for windage) and the three-dot system. Wood handles also are available to replace the standard composition handles supplied with the various models.

It is unlikely that any of the SIG Sauer pistols is about to win a beauty contest — they are not what one might call "pretty" pistols. They are not ugly, either, but they simply are not cosmetically graceful. That's because they are business all the way. This reality sinks in instantly when a shooter grasps one of them and takes over at the controls.

Speaking of controls, there are not a lot of them, and those which are in evidence are where they should be and are both easy and quick to operate.

The magazine release button, for example, is a la 1911 design — at thumb level just aft of the trigger well. The trigger, of course, is also one of the controls, and it is located in the traditional spot, as well.

At the top of the handle on the left side of the pistol are the two main controls — the slide release lever and the decocking lever. The slide release lever is the smaller of the two controls, and is the most rearward. When the slide is locked to the rear, simply depress the lever and the slide slams forward.

The decocking lever is in exactly the right spot, and gives the whole line of handguns its signature identity. Whenever the pistol is cocked and the shooter wants to put it back into a safe mode, all that he or she needs to do is to depress the

The design of the P226's grip and trigger guard, gives the shooter an extra edge.

decocking lever, and the pistol is safe. However, to fire, all that needs to be done is to pull the double-action trigger and it goes bang. How quick. How handy.

Disassembly of the SIG Sauers also is quick and simple. First, assure that the pistol is not loaded. Then, remove the magazine and pull the slide to the rear, locking it rearward by pushing upward on the slide release lever.

Next, rotate the take-down lever (located on the left side of the frame just above the trigger) clockwise until it stops. Then,

when the slide release lever is depressed, the slide can be moved forward and off the frame (hold onto the slide, or it may go sailing across the room).

The recoil spring and guide are removed a la any P-35 or its derivatives. Grasp the spring and base of the guide where they rest against the bottom of the barrel, pull back slightly, then guide the spring and guide up and out of the bottom of the slide. Next, jiggle the barrel up and out of the slide. That's as far as the pistol normally needs to be disassembled for routine

The SIG Sauer P228 is a high-capacity compact that is popular for plainclothes as well as off-duty carry.

The P-210-6 is the first SIG auto. Any discussion of firearms with SIG in its name must mention this gun.

cleaning and maintenance.

It was the SIG Sauer design which brought an exciting variation of an old theme to the gun industry. This design really doesn't have a classic ejection port as did semi-auto and auto pistols which preceded it. Rather, empty casings are ejected through a square cut which extends all the way across the top of the square-profile slide, and down a bit on the right side.

This squared cut in the top of the slide not only serves as an ejection port, but it is an integral part of the locking mechanism. Corresponding shoulders in the breech area of the barrel lock into the slide via this huge cut/ejection port. This form of lockup has been copied by other companies in the 9mmP pistol business since — and why not? It works.

A close look at the recoil spring bespeaks the amount of thought and attention to detail which are common with the SIG Sauer line. It is a compound spring, comprised of two strands of spring steel wrapped around each other as they were formed into an elongated coil. Why did they do that? A number of reasons, actually, but primary among them is the fact that the pistol works more reliably in extremely cold weather as a result.

In fact, there is that level of attention to detail extant throughout each of these pistols. Where they need to be precise, they are. Where the metal needs to be hardened, it is. The result? They shoot, and shoot, and shoot and then keep shooting some more.

But longevity is not the only concern one would have when considering a 9mmP handgun. Frankly, it is the way in which these pistols, individually or as a group, feel, fit and hit the target which is most impressive.

Indeed, they are world class pistols, and are among only a handful of designs which one might consider totally appropos to take into a gunfight.

Although this entire line is now known as the SIG Sauer offering, that combination of names may give pause to some of the old timers. An understandable degree of confusion might result. Yes, there are SIG firearms, there are Sauer firearms — and there are SIG Sauer firearms.

THE P-210

SIG firearms are made in Switzerland. By far, the most famous of the SIG pistols is the original P-210-1 which was introduced in 1949. This is a single-action semi-auto offered in .22 long rifle, .30 Luger and 9mmP. It has a polished blue finish, 4 3/4-inch barrel and is 8 1/2 inches long overall. It weighs 35 ounces in .30 Luger and 9mmP, and 33 ounces in .22 rimfire. Checkered wood stocks are standard.

There are several sub-models of the P-210. For example, the P-210-2 is similar to the P-210-1, except the finish is dull and it has plastic stocks. The P-210-5 Target model is similar to the P-210-1, except it has a six-inch barrel, adjustable trigger stop, adjustable rear sight and target front sight. And, the P-210-6 Target model is similar to the P-210-2, with the target features. For owners of any of the P-210 pistols, there also is a .22 conversion unit so the pistol can be used as a rimfire. It consists of magazine, slide and recoil spring for the caliber.

While SIG is a Swiss operation, Sauer is a German company. Originally located in Suhl, but now in Eckenforde, the move had to do with the division of Germany following World War II, but any such concerns would be moot now due to the fact that Germany has been re-united.

J.P. Sauer u. Sohn is a famous gunmaker, and has produced some of the world's fine handguns, shotguns and rifles. On the pistol front, Sauer was best known during the early part of the 20th Century as a maker of a number pocket pistol models, beginning with the Model 1913 which was chambered for the .32 Auto cartridge. Next came the Model 1930, also chambered for the .32 Auto. The Model H double-action auto (made from 1938 until 1948 and designated Model 38 when issued during wartime) was offered in .25 Auto, .32 Auto and .380 ACP. Also, the company offered a Pocket 25 Automatic Pistol, which was chambered for the .25 Auto.

Couple those models with the many classic side-by-side shotguns, combination guns and bolt-action rifles produced by Sauer over the years, and the name quite literally stands for quality — high quality all the way.

Hence, the combination of the effort involving both SIG and Sauer into the SIG Sauer lineup means top notch all the way. These are major league firearms intended for use under any conditions anywhere in the world at anytime.

CHAPTER *Fourteen*

A FAMILY CALLED GLOCK

This Unusual Design Has A 9mm To Meet Various Needs!

Rick Kennerknecht puts a Glock 19 pistol in 9mmP through a range test. This is a handy-size pistol that performs well.

TO A LARGE degree, Glock pistols have redefined the way many shooters and representatives from the law enforcement community view working handguns.

Perhaps the best way to describe the entire Glock line of handguns is to say they are 1980s pistols. Literally, they came out of nowhere in the gun world, and have taken a large segment of it by storm.

However, in much the same way that books banned in certain places enjoy added sales activity generally, the controversial beginnings for Glock did nothing but help make the firm a household word. That controversy erupted when naysayers shook in imagined horror that these "plastic guns" would be able to defeat airport security.

To put it all into perspective, the early 1980s were a time when the world was keenly aware of atrocities foisted upon the world by international terrorists. The fact that many of the parts of the Glock pistols were made of polymers (plastics) made the anti-gunners go ballistic. Actually, Glock handguns are no more or less identifiable by airport security systems than about any other kind of firearm. But for those who would allege that the sky was falling, Glocks represented handguns from hell.

Granted, the false claims by the antis may have been unfair and unjustified, but they were not all bad for Glock, as it turned out. As mentioned above, the notoriety ascribed by the alarmists gave the Glock instant identity — something that could easily have taken several more years under more normal circumstances.

Gaston Glock, an Austrian engineer, formed Glock Ges.m.b.H. in Deutsch-Wagram, Austria in 1963 with the manufacturing of commercial appli-

The Glock 17 is the pistol that made Glock famous. Its length is 7.21 inches with a weight of 21.91 ounces.

Above, the Glock 19 is a compact in 9mmP. Left, the Glock 17L competition model is serious equipment.

The Glock 9mmP line is composed of three models. From left, they are the Model 17L, Model 17 and Model 19.

ances for the Austrian market. Later, Glock developed a variety of military and police-related products, including military knives, training and fragmentation hand grenades, non-disintegrating machine gun belts and entrenching tools.

In 1980, the Austrian army was searching for a modern state-of-the-art 9mm semi-automatic pistol to equip their troops with by 1983. Using modern manufacturing methods and non-strategic materials such as polymer, Gaston Glock was able, in 1982, to offer to the Austrian army test samples of a cost effective 9x19mm semi-automatic pistol.

After passing stringent testing procedures against domestic and international competitors, the Glock was purchased by the Austrian army as their new service pistol. In 1984, the Glock 17 pistol also surpassed all prior NATO (North Atlantic Treaty Organization) durability and strength standards and was chosen by the Norwegian Army as their standard sidearm.

In late 1985, Glock, Inc., was formed in Smyrna, Georgia — an Atlanta suburb — to begin servicing North American law enforcement agencies and sport shooters alike with the new NATO-proven Glock 17 pistol.

Five years later, by November 1990, more than 2,700 U.S. law enforcement agencies on federal, state and local levels had issued or authorized Glock pistols for duty use by their law enforcement personnel. In October, 1990, a Miami police officer, Armando Vales, captured the world title of the I.P.S.C. World Stock Gun Championship in Adelaide, South Austra-

lia, with a stock 9mm Glock 17L competition model.

With their square, boxy design and flat black finish, Glock pistols are easily identifiable in the field, but it wasn't their looks which made them famous. Quite simply, the Glock pistol was the first in an increasingly long line of "goof-proof" handguns which are simple to use.

Glocks incorporate the double-action-only concept, although they are not actually true double-action pistols. It might be more correct to use another Glock term to describe the actions. They are Safe Action pistols.

Perhaps the best way to describe differences between Glock pistols and most others on the market is that the Glock is not a double-action version of a design which began life as a single-action mechanism. For example, there is no long trigger pull which cycles a hammer, as is the case in the more traditional designs. Rather, the Glock incorporates a striker mechanism with multiple safety devices which are built-in and automatic.

Evidence of the design difference is apparent on the outside of the Glock itself. There are only three "controls" on the gun — the slide release lever, located on the left side of the frame just above the grip area, and the double-duty trigger. Add the magazine release button located just aft of the trigger housing, and that's it.

The first of the safety features is the trigger safety. It is the small sub-trigger or lever protruding through the middle of the

The Glock 17L has a dot on the front sight and a white outline on the rear sight.

trigger itself. When the trigger finger starts to depress the trigger, the trigger safety goes rearward and becomes flush with the face of the main trigger.

Next on the safety front is the firing pin safety which blocks the firing pin until the trigger is pulled completely to the rear. Finally, there is a drop safety which prevents the pistol from firing if it is dropped. It, too, is disarmed as the trigger is pulled fully to the rear. Further, the striker assembly is not fully cocked until the trigger is pulled completely to the rear, so this feature is an added safety function.

All of this results in a trigger pull which is longer than a traditional single-action design, but shorter than the normal double-action variety. Trigger pulls on production Glocks shot by the author tend to be quite uniform from one handgun to another. Glock Models 17 and 19 tend to have seven-pound pulls, and the Glock 17L competition model has a trigger pull right at five pounds out of the box.

Granted, Glock pistols are not likely to win any beauty contests. However, they do have an appeal for many shooters which transcends surface looks. They tend to shoot and shoot and shoot without problems, and they generally are satisfactorily accurate for their intended purposes. Those are certainly two gigantic areas of concern for such hardware. To put it another way, they go "bang" when the trigger is pulled, and they probably will hit the target, if the shooter does his or her part.

To make their point about reliability, the folks at Glock showed up at the Raahauge Shooting Sports Fair near Norco, California, on Saturday, May 19, 1990, with 20 Glock 17 pistols. That sports fair draws about 25,000 people during its

The Glock 17 has only three controls: the slide release, located at the top of the frame above the slide grip panel; the trigger and the magazine release button.

The Glock 17 has vertical striations and checkering on the backstrap of the grip.

Glock pistols are noted for holding up to extended use. To demonstrate this, Glock assembled a Model 17 from parts of 20 pistols and conducted a marathon test. The pistol fired 10,140 rounds in three hours, 47 minutes.

three-day run each year, with over 10,000 spectators on the grounds at the time of the Glock demonstration.

Before the shooting began, all 20 pistols were disassembled, and their parts thoroughly mixed. Then, starting with G-17 serial number MU 421 US (frame), a complete pistol was assembled from the piles of parts. What that meant was that the test gun would have been made of random parts — not parts specifically fitted for the purpose.

Shooting was performed by members of the California Rangemasters Association and represented eight different law enforcement agencies. During the next three hours and 47 minutes, that one handgun was fired 10,140 times, using Federal Hi Power 9mm ammunition (stock #9AP).

The time period included mandatory range cease fires for target replacement, as the test was conducted on the same firing line as the public shooting at the fair.

Only one malfunction attributable to the pistol was experienced. At approximately 4,500 rounds, a trigger spring broke. A replacement part was drawn from the existing leftover parts, installed in less than one minute, and the test continued.

Also, at every 2,500-round interval, the pistol was field stripped so the chamber and breech face could be cleaned. No other maintenance was performed during the entire test.

In 9mmP, the Glock lineup is represented by three models. There is the basic Glock 17 standard pistol, the Glock 19 compact and the Glock 17L competition. By model, the specifications are:

GLOCK 17

Overall length is 7.21 inches; height, (with sights), 5.16 inches; width, 1.18 inches; length between sights, 6.5 inches; barrel length, 4.49 inches; rifling, hexagonal profile with right-hand twist; rate of twist, one turn in 9.84 inches; magazine capacity, 17 rounds standard, (optional 19-round mag.); weight, 21.91 ounces without magazine, (empty magazine is 2.08 ounces, or about 9.5 ounces fully loaded.

The Glock 17L is delivered with an extra magazine and a handy magazine loader.

GLOCK 19

Overall length, 6.74 inches; height, (with sights), 4.92 inches; width, 1.18 inches; length between sights, 5.98 inches; barrel length, 4.02 inches; rifling, hexagonal profile with right-hand twist; rate of twist, one turn in 9.84 inches; magazine capacity, 15 rounds standard, (optional 17-round mag.); weight, 20.99 ounces without magazine (empty magazine is 1.98 ounces, or about 8.55 ounces full).

GLOCK 17L

Overall length, 8.77 inches; height, 5.16 inches; width, 1.18 inches; length between sights, 8.03 inches; barrel length, 6.02 inches; rifling, hexagonal profile with right-hand twist; rate of twist, one turn in 9.84 inches; magazine capacity, 17 rounds standard, (optional 19-round mag.); weight, 23.35 ounces without magazine; (empty magazine is 2.08 ounces, or about 9.5 ounces full).

During range testing, the Glock 17 performed well. It pointed quickly, and the simple combat-style sights made target acquisition both quick and easy. Hitting random four-inch targets at unknown distances ranging from five feet to seven yards was boringly routine. There was also no trouble hitting the same size targets at will at distances up to 25 yards. Trigger pull was consistent, and did not seem to be a factor in hitting the targets.

The Glock 19 performed similarly to the 17 and did not seem to be a "compact" in use. Rather, it performed much the same way one would expect a full-size model to do. However, recoil was slightly more noticeable with the 19, as compared to the 17. That difference, however, did not affect tactical performance adversely.

Because of its longer barrel and slide, the Glock 17L handled a bit more steadily than did either the 17 or 19. Its tactical accuracy was so good that it was almost scary. I merely needed to point it at the various targets, pull the trigger and hit them.

From a tactical perspective, all three models were superb.

The 17L, however, did demonstrate that it had an edge when it came to bullet placement.

One factor, however, was noticeable each time the Glocks were shot. Perceived recoil is greater with them than with most of the more traditional 9mmP handguns. This seemed to have little, if anything, to do with the size and overall shape of the grips. They were generally fist-filling and ergonomically correct.

I suspect the material from which the grip frame is made, coupled with the relative light weight of the pistols, are the reasons for the increased felt recoil.

Simply put, the grips are hard — made of a hard polymer. Checkering and vertical striations are moulded into the front and rear of the handle, as well as on the face of the trigger guard. Grip side panels are stippled. All of these features contribute nicely to a non-slip grip formula.

But the hard surface of the grip area certainly transmits the rather sharp recoil of the 9mmP with aplomb. I would not term this felt recoil to be overly objectionable, but some form of softer covering would be nice for extended range applications.

Meanwhile, law enforcement agencies all over the place are switching to Glocks, whether the cartridge of choice is the 9mmP or something else. Acceptable reliability and accuracy, of course, are big factors which help the various departments decide.

However, accidental shootings are things which simply don't cut it in society these days. And, the Glock's goof-proof design is a major plus factor here. Simply put, a shooter has to want to shoot the Glock for it to go off. Yet, when the decision is made, it goes off every time.

Those are the sorts of things law enforcement administrators weigh heavily when it comes to choosing a handgun. In fact, the Glock design is really good for people who are not constant and serious shooters. The simplicity of the design and operation means the handguns can be shot effectively by people who are not serious pistoleers.

There is no effort here, though, to suggest these pistols are

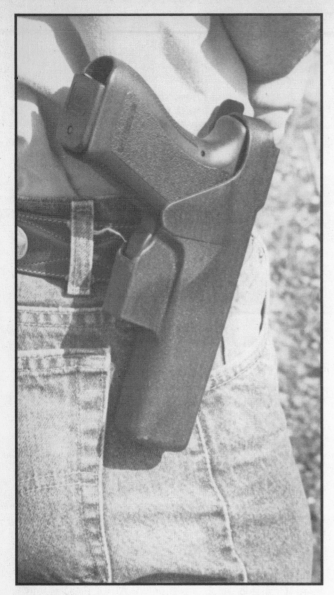

This Model 17 is carried in a Glock holster which is made of synthetic material impervious to weather.

This open-bottom, one-piece holster from Glock places the Glock 19 in a high carry. The holster is ultra handy.

not serious handguns. They are, but they lack the aesthetic appeal of the various "pretty" guns. With such an appearance and feel, these handguns are nothing more or less than their designer intended: tactical performers.

Although Glock pistols are not as maintenance-intensive as some handguns, they do require periodic cleaning. To disassemble any of the three Glock 9mmP handguns, the same procedure is used.

First, remove the magazine and assure there is no ammunition in the pistol. Next, remove the slide. To accomplish this, first pull the trigger, then grasp the pistol in either the right or left hand in such a way that four fingers rest over the slide and the thumb rests on the rear side of the receiver.

Using the fingers, draw back the slide about 0.12-inch, and pull the slide lock downward with the thumb and index finger of the right or left hand. A special note here will help eliminate a certain degree of potential frustration.

The slide lock has a small, checkered "button-like" head protruding from both sides of the receiver just above the trigger housing. Both side of the slide lock need to be pulled downward simultaneously for the slide to be removed.

Once the slide lock has been depressed, push the slide forward and separate it from the receiver.

The slide removed, taking out the barrel comes next. To accomplish this, push the recoil spring tube somewhat forward with the thumb. Be careful, because the spring is under tension. Then, remove the recoil spring tube with recoil spring from the slide and separate them if necessary.

Now grasp the barrel on the barrel locking cams, push it slightly forward, raise it and pull it backward and out of the slide. This completes the basic field stripping procedure for the Glock handguns. Reassembly is the reverse procedure.

Glock's 9mm Machine Pistol And The Law

Oregon sheriff's deputy Dwes Huston has a string of expended cases in the air as he fires full-auto with the Glock 18. In this instance, the officer is using the extended 33-round magazine, but it is hidden by the hand-hold he is using.

IF YOU LIKE things presented in orderly fashion, you probably have noted that there is a hole in the lineup of Glock 9mm handguns. There is the Glock 17, of course, and there is the Glock 19, but what about the Glock 18?

It's there, too, but it might be said that this particular Glock designation is in a world of its own. It's not one you'll find on the firing line at your gun club or even in most law enforcement weapons inventories at this point. The Glock 18 is a machine pistol that has a selective-fire capability.

At first glance, the Glock 18 does not look all that different from its immediate numerical predecessor, the Glock 17. It has the same general exterior design contouring, except that there is a selector switch on the left side of the Glock 18.

The term "machine pistol" is really sort of all-inclusive. The Germans who developed the concept tend to think of all submachine guns as machine pistols, since they are relatively small and fire pistol ammunition. The venerable broomhandle Mauser, for example, was reworked in the era of World War I to handle sustained fire.

In the period following the War To End All Wars, several Spanish arms manufacturers adopted the design and found immediate takers in China, where the war lords still held power despite the fact that revolution was brewing. Noting the success of the broomhandle selective-fire design, several other European manufacturers entered the market with their own version.

Various other makers came up with machine pistol designs. For example, one developed by Star, the Spanish company, shortly before World War II, was little more than a direct copy of the Government Model 1911 auto that incorporated a selective-fire capability.

As one might expect, this particular model was chambered for the .45 ACP cartridge instead of the 9mm Parabellum. Offered with detachable stocks and extended magazines, it found a ready market in Latin America. The Soviet Union, seemingly impressed with the concept, developed its own machine pistol, the Stechkin, which was chambered for the 9mm Makarov cartridge.

You can see that the machine pistol dates back in history and that the Glock 18 is hardly a new concept, but it does take

The Glock 18 with its 19-round magazine looks much like the Glock 17, except for full-auto selector switch on its left side.

Chuck Karwan had the chance to fire several hundred 9mmP rounds, mostly full-auto, with the Glock 18 machine pistol and found he appreciated it.

advantage of some interesting modern technologies.

Combat handgunnery expert Chuck Karwan had heard of the selective-fire Glock pistol about the time it was introduced and admits he had serious doubts as to its usefulness in combat and specifically for law enforcement use.

"With its light weight and high rate of fire, I felt certain the Glock 18 would be too difficult to control in the full-auto mode to be of real use in a law enforcement situation," he recalls.

He did have a chance, however, to check out one of the Glock 18 pistols that had been acquired by an Oregon sheriff's department. Deputy Jim Main was in charge of training

personnel of the Douglas County Sheriff's Department in the use of the newly acquired machine pistol.

According to Main, training with the Glock 18 for personnel of his department has been devoted primarily to use of the gus as an entry weapon when officers are involved in drug busts and similar fast-action efforts. The weapons used previously by the Douglas County Sheriff's department when going up against drug dealers and others in the illicit trade had been the Heckler & Koch MP5 submachine gun, so the use of full-auto weaponry was hardly a novelty to the department's entry-team personnel.

Another plus for this particular law enforcement agency was the fact that deputies had been issued the Glock 17 as the official duty handgun. The similarity in feel, balance and controls between that and the Glock 18 simplified training, according to Deputy Main. The only difference is the selector switch on the left side of the Glock 18. It is possible to even use the same holster and magazines of the Glock 17 with the selective-fire version.

Chuck Karwan was able to fire the Glock 18 on three different occasions, expending several hundred rounds in the full-auto mode. He also was able to observe the training of department personnel in use and application of the machine pistol in the field.

"One of the best applications for a machine pistol either for the military or police is as a room-entry weapon, particularly for the first person through the door," Karwan wrote in his DBI volume, The *Gun Digest Book of Combat Handgunnery, Third Edition*. The machine pistol "has several advantages in that role. First, it can be operated with one hand just like a handgun if it becomes necessary. It can be secured quickly in a belt holster should both hands be needed. It also is far easier to maneuver in tight quarters than a shotgun, assault rifle or the

Deputy Dwes Huston of Oregon's Douglas County Sheriff's Department gets field training from behind a portable barricade utilized in forced entry exercises.

other machine pistol with which they had experience. Chuck Karwan agreed, comparing it to machine pistols from his own experience that fire only .22 rimfire ammunition or, perhaps, the Astra Model F machine pistol. The latter is equipped with a rate-of-fire reducer, which is meant to make that particular gun easier to control.

Conjecture among those sheriff's deputies being trained with the Glock machine pistol was that ease experienced in controlling the gun in the full-auto mode was born primarily of the basic design of the entire Glock line, which seems to position the gun's bore line immediately over the top of the shooter's hand.

This means, of course, that the resulting recoil is straight to the rear, with far less tendency for the gun's muzzle to rotate upward, as is the case with other pistols and especially full-auto weapons.

"The tendency of the muzzle to rise is controlled with

Chuck Karwan was justly proud of the silhouette target he fired full-auto with Glock 18's 33-round magazine.

conventional submachine gun."

In firing the Glock 18, Karwan found it operated perfectly. He also observed members of the sheriff's department entry team, as they fired several hundred rounds from the pistols. The only problem noted — not one that could be considered a malfunction — lay in the fact that, at about the point that 300 rounds or so had passed through the gun, fouling was beginning to gum up the works. This manifested itself in a failure of the slide to remain in the locked-back position after the last round had been fired from the magazine.

"Obviously, if kept clean, there is little likelihood of the Glock 18 being involved in any extended engagement that would result in enough shooting to cause problems of reliability," Karwan opines.

Those deputies who had fired other machine pistols in the course of their work or training found that firing the Glock 18 amounted to a series of surprises, even revelations. All agreed that the Glock was far easier to control and handle than any relative ease, when using a solid, two-handed grip," Karwan discovered.

"Shooting one-handed with the gun in its full-auto mode is another story," he admits. "The muzzle rise is rapid, even though it is easier to control than with other machine pistols I've had the opportunity to check out on the range." Rate of fire of the Glock 18, with the selector switch set for full-auto, is in the vicinity of 2,000 rounds per minute.

In Vietnam, where most troops were armed with the selective-fire M16 rifle, we no longer could boast of being a "nation of riflemen." We had become a "nation of sprayers" and the ammunition bills paid by the U.S. Government substantiate that accusation.

In an effort to reverse that trend, the Pentagon now is having the M16 built with a three-shot burst capability.

There also are some machine pistols that feature a three-shot burst. In fact, the VP-70, produced by Heckler & Koch in the Seventies was limited to a three-shot burst and semi-auto fire only. There was no full-auto capability for that specific model.

There is no three-round burst limitation incorporated in the Glock 18's design, but that is one of the techniques being taught these days in use of selective-fire arms. With extensive military and civilian experience with full-auto armament, Karwan has attempted, over the years, to school his trigger finger to handle a three-round burst without benefit of a mechanical cut-off. His comment: "It is easier to fire more rounds than three with the Glock 18, but damned hard to fire less!"

This particular expert, incidentally, does not favor the burst-control device that has been incorporated in some arms designs. "Burst-control devices are a mechanical solution to a training problem," he contends. "They tend to complicate a firearm's mechanism unnecessarily and to compromise its reliability and durability.,"

A great advantage in design of the Glock 18 is the fact that

Some of the sheriff's deputies undergoing training with the machine pistol favored this type of two-hand grip, allowing them to use lower area of the longer magazine.

it uses the standard 17- and 19-round magazines of the semi-auto Glock 17. However, the Georgia distributor for the guns also can offer a 33-round stick-type magazine. It fits the magazine well in the same manner as the shorter standard magazines, protruding about two inches below the bottom of the mag well.

"This extra length can be used to advantage, however," Karwan found, "as it can be used as a handle for the weaker hand in la two-handed firing position."

Deputy John Strickland was proud of the skill he acquired with the Glock 18 during his department's training sessions. He favored a low-torso hold so that any high shots still would be in kill zone on the target.

Deputy Dwes Huston favored the two-hand hold with left hand on lower section of the 33-round magazine. This system helped a credible score for full-auto fire.

One of the Oregon deputies with whom Karwan was shooting favored this particular position, claiming that the extra leverage helped him to control the machine pistol when firing full-auto. This individual's use of the long grip made it possible for him to fire an entire magazine of 33 rounds into the chest area of a silhouette target at combat distances. Karwan, however, found the hold awkward when he tried to emulate the deputy's performance.

"When shooting at multiple targets with the Glock 18, I could put a three-round burst into each target nearly as quickly as I could put one round into each target while firing semi-auto," Chuck Karwan reports. "This, of course, gives the gun/ammunition combination a far higher probability of delivering an incapacitating wound than does the conventional semi-automatic pistol."

It is his contention that one of the better 9mm jacketed hollow-point loads offers a 90 percent probability of a one-shot stop with a single torso hit. "A three-round burst to a felon's torso with the same load should have the probability of 99.9 percent for a stop. It just doesn't get any better than that!"

Chuck Karwan feels the best method of employing the Glock 18 machine pistol is with the three-shot burst. What this amounts to is that the shooter aims only once to send three rounds downrange. It becomes a "triple-tap" in effect, but with one pull of the trigger. His experience shows that a shooter who has practiced considerably with this particular handgun can get consistent hits on a torso-size silhouette target at 20 yards or so.

However, Karwan doesn't discount the continuous burst potential for the Glock 18. "I found that if recoil caused me to track off the target, it was possible to bring the gun back on target in mid-burst just by getting into equilibrium with the recoil," he explains. "With a lot of practice, one can keep the gun pretty much on the target at a combat range of seven yards or so, even if firing the entire 35-round magazine."

In firing into a pond from an elevation, Karwan had the opportunity to see where his bullets were landing during extended firing of the entire magazine. In this instance, he was firing at a range of approximately 25 yards. He feels, based upon this observation, that he would miss a silhouette target few times during a full-magazine burst — even as impractical as that type of firing might be.

"The biggest problem with firing extended bursts is the fact that the gun's sights seem to disappear in the resultant blur as soon as the trigger is pulled." He feels that, for close-range combat situations, a laser sight might offer an advantage in helping to hold the rounds on the target in a combat situation.

While most machine pistols of the past have been designed to handle the capability of adding a shoulder stock, this is not the case with the Glock 18. There is no such provision. Karwan doesn't feel it needs such a stock, since he sees its primary role strictly as a pistol for entry teams where the officer probably would want one hand free in any case.

"With the exception of the full-auto selector, this pistol really is a Glock 17 in nearly every way," Karwan points out. "In normal use, it would be used in the same manner as the Glock 17, saving the full-auto capability for special needs and situations..

One exception between the two models is the slide, Karwan's investigations showed. They do not interchange, because the slide rails differ in dimensions. There also are some dimensional differences in the frames of the two pistols, as well as several other parts, a requirement to allow selective fire for the Glock 18.

Needless to say, you are not going to find the Glock 18 at your corner sporting goods emporium. Sales are limited strictly to law enforcement agencies and selected military organizations.

"Not every entry team will pick such a weapon," Karwan states in his final evaluation. "For instance, it probably would not be appropriate in a hostage rescue mission. However, even in that situation, it would be simple just to switch to semi-auto fire and use the weapon as a conventional semi-auto pistol.

"It is not a gun for a person who has not been trained to use it," he opines, "but those who are trained properly can provide a big nightmare for any bad guy!"

CHAPTER
Fifteen

THE 9mms OF HECKLER & KOCH

This German Maker's Lineup Is Short — But Adequate

The MP5K-PDW (top), with its stock folded, is compared to the Beretta M9, the U.S. service pistol.

HECKLER & KOCH is among the world's better known producers of 9mmP firearms, yet actually has relatively few models in that chambering. It is a situation of quality rather than quantity. Yet, as this book was being written, HK was in the process of bringing out a whole new design in semi-auto pistols called the USP — the letters standing for "Universal Self-loading Pistol."

This is truly a new pistol in a number of respects, starting with the fact that it is the first HK firearm designed specifically for the American market. Before exploring the USP further, it might be prudent to look back into the recent history of HK firearms and how they have fit into the overall picture.

For many Americans, the name HK has been synonymous with expensive. Generally, HK firearms in the United States have been priced at two to three times the amount of other firearms on the market. Hence, they never have been a high-volume proposition. Further, the high standards of quality are well established and virtually never questioned.

On the 9mmP front, however, HK has had only a short lineup of models. Certainly, there has been the famous MP5 submachine gun, but for most shooters, such a firearm is far from ever being a reality. Rather, it is a law enforcement/military proposition.

For civilians, there have been the P9, VP70Z, SP89 and the P7 series. That's really a short lineup, but there are some outstanding handguns among them. At this writing, only the SP89 and P7 models remained in production.

HK P9

The HK P9 was manufactured for seven years, ending in 1984. It was a single-action semi-auto with four-inch barrel, fixed sights and a Parkerized finish. In addition to 9mmP, the P9 was available also in .30 Luger (7.65P) and (designated P9S) in .45 ACP.

HK VP70Z

Also discontinued in 1984 was the VP70Z, which was a double-action semi-auto pistol with 4-1/2-inch barrel. It also featured a double-column magazine that held 18 rounds.

HK SP89

Although the SP89, introduced in 1989, is technically a semi-auto handgun, it has the looks of a stockless "hand rifle." Barrel is 4-1/2 inches, but the firearm weighs 4.4 pounds, and is 12.8 inches long overall. It is quite similar in many respects to the HK94, which is a semi-auto rifle in 9mmP (a 9mmP variant of the famed HK91 in 7.62mm NATO). Magazines for the SP89 pistol hold 15 or 30 rounds.

Heckler & Koch MP5A2 subgun might be considered a distant cousin of the current crop of the maker's handguns inasmuch as both fire the 9mmP round.

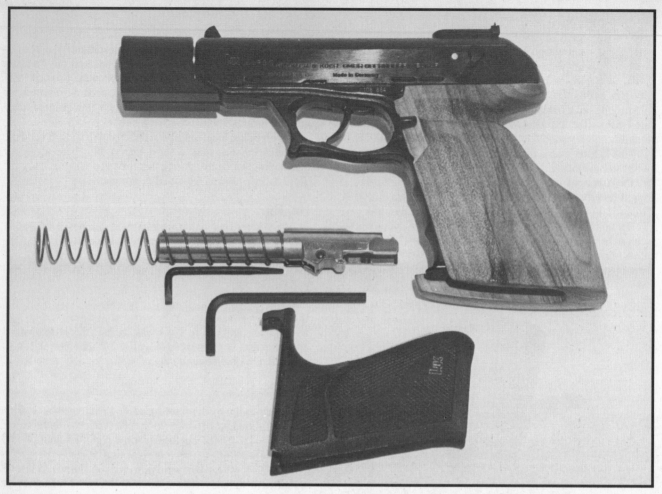

This P9 has a compensator and target grips. While no longer in production, there are many P9s still being used.

HK P7

Despite the fact that the models mentioned above have been well known among several segments of the shooting public, it has been the variants in the HK P7 lineup which have established a mental image for what HK pistols are — an image which focuses immediately upon the unique firing system incorporated into these handguns. For lack of a shorter description, these pistols incorporate a "squeeze-cock" mechanism which, among other things, happens to make them among the safest of the world's handguns to use, and some of the most effective service/combat models ever made.

It all started with the P7PSP, which also was discontinued in 1984. However, it had the now-famous "squeeze-cock" system which has typified HK on the American market. That system includes a hinged (at the bottom) front grip strap which can be "squeezed" backward by the shooting hand. That pressure and resultant movement "cocks," or moves the striker into battery, which arms the pistol. Then, a simple single-action pull on the trigger fires the handgun.

This system affords a level of carry safety which at least matches (some feel it surpasses) any double-action design, yet allows the comparatively light and easy trigger pull of a single-action on every shot. A live round can be carried in the chamber safely in such a design, because the action is not cocked until the grip is squeezed by the shooting hand.

Following the P7PSP was the P7M8 which is being offered

currently. It incorporates the squeeze-cock design, and the magazine holds eight rounds. Barrel length is four inches.

The P7M13 is similar to the P7M8, except it has a double-column magazine. Capacity is 13 shots.

For this writing, the author checked out the P7M13 with nickel finish. This is the sort of handgun which becomes more interesting and effective with use. The more one shoots it, the more one appreciates its many features. And, the more one shoots it, the more one realizes that it truly is among the world's finest ever 9mmP handguns. It is not a target handgun. Rather, it is the sort of 9mmP one would opt to take into a gunfight if he had total choice in the matter.

At first glance, the P7 profile is not what one would be tempted to call pretty. It is not ugly, either, but is more in line with the "functional" look when it comes to an aesthetic school of design. This is typical of many mechanical objects which originate in Germany.

Add to that the level of fit and precision one would expect from firearms emanating from Oberndorf, and the idea that it works and works well begins to take form. This may be where many gun designs end. However, with the P7, it is where everything begins. From this point, things become more and more interesting.

For example, the design features a fixed barrel with polygonal rifling that is hammer forged. It is easier to

The P7M8 is the first HK to have the squeeze-cock grip.

accomplish accuracy with any of the above features, but put them all together in one pistol, and it would be difficult to make one that didn't shoot at least okay. But there is more.

Like other firearms in the HK lineup, the P7 has a fluted chamber. In addition to putting lines on the sides of spent brass, the fluting serves a functional purpose. It causes the handgun to extract and eject empties, even if the extractor should break or be missing from the handgun entirely. In fact, the only real purposes for the extractor are to serve as a loaded chamber indicator and to make extraction totally smooth and consistent.

But there is more. The pistol design also incorporates a gas system which uses the gases from the burning powder to help retard the rearward movement of the recoiling slide when a round is fired. This eliminates the need for a heavy slide or a more conventional form of locking mechanism. Functional reliability is what this is all about.

Add to all of this the 110-degree grip angle and weight distribution of the pistol, and the shooter ends up with a firearm that functions flawlessly and points naturally. In any tactical situation, those are, of course, two of the most important features any firearm can offer.

Although the exacting manufacturing process necessary to produce the P7 pistol results in a price tag that blows away many prospective buyers, it also affords the creation of a handgun that will last virtually indefinitely if treated at all respectfully. When it comes to the finer firearms, the differences often are so subtle that they are appreciated by relatively few shooters. For example, even the magazine for the P7M13 is something to talk about.

First, these magazines are made of much thicker steel than virtually any others on the market. And, the design, which goes from staggered double-column at the base to single-column at the top, accomplishes a number of intriguing things all at once.

Because of its shape, the magazine can be inserted into the grip quickly and smoothly. The shooter need not look at the pistol or magazine when inserting the mag into the gun. When the ambidextrous magazine release lever behind the trigger area is depressed, the magazine literally pops out and free from the pistol. That also is nice.

But what approached mind-boggling attention to detail was the way the 13-round magazine loaded. It was so mystifying that I had to disassemble the magazine for closer study to figure out how the reality had been accomplished.

For those who are unaware, high capacity magazines can be thumb-busters to load — especially those rounds which are inserted when the magazine is already about half full. The procedure is tough enough that there are a number of little devices available which help the shooter save skin on thumb and forefinger (and preclude blistering when the procedure is performed numerous times in short order).

However, when loading the magazine for the HK P7M13, it became apparent quickly that it was not noticeably more difficult to load the thirteenth round than it had been to load the first one. How does that happen? Simple. The answer is a combination of the spring and the double-to-single column housing design. This system is just one more example of the degree to which everything about these pistols has been thought-out and executed properly. These are the subtlies that

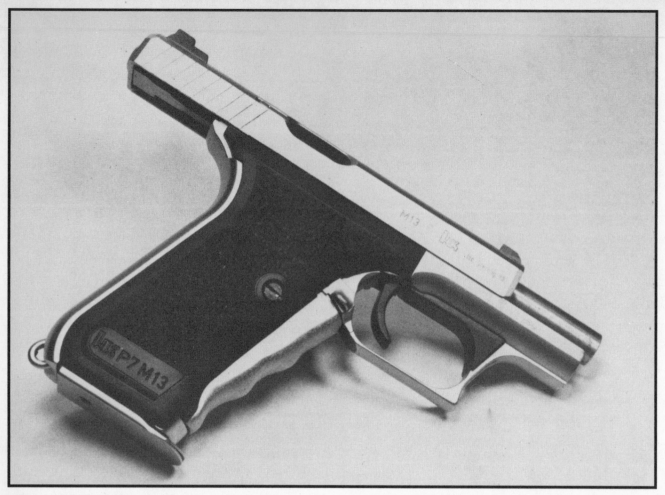

Author used this P7M13 while writing this book. He considers it to be one of the finest 9mm handguns ever made.

separate world class pistols from other guns.

The nuances of the design may be legion, but when executed into the final product, they make for an extremely simple handgun to clean and maintain. Disassembly and reassembly are incredibly simple and easy.

After assuring that the pistol is not loaded, remove the magazine and allow the slide to snap forward (whenever the slide is locked to the rear, snapping it forward is as simple as squeezing the cocking lever, which is the entire front of the grip). Next, push the slide retaining button at the left rear of the frame while pulling the slide back about three-quarters of an inch.

With the slide pulled that distance to the rear (there is a "feel" when it reaches that point), lift up the rear of the slide and then allow it to move forward and away from the muzzle of the barrel. Once the slide has been removed, the recoil spring slides off the barrel, and the pistol is ready for routine cleaning and maintenance. Reassembly is the reverse process.

However, there are a couple of notes to make the process slick and quick. When replacing the slide, make certain that the gas piston, which is attached to the bottom front of the slide, is aligned with the gas cylinder so it will slide into place smoothly. Then, it is simply a matter of angling the slide so it will move backward against the pressure of the recoil spring until it is far enough to the rear to be rotated down and into

place. It clicks into place easily, and the pistol is reassembled. Frankly, it is so quick and slick that after a couple of practice runs, it can be done without conscious thought.

Further cleaning and maintenance can be done on the firing pin assembly and bushing, which is removed from the rear of the slide. To accomplish this disassembly, merely depress the cocking lever until the end of the firing pin is flush with the slot in the firing pin bushing. Then, with a finger or coin (I found the finger works fine), rotate the bushing 90 degrees clockwise and it comes loose. Depressing the cocking lever fully pushes the bushing far enough out of the slide so it can be grasped and pulled all the way out.

This is all the further one has to disassemble this part of the pistol for cleaning. The firing pin assembly does disassemble further, but it is not recommended to do so on a regular basis. Care must be taken to assure that the assembly is put back together properly should it be further disassembled, however.

Following extended amounts of firing (like after 500 rounds or about every year), there are some other more detailed cleaning procedures recommended for the pistol. They are all simple, straight-forward operations, and involve cleaning detail work to keep dirt and sludge from building up in critical spots and causing malfunctions.

The author fired many more than 500 rounds through the test pistol, using a wide variety of factory ammunition and

Above is a P7M13 service-grade handgun with its distinctive squeeze-cock feature. Below is the gun's magazine.

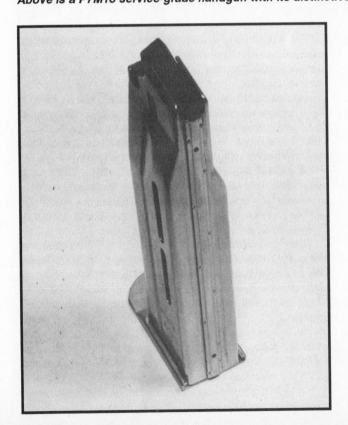

handloads. All functioned flawlessly, and the general level of tactical accuracy was incredible.

From the bench, the pistol fired groups of two inches or less at 25 yards with virtually all ammo fed to it. Some groups were in the 1-1/2-inch category, but rarely were five-shot groups smaller. However, within the groups, it was common to have two or three holes touching each other.

The author credits the achieved level of accuracy more to pilot error than anything else. The feeling was that the pistol is probably capable of one- to 1-1/2-inch groups with high quality ammunition.

But the P7 is not a target handgun, so that type of accuracy is more academic than anything else. The accuracy in a service pistol is that which is delivered under tactical conditions. It was in this category that the author was totally amazed. It is difficult to miss a six-inch plate at random distances from several feet to 25 yards with this gun.

Sights on the test pistol were simple — front post, notch rear. The rear sight was drift adjustable for windage. The three-dot system was in place, but could be eliminated with a felt tip pen for those who like real sights. However, the sights on the P7 are, in a way, almost academic when it comes to tactical shooting. They, like the extractor, contribute to consistency, but are essentially unnecessary for successful use.

The secret of using the P7 is to forget many of the habits one has created with other designs, put the mind into auto-pilot,

The HK USP (Universal Self-loading Pistol) was originally designed for the .40-caliber but it also is available in 9mm.

point the pistol at the target and hit it. It really is that simple.

The P7 design points so naturally that the author was able to look only at the target (paying no attention to the pistol) and, while concentrating visually on the target, point the handgun and squeeze the trigger, hitting the target every single time. That's impressive. But even more impressive is the fact that this same procedure can be done instantly when turning and spotting a target, and it can be done with rapidly repeated shots.

Granted, it does take some degree of familiarization with the squeeze-cock design before shooting the P7 becomes smooth and quick. But once the shooter is so familiarized, the operation becomes second-nature. Oddly, this is the sort of a pistol which could be functionally mastered more quickly by a new shooter than by a shooter who had become familiar with other designs. For veteran shooters, it is a matter of re-education.

The pistol comes in a hard box with spare magazine, cleaning rod and cleaning brush. The HK P7 is not a pistol for everyone. But for those who can appreciate and make use of its many unique features, it truly is a world class 9mmP handgun.

However, HK happens to be a viable commercial enterprise, and selling firearms is its business. Given the widespread availability of 9mmP handguns in the United States at more affordable prices from other manufacturers, HK found

itself in a position of offering a fine handgun, but one which had a built-in limitation on sales — price. It simply costs a lot to make a pistol like the P7. Devaluation of the U.S. dollar also has had its effect.

Also, there are other matters of concern when it comes to the general pistol market in the United States. Certain types of features are considered necessary by many individuals and agencies, and certain features are required for some of the various kinds of shooting games conducted here.

To address that situation, HK went back to the drawing boards and came up with that whole new design which it calls the USP (Universal Self-loading Pistol). Of course, if one were to be globally parochial, the USP also could be considered to stand for "United States Pistol." How vain!

This pistol was introduced officially at the 1993 Shooting, Hunting, Outdoor Trades (SHOT) Show in Houston, Texas, but has not yet been available on a production basis in 9mmP at the time of this writing. The design was offered first in .40 S&W, to be followed quickly by production handguns in 9mmP.

The author had an opportunity to fire several of the prototype USP pistols in both 9mmP and .40 S&W during a trip to a local Houston range the day before the SHOT Show opened, and it truly is a fine handgun.

For lack of a better way to describe it, the USP has all of the "whistles and bells" one would expect from a state-of-the-art pistol, and it is made of the latest high-tech materials. Also, it is to be priced more in line with the affordability factor than is the P7.

"The HK USP is the first HK pistol designed especially for American shooters," the company reported when the new model was introduced. "Features favored by U.S. civilian, law enforcement, and military users provided the design criteria for the USP. Its controls are uniquely American, influenced by such famous and successful designs as the Government Model 1911 pistol.

"The USP can be safely carried 'cocked and locked.'" HK noted. "The control lever, a combination safety and decocking lever, is frame mounted and quickly accessible....The USP control lever has a positive stop and returns to the 'fire' position after decocking."

An interesting factor about the USP is that it was designed from the ground up as a .40 S&W handgun. This is the reverse of many gun designs which were first 9mmP propositions, then altered to handle the more powerful .40 S&W. In 9mmP terms, this means it is a handgun which should be able to handle the 9mmP forever.

The frame of the USP is made of polymer (plastic) and metal components are shielded by special corrosion resistant

Even after intentional testing abuse, the HK USP still continued to fire tight groups from 25 yards away.

SPECIFICATIONS	USP9 (9mm)
CALIBER	9X9mm Parabellum
OPERATING PRINCIPLE **ACTION TYPE**	Short recoil Modified Browning type, linkless
SIGHT	Fixed patridge style, adjust able for windage an elevation. Standard 3-dot or optional tritium.
TOTAL LENGTH	194 mm (7.64 in.)
BARREL LENGTH	105 mm (4.13 in.)
SIGHT RADIUS	158 mm (6.22 in.)
TWIST LENGTH	250 mm (9.84 in.)
HEIGHT (Total)	136 mm (5.35 in.)
WIDTH	
Slide	29 mm (1.14 in.)
Frame	32 mm (1.26 in.)
WEIGHT	
Total w/o Magazine	752 grams (26.52 oz)
Empty Magazine	55 grams (1.94 oz)
Cartridge	9.92 grams (.35 oz)
SLIDE FORCE (to retract slide)	8 kg (17.64 pounds)
RIFLING	6 lands and grooves, constant right hand twist
MAGAZINE CAPACITY	12 cartridges (does not include cartridge in chamber)

SAFETIES
1. Manual safety lever (applicable models only)
2. Double-action mode with hammer intercept notch
3. Firing pin block
4. Disconnector

Hostile Environment (HE) finishes. Outside metal surfaces are protected by an extremely hard, nitro-gas carburized black oxide finish. Internal metal parts, including springs, are coated with a special Dow Corning anti-corrosion process that reduces friction and wear.

"By using a modular approach to the internal components, the control lever of the HK USP can be switched from the left

The HK SP89 is a high-capacity, 9mm handgun patterned after the legendary, highly successful HK assault rifle series.

to the right side of the pistol for left-handed shooters," HK reported. "The USP also can be converted from one type of trigger/firing mode to another. This includes combination double-action and single-action (DA/SA) modes and double action only (DA-Only) modes."

In all, the USP will be available in seven different trigger/firing mode configurations. That's versatility!

"In addition to a wide selection of trigger/firing modes, the USP has an ambidextrous magazine release lever that is shielded by the trigger guard from inadvertent actuation," HK reported. "The grip of the USP is stepped at the rear and combined with the tapered magazine well, makes magazine changes fast and precise. The sides of the grip frame have finger recesses that also aid in magazine removal."

"An extended slide release lever is positioned to allow easy operation without changing the grip of the shooting hand," HK explained. "And the HK USP does not have a magazine lock-out feature. You can still fire a chambered round even with the magazine removed.

"One of the most important unique design features of the HK USP is the mechanical recoil reduction system," HK continued. "This system is incorporated into the recoil/buffer spring assembly located below the barrel. Designed primarily to buffer the slide and barrel and reduce recoil effects on the pistol components, the system also lowers the recoil forces felt by the shooter.

"This recoil reduction system was tested and proven in the HK .45 ACP handgun designed for the US Special Operations Command in 1992," HK stated. "Using the same system as the USP, the HK 'SOCOM pistol' fired a steady diet of more than 27,000 +P cartridges without damage to any of the components, including the polymer frame."

Suffice it to say that the USP comes onto the market with high expectations — something typical of firearms from the German manufacturer.

Specifications for currently produced HK 9mmP pistols are:

USP9

This is a short recoil, modified Browning action design with magazine capacity of 16 rounds. Sights are of the three-dot type. Barrel length is 4.13 inches, making the pistol 7.64 inches long overall. Weight is 1.66 pounds empty, and height is 5.35 inches. It features a polymer receiver with integral grips.

P7M8 *(Nickel or Blue)*

The action is recoil-operated with retarded inertia slide. Magazine capacity is eight rounds, and sights of the three-dot style. Barrel length is 4.13 inches, and overall length is 6.73 inches. Weight is 1.75 pounds, and height is 5.04 inches. Grips are plastic.

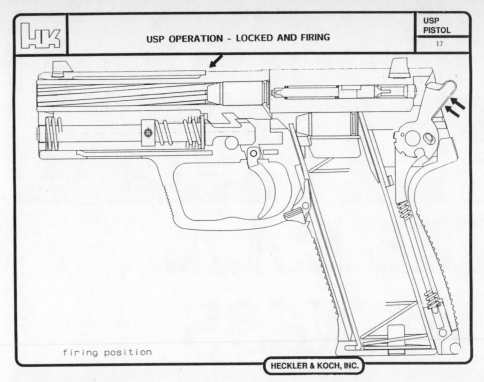

firing position

HECKLER & KOCH, INC.

This diagram of the USP illustrates the pistol in the locked and firing position.

Below: The H&K MP5KA1 has the look of an assault handgun, but is descended from the MP5 subgun and is selective fire.

P7M13 *(Nickel or Blue)*

The action is recoil operated with retarded inertia slide. Magazine capacity is 13 rounds and sights are the three-dot style. Barrel length is 4.13 inches, and overall length is 6.9 inches. Weight is 1.87 pounds empty, and height is 5.3 inches. Grips are plastic.

SP89

This firearm features a delayed roller locked bolt action. Magazine capacity is 15 rounds, and sights are square notch rear and hooded front. Barrel length is 4.5 inches and overall length is 13 inches. Weight is 4.4 pounds empty, and height is 8.26 inches. Grips are synthetic.

CHAPTER
Sixteen

THE E.A.A.
WITNESS

In Two Configurations, The 9mm Autos Are Excellent Defense Guns!

EAA offers two basic 9mm pistol designs, the Witness (top) and Compact Witness.

While the EAA Witness is a full-size, high-capacity 9mmP, it still fits comfortably in the author's hands.

The checkered rubber stocks on the two Witness models are thicker than most wood ones, providing a sure grip.

EUROPEAN AMERICAN Armory, located in Hialeah, Florida, is a big name in the 9mmP business, famous for the Witness line of semi-auto handguns. EAA's Witness pistols, available in several chamberings, including the 9mmP, are imported from Italy and have become some of the favorites among shooters of various action or shooting gallery types of target disciplines.

Although the designation of Witness was introduced in 1991, the general design of these pistols is quite a bit older than that. They are the Tanfoglio pistols which, in another life, were called TZs — interesting, because of their similarities in design with the Czechoslovakian CZ handguns.

Before anyone gets totally concerned about finer points in the lineage of this design, it is proper to note that they are modern variants of the John Moses Browning-designed P-35 (aka Hi-Power). But there is a major difference, and it is that difference which has made this design so popular in many of the shooting disciplines: Unlike its P-35 ancestor, the Witness is double-action/single-action (meaning the first shot can be double-action, followed by single-action firing).

Essentially, there are two basic 9mmP models in the Witness line. They are the standard and the compact. Specifications are:

STANDARD WITNESS

Barrel length	4.5 inches.
Overall length	8.12 inches.
Weight (empty)	35 ounces.
Height	5.5 inches.
Magazine	Double column, 16-round capacity.

COMPACT WITNESS

Barrel length	3.5 inches.
Overall length	7 inches.
Weight (empty)	30 ounces.
Height	4.5 inches.
Magazine	Double column, 12-round capacity.

Stocks on both models are made of checkered black rubber. Sights are a blade front and windage-adjustable rear (three dot system also present). The trigger guard is squared-off for two-hand hold.

In addition to a number of chamberings, there is a variety of finishes available, as well. However, whether the pistol is a basic Witness or a full-on race gun, the operation is the same. The only major difference between the standard and compact models is size.

The long tang extension on the rear of the EAA Witness' frame prevents the hammer from hitting the shooter's hand.

Witnesses are real guns. By that, I mean they are made of steel and are designed to last a long time and go through a lot of ammunition. It is in the shooting and handling of the Witness pistols that one acquires an appreciation for their many features and characteristics. How did they perform for the author?

STANDARD WITNESS

This is one of the most natural pointing 9mmP pistols investigated during the formulation of data for this book. This characteristic came as no surprise, however, considering its lineage — the P-35 having established a pointability standard by which many other handguns are measured.

Considering that this, in its basic configuration, is a service grade handgun and not a bullseye target model, accuracy was okay to good, depending upon the ammunition fired. For most loadings, groups off the bench were in the two- to three-inch category, with the larger groups coming from 147-grain bullet ammunition. Most of the factory loads and handloads used with 115- or 124-grain bullets grouped at two to 2 1/2 inches off the bench at 25 yards.

The Oehler 35P chronograph, with triple sky screens placed 15 feet from the muzzle, showed that the Witness delivered expected ballistic performance for a pistol with its barrel length.

For example, for a five-shot string, PMC's 115-grain FMJ loading produced a high of 1162 feet per second and low of 1091. That gave a median of 1126, with an extreme spread of 71 and standard deviation of 31.

Federal's 125-grain American Eagle Metal Case loading registered a high of 1095 and low of 1050 for a median of 1070 feet per second. Extreme spread was 45, and standard deviation was 19.

Winchester's USA 115-grain ball loading registered a high of 1189 and low of 1129 for a median of 1157 feet per second. Extreme spread was 60 and standard deviation was 27.

Remington's UMC 115-grain metal case loading registered a high of 1072 and low of 1042 for a median of 1060 feet per second. Extreme spread was 30 and standard deviation was 11.

The most consistent loading was the author's handload comprised of Hansen brass, CCI small pistol primers, 5.0 grains of Hercules Unique powder and 125-grain hardcast bullets. That loading registered a high of 1169 and low of 1142 for a median of 1155 feet per second. Extreme spread was 27 and standard deviation was 10.

Through repeated sessions at the range over a period of several months, the standard Witness performed flawlessly with all ammunition fed to it — and that included a lot more loadings than were chronographed.

After some of the more formal paper-punching rituals were performed to establish baseline accuracy expectations, the Witness was shot at random targets located at random distances, stretching from five feet to 40 yards. Smallest of the targets were six-inch-diameter paper plates, and largest of the targets were 8 1/2x11-inch computer paper. None of the targets was missed when shot at quickly and randomly out to the 25-yard line. Very few of the targets between 25 and 40

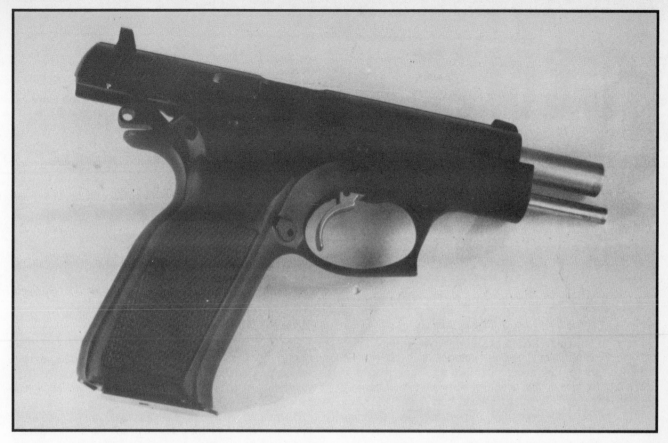

With the slide locked to the rear on the full-size EAA Witness, the recoil-spring guide is exposed below the barrel.

yards were missed, and virtually all of those misses could be credited with breakdowns in basic shooting technique by the pilot.

On one occasion, it became apparent that the pistol was pointing naturally enough to study hit probability should the pistol and its sights be totally ignored while shooting. The author concentrated only on the target, keeping eyes glued to the target and not even consciously seeing the pistol when firing. It was totally instinctive shooting, and the hits were routine at targets from five feet to 10 yards. Beyond 10 yards and out to 25 yards, six-inch paper plates were hit about half of the time using this technique. Few handguns were able to duplicate that kind of performance for the author.

There were several reasons credited for the good, overall tactical performance. First, the basic design is excellent. But beyond that, the checkered, black rubber stocks on the pistol are slightly fatter than the wooden counterparts occurring on a number of other handguns with the same general configuration. This beefiness seemed to fill the author's rather large hands with long fingers well, which meant more meaningful control of the pistol (the only valid form of gun control, by the way).

The Witnesses have thick grips to accommodate the staggered 9mmP magazine.

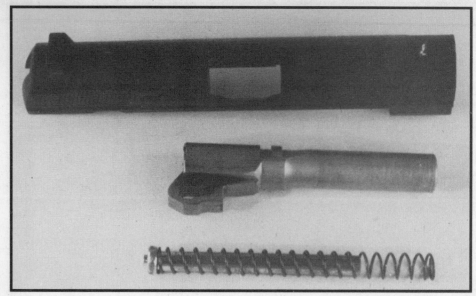

The Witnesses are the same except for the length of the slide, and its components.

Best accuracy, of course, was achieved when shooting the Witness in the single-action mode. However, results were totally acceptable when shooting double-action. In fact, groups generally grew by only about a half-inch at 25 yards when the shooting was done double-action with a two-hand hold, compared to single-action with a two-hand hold.

Tactical accuracy when the Witness was fired double-action with a one-hand, extended arm hold was considerably less than when the same pistol was fired in the same manner in the single-action mode. The author credited that phenomenon with the noticeably gritty characteristic of the long pull when the pistol was fired double-action. It simply was more difficult to control the pistol with one hand under those conditions. However, a six-inch plate was not missed as a result, so tactical accuracy remained credible in any of the many modes of firing.

COMPACT WITNESS

The compact Witness may be nothing more or less than a small sibling of the standard model, but the handling dynamics were so different as to make one wonder if they weren't two entirely different handguns from two entirely different makers.

Performance of the compact, however, was on par with the standard model. And, for a shorter pistol, the smaller Witness retains a pleasurable level of pointability.

Also, in a similar manner as its full-size stablemate, the compact Witness demonstrated no outrageous preference or dislike for any particular kind of load. For example, groups from the bench at 25 yards were quite similar between the two pistols with the various kinds of ammo used. The compact delivered groups ranging from two inches to four inches, with the four-inch groups involving 147-grain loadings.

The extended toe on the magazine plate of the 9mm compact Witness helps the shooter to control the pistol.

The stubby dimensions of the compact Witness (top) make it easy to carry. The compact (below) is fairly thin despite a big magazine.

The difference in barrel length, however, made for some rather interestingly different ballistic performance with the various loadings.

PMC's 115-grain FMJ loading registered a high of 1149 and low of 1036 feet per second for a median of 1102. Extreme spread was 113, and standard deviation was 33.

Winchester's USA 115-grain ball loading registered a high of 1114, low of 1077 and median of 1093 feet per second. Extreme spread was 37 and standard deviation was 15.

Remington's UMC 115-grain metal case loading registered a high of 1149 and low of 1104 for a median of 1118. Extreme spread was 45 and standard deviation was 19.

The author's handload (from the same batch and fired within minutes under the same range conditions) featuring the 125-grain hardcast bullets registered a high of 1150 and low of 1094 for a median 1120 feet per second. Extreme spread was 56 and standard deviation was 23.

A quick comparison of this data, compared to the data from the standard Witness, reveals what shooters mean when they insist that different firearms handle ammunition differently. For example, the author's handload had more than twice the standard deviation with the compact gun as it had with the standard Witness. Interestingly, the standard deviation for the Winchester USA loading was almost twice as much with the standard model as it was with the compact (cartridges all came from the same 50-round box).

Certainly, the burning rates of the various kinds of powders played some role in the outcome. But other more subtle differences, like the smoothness and concentricity of the insides of the barrels, also come into play in such situations. That is why the author did not attempt to perform a detailed ballistics rundown on each and every 9mmP handgun used for

The concave profile on the front of the trigger guard is helpful for controlling the sharp recoil from the small Witness (left). The fixed three-dot sights are standard on EAA 9mmP Witnesses.

this book. Frankly, there can be great differences between two seemingly identical pistols, so precisely what the author experienced with the specific test guns might or might not be really valid for other shooters with other pistols, even though the pistols may be the same make and model. Suffice it to say that such details are akin to a window sticker on an automobile in car lot — they are based upon which general comparisons can be made and provide a starting point for further consideration.

The only way to determine precisely how any specific firearm is going to handle a specific loading is to run that loading through that firearm and measure the results.

Back to the handling characteristics of the compact Witness. It carries nicely, but is not equal to the standard Witness in the overall tactical accuracy department.

For example, there were periodic misses of six-inch plates at distances beyond seven yards. Hits were still routine all the way to 25 yards, but out of 10 shots, the author missed an average of two plates at the 25-yard line. Still, this is excellent performance.

The problem, as was demonstrated during the controlled bench shooting, was not so much with the pistol itself as it was with the interaction between the pistol and the pilot. The shorter grip of the compact simply did not fit the author's large hand quite as well as the standard Witness.

In fact, the difference in fit was enough that there was no need to try the "no sights" instinctive shooting with the compact.

For what it is, however, the compact is a good performer. How can one go wrong with a smallish pistol that can put holes within a six-inch circle every time out to the 10-yard line? For defensive shooting, that is about as far as anyone would care to take the issue anyway.

Certainly, the compact Witness functioned as well as did the standard size model. There were no jams or hang-ups with any of the ammunition used.

The trigger pull felt similar on the compact version, but because of the slight change in the angle of the muscular pull in the shooting hand, let off was not quite as positive and

repeatable with the smaller pistol — again, that was a factor of the author's hand size, and not of the pistol itself.

This point, however, should be considered as one of the supreme considerations whenever the subject of handgun acquisition comes to the fore. How a particular pistol fits into a specific shooter's hand is of paramount importance. The better the fit, the better the pistol will perform for that person. That is why it is impossible for anyone to suggest an all-round "perfect" 9mmP handgun for everyone. There simply is no such thing. Handgun performance is a very personal thing.

The Witness pistols feature the same general barrel/slide lockup design as the P-35. And disassembly is accomplished in the traditional fashion. First, remove the magazine and clear the chamber to make certain the pistol is unloaded.

Next, pull the hammer to the full-back position and align the two takedown marks (dots — one at the rear left of the slide and one at the rear left of the top of frame). This requires the slide to be moved rearward about 1/4-inch. While the two dots are aligned, remove the slide stop/takedown lever which is

With slide locked to the rear, the compact Witness from EAA is ready for loading. Controls are in the normal places.

located on left side of the frame just above the trigger. To get the lever started, it sometimes helps to push on the lever's crossbolt extension on the opposite side of the frame. On the test pistols, the fit was snug, so it might require a solid push to get it started. However, the manufacturer warns against using any tools like a mallet or screwdriver for this purpose. Once the lever is lifted out a fraction of an inch, it can be jiggled out the remainder of the way with the thumb and forefinger.

By sliding the slide and barrel assembly forward, it can be removed from the frame in a single unit. Next, hold the slide upside down and remove the recoil spring and guide. Once the recoil spring and guide are removed, the barrel can be lifted up and out of the slide. This is as far as the pistol normally needs to be disassembled for cleaning and routine maintenance. Reassembly is the reverse process.

Although the Witness is similar in design to the P-35 and other like handguns, there are some differences. For example, they lock up similarly, but the camming mechanism on the bottom of the barrel is slightly different. It operates under the same prinicple, but is executed a bit differently.

Because the Witness has an integral feed ramp in the breech end of the barrel, it offers a high level of cartridge support (unlike the Model 1911-type designs). Although this feature is not particularly critical when standard factory loads are used, it can make a big difference with some handloads as well as with some of the hotter factory-loaded ammo which is available in 9mmP — a cartridge which is loaded all over the world and for a wide variety of firearms, including submachine guns. The Witness design is of the stronger variety and is made to handle the relatively high working pressures encountered with much of the 9mmP ammo.

Another factor which has contributed to the popularity of the Witness is the way it lends itself to "smithing." This pistol is the basis for many of the high-tech, high performance "race" guns used by serious competitors.

That means there are a lot of aftermarket options available, and it means that many of the better pistolsmiths are set up to do all kinds of procedures, depending upon the specific desires of individual shooters.

European American Armory itself offers a number of upgrade and custom options.

However, the basic service grade Witness pistol, whether it is the standard or compact model, continues to offer a lot of performance in a sturdy, well-made package.

Witness pistols are priced mid-range for their genre, which means they also represent a good value. Overall, the Witness pistols from EAA are excellent performers for any 9mmP application.

CHAPTER
Seventeen

ACTION ARMS & THE CZ

This Importer Now Has A Corner On This Top-Selling Czech 9mm Pistol

The CZ75 (top) and CZ85 are the two full-size service-grade autos offered by Action Arms.

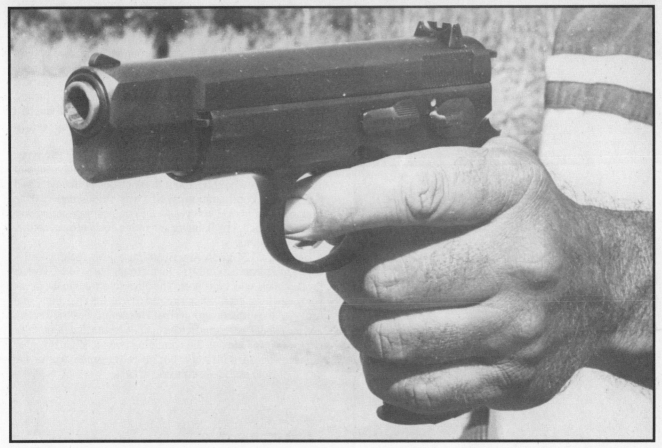

The CZ75 9mmP, imported from Czechoslovakia by Action Arms, is noted for its natural pointability and reliability.

O F THE WORLD'S major gunmaking centers, Brno in Czechoslovakia is among the better known. Both military and civilian firearms from this area in Southeastern Europe have set the pace for both quality and function for most of the 20th Century.

Currently, there are two CZ 9mmP pistol models available from this famous Czech area. They are the CZ 75 and CZ 85 double-action semi-autos. Actually, the pair of 9mmP offerings might be considered as one basic model — the CZ 75 — and an updated variation of it — the CZ 85.

For practical purposes, the CZ 75 might be described as a totally successful double-action descendant of the John Moses Browning-designed P-35 (aka Hi-Power). Although there are a number of differences between the P-35 and the CZ 75, both pistols share the same basic design and function, and their overall configuration and feel are similar enough to bear witness to the familial relationship. Dimensions for the CZ 75 are:

Barrel length	4 3/4 inches.
Overall length	8 inches.
Weight *(empty)*	35 ounces.
Sights	Fixed.
Magazine capacity	15 rounds.
Stocks	Checkered wood.

The CZ 85, introduced in 1986, is essentially the same pistol as the CZ 75, except the CZ 85 features an ambidextrous safety and slide release.

Pointability of these two pistols is superb, and function throughout extensive testing was flawless. And, this was no surprise, given the quality of materials and workmanship. To put it bluntly, these are full-size, real guns. They are manufactured of steel and made well enough to last a lifetime, even if there is a lot of shooting to be done.

High quality in both materials and workmanship is an assumed standard for firearms out of Brno. Consider the fact that it was the Brno magnum Mauser bolt-action which was used for some of the more famous African hunting arms.

In addition, the military Mauser rifles made at Brno earlier in the century were among the more sought after surplus rifles to be used for custom sporters during the golden age of such activity in the 1950s. Expect that phenomenon to repeat itself during the 1990s as more and more of the Brno surplus Mausers are finding their way back onto the market.

Other famous firearms from Brno have included an array of fine shotguns and combination guns — longarms with multiple barrels which fire both centerfire metallic cartridges and shotshells.

With all of that tradition in mind, I had high expectations for the CZ pistols which are imported into the United States by Action Arms, Ltd. Those expectations were not cut short during extended range sessions.

Representative groups fired with a variety of factory ammunition types and handloads divulge the level of performance one might expect from the CZ pistols. All groups were fired from the bench at 25 yards, and were five-shot strings. Results included:

Winchester's USA 115-grain FMJ loading produced an almost perfectly circular concentric group which measured 1-1/4 inches. This is superb performance for a service-grade 9mmP semi-auto, and the group was repeated several times during the various sessions at which the CZ 75 was used.

PMC's 115-grain Starfire loading produced a vertical string for a group, and the string measured three inches. Interestingly, PMC's generic 115-grain FMJ load produced a horizontal string measuring 2-1/8 inches. Both groups shot to essentially the same point of impact.

Does that mean that if a person were to load the two types of PMC ammo alternately in the magazine that the resultant 10-shot group would be about three inches in diameter and concentric in configuration? Well, I was curious, and tried the exercise. The answer was yes — the composite grouping was about three inches in diameter and rather concentric in nature. Very interesting.

Federal's 124-grain American Eagle FMJ loading delivered a most impressive 1-1/4-inch group. Three of the bullets produced a single, large hole. The other two holes in the target were touching each other slightly above the first three and provided the ultimate group size. This ammo was tried again, and the results were almost identical. Why the first three shots are to one big hole and the remaining two are slightly higher is somewhat of a mystery, but given the small size of the group, it is an academic concern, at best.

Like the Browning Hi-Power, the CZ75 doesn't have a separate barrel bushing (left), a feature found on the Colt 1911. The CZ75 comes with a fixed front sight and rear sight drift-adjustable for windage (below).

Not a compact, the CZ75 is a full-bodied, high-capacity 9mmP that is designed for extended and tough service.

Remington's UMC 115-grain metal case loading provided a vertical string for a group, which measured exactly two inches. Three of the five holes touched each other, which means that the group actually was rather impressive.

One of the author's handloads, which featured a 124-grain Winchester FMJ bullet, 5.0 grains of Hercules Unique powder, CCI small pistol primer and Hansen case, produced a horizontal string for a group. It measured 2-1/4 inches. Again, the first three holes touched each other, providing a three-shot group of one half-inch center-to-center.

A second handload then was attempted with disappointing results. It was the 125-grain hardcast bullet with the same quantities and other components used in the first handload recipe. It was close to being a non-group, with four of the five rounds providing a vertical string of 4-1/4 inches. The fifth shot went to the left, roughly 3-1/2 inches from the center of the vertical string. More shots were fired, and they confirmed that this particular loading was not workable in this particular pistol. No cohesive group was ever achieved. Obviously, the pistol did not like that particular handload.

However, given the performance the CZ 75 exhibited with some of the factory loadings, it is safe to declare that this is one great-shooting, service-grade handgun.

Other shooting with the pistol at random targets located at random distances from five feet to 25 yards during quick shooting sessions revealed that the CZ 75 is as credible under "street" conditions as it is off the bench. Six-inch targets were hit so routinely that the pistol became somewhat boring to shoot. It was just one of those point the pistol, pull the trigger and hit the target routines. That is a fulfilling way to be bored.

THE CZ 85

During a range session on the same day, and immediately following the session with the CZ 75, the CZ 85 was put to the test. Results were satisfying.

PMC's 115-grain FMJ loading produced a rather concentric group which measured 2-1/8 inches. The first three shots produced a group which measured 1-1/4 inches, and the last two shots hit within a half-inch of each other.

Does this sound somewhat familiar? Indeed. It seemed as though both the 75 and 85 would put the first three shots into a truly small area, then expand the group with the next two shots. I attempted to short-stop the mystery by following with a 10-shot group, just to see what would happen as the barrel got hotter and hotter with successive shots.

Interestingly, the first three shots were close, the next three also were close, but about an inch away, then the group began to fill in the space between. What resulted was a group of about 2-1/2 inches which was rather concentric. So, it is assumed that one could shoot the pistol repeatedly and expect extremely tight grouping for the first three shots, with good grouping regardless how many shots were fired. That is comforting.

Remington's UMC 115-grain FMJ loading provided a rather curious group. The first two shots were overlapping. The next two shots were almost touching, but located 2-1/4 inches lower on the paper. The fifth shot was a flier 4-3/4 inches low and to the right of the initial two shots. The author did not attempt to explain the phenomenon.

Winchester's USA 115-grain ball loading produced a

The CZ85 fills the shooter's hand. Its grip size and angle are ergonomically correct.

vertical group which was 3-1/2 inches high. The first four shots provided a rather square group which measured 2-1/4 inches, with the five-shot group expanded to its size by the fifth shot which went high.

Federal's American Eagle 124-grain FMJ loading produced a horizontal string 3-1/4 inches wide. The first three shots were also horizontally strung, and measured 1-1/4 inches, with the ultimate size of the group expanded by the last two shots.

The author's 125-grain hardcast handload provided a concentric, large group. It measured 3-3/4 inches.

Hence, it might be assumed that the test CZ 75 shot somewhat better than the CZ 85. However, they both shot quite well. The tendency of both pistols to put the first three shots into extremely small groups, then expand group size on successive shots causes reasons for wondering whether it is a situation which could be addressed with some retro-work.

With a little fine-tuning, it might be expected that the pistols would put five-shot groups into about the same space

as they put the first three shots when used right out of the box. Even if they didn't, the performance was interesting, because the best grouping was always with the first three shots. That would mean that the first three shots would certainly hit any reasonable target — and that is totally comforting.

So how did the two pistols handle the various loadings ballistically? Very similarly, according to the Oehler 35P chronograph. The triple sky screens were placed 15 feet from the muzzle for the shooting sessions. By pistol, the chronograph results were:

The CZ 75, with Remington's UMC 115-grain metal case loading produced a high of 1193 and a low of 1176 for a median of 1183 feet per second. Extreme spread was 17, and standard deviation was 5.

Winchester's USA 115-grain ball loading produced a high of 1159 and a low of 1126 for a median of 1146 feet per second. Extreme spread was 33, and standard deviation was 13.

Federal's American Eagle 124-grain metal case loading

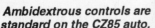

Ambidextrous controls are standard on the CZ85 auto.

The front of the CZ85 (left) trigger guard is squared and checkered for added control. Below, the no-glare rib is a special feature of the CZ85.

produced a high of 1093 and a low of 1074 for a median 1082 feet per second. Extreme spread was 19 and standard deviation was 6.

PMC's 115-grain FMJ loading produced a high of 1150 and a low of 1121 for a median 1138 feet per second. Extreme spread was 41, and standard deviation was 18.

Overall, this is extremely good consistency.

With PMC's 115-grain FMJ loading, the CZ 85 produced a high of 1139 and a low of 1115 for a median 1129 feet per second. Extreme spread was 24, and standard deviation was 10.

Federal's American Eagle 124-grain metal case loading produced a high of 1110 and a low of 1092 for a median 1099 feet per second. Extreme spread was 18, and standard deviation was 7.

Winchester's USA 115-grain ball loading produced a high of 1163 and low of 1132 for a median 1149 feet per second. Extreme spread was 31, and standard deviation was 12.

Remington's UMC 115-grain metal case loading produced a high of 1169 and a low of 1137 for a median 1160 feet per second. Extreme spread was 32, and standard deviation was 13.

My own 124-grain hardcast handload produced a high of 1294 and a low of 1247 for a median 1262 feet per second. Extreme spread was 47, and standard deviation was 18.

Again, considering the wide range of makers and loadings, this is extremely consistent performance. This not only speaks well of the quality of ammunition being marketed by the major manufacturers these days, but speaks well of the pistol which puts them downrange without drastically affecting the inherent performance of the ammo.

Overall, I felt that, as individual firearms, the test CZ 75 was slightly better than the CZ 85. This is not to suggest that, generally, the CZ 75 pistols are better than the CZ 85 models. Rather, it was felt that the slight difference had to do with individual firearms.

What this means is that there would likely be as much of a difference between two CZ 75 pistols or two CZ 85 pistols as there was between the two models in the tests.

With that in mind, it is safe to suggest that either model is a good bet for general 9mmP use. The real question is whether the ambidextrous feature of the CZ 85 is necessary for the individual shooter. If so, then it is the better bet. If not, the CZ 75 is a good bet.

Simply put, it was felt that with either model it is a can't-go-wrong proposition. These are well designed and well made handguns which can hold up over a lifetime or more of shooting.

CHAPTER
Eighteen

TESTING THE TAURUS

All Of These Models Perform Better Than Just "Well"!

In testing the various Taurus pistol models, Steve Comus discovered that they performed above his expectations.

The only difference between the Taurus PT 92 (right) and the PT 99 model (below) is that the latter pistol is equipped with adjustable sights.

TAURUS IS a big name in the handgun business, and that includes pistols which shoot the 9mmP cartridge. These Brazilian-made pistols bear a striking resemblance to models from Beretta in Italy, function under the same principles and are disassembled and reassembled in the same manner.

MODEL PT 92

At the heart of the Taurus 9mmP line is the Model PT 92, a full-size, 15-shot service grade handgun. It has a 4.92-inch barrel, is 8.54 inches long overall and weighs 34 ounces. Stocks are of Brazilian hardwood, and sights are fixed (the-three dot system is also incorporated).

This is a double-action/single-action design, which means the first shot can be taken double-action, followed by subsequent shots in single-action. Or, the exposed hammer can be cocked manually for single-action shooting throughout. The PT 92 is available in three finishes: blue, nickel and stainless steel.

Shooting the Model PT 92 Taurus is a joy. The pistol's grip is large enough in every respect to fill the hand, and that means the right kind of gun control. Out of the box, the test model performed well with every kind of ammunition fired through it.

Most impressive was the group from the Sure Fire 115-grain full metal jacket loading. Shot at 25 yards from an unsupported bench position (elbows on the bench), the handgun delivered a group of just over two inches. Three-inch groups were the rule for most other loads. Other ammunition tested included Hansen's NATO Military 123-grain full metal jacket offering, PMC Starfire 124-grain jacketed hollowpoint and Winchester's 147-grain Black Talon jacketed hollow-point. Both the Black Talon and Starfire loadings delivered 2-1/2-inch groups at 25 yards, and the points of impact were nearly exactly at the point of aim. Bullet placement with other loads was three to five inches under point of aim, but horizontally in line.

Overall, the full-size PT 92 was the author's favorite among the Taurus 9mmP pistols tested. It certainly is a credible pistol, and feels good when it is shot.

The PT 92 works well when fired from one or two hands. In fact, a two-hand hold is enhanced as a result of the concave configuration of the front of the trigger guard. Controllability also is eased by the vertical striations on the front and back of

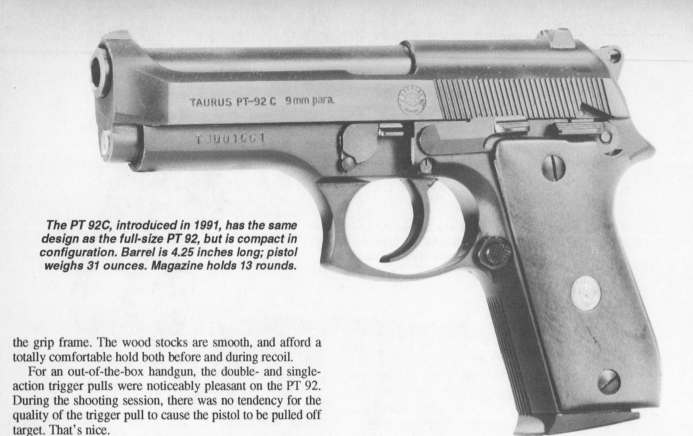

The PT 92C, introduced in 1991, has the same design as the full-size PT 92, but is compact in configuration. Barrel is 4.25 inches long; pistol weighs 31 ounces. Magazine holds 13 rounds.

the grip frame. The wood stocks are smooth, and afford a totally comfortable hold both before and during recoil.

For an out-of-the-box handgun, the double- and single-action trigger pulls were noticeably pleasant on the PT 92. During the shooting session, there was no tendency for the quality of the trigger pull to cause the pistol to be pulled off target. That's nice.

MODEL PT 99

Taurus also offers the Model PT 99, which differs from the PT 92 only in that it is furnished with adjustable sights.

MODEL PT 92C

Essentially, this is the same design as the full-size PT 92 except in compact configuration. The barrel on the PT 92C is 4.25 inches long, making the pistol 7.5 inches long overall. Weight is 31 ounces, and magazine capacity is 13 shots. The compact version was introduced in 1991.

The test pistol wore a nickel finish and is a handsome handgun. It may be a compact by definition, but I felt its size put it between what might be considered a true "compact" and a full size service pistol. For example, the Taurus PT 908, which will be discussed later, is what I would classify as a true compact.

Semantics aside, the PT 92C offers a lot of performance for its abbreviated size. It feels good in the hand and is easy to control. Groups fired with it were good, but on average about an inch larger than those achieved with the full size Model 92. Most, if not all, of the accuracy difference was assumed to be due to pilot error. The author had the impression while shooting this handgun that it was performing well.

Certainly, it preferred the Sure Fire loads better than any of the others, and not because of accuracy. It shot all loads at least as well, some a little better than others. Sure Fire loads are full power, and that means they make autoloaders cycle as well as the design can cycle.

There's no question that with a 100- or 200-round break-in period that the PT 92C would cycle even the lightest of loads well. However, it was slightly sluggish with some of the less potent loadings. As with the full-size Model PT 92, the "C" version shot all loads close to point of aim. The Sure Fire,

Black Talon and Starfire offerings putting the bullets the closest to the point of aim.

Overall, this was seen as a fun gun to shoot, and one which could perform well in some of the more serious applications.

The trigger pull in double-action was a bit gritty at first, then smoothed out. In single-action, the trigger pull was deliciously nice. In fact, for shooters with normal or slightly smaller than normal hands, this version could be the perfect size. It has all of the same good features of the full-size model, and simply offers them in a slightly smaller package.

MODEL PT 908

The PT 908 is somewhat different from the other 9mmP handguns marketed by Taurus in that it features an eight-round, single-column magazine, is compact in size and does not have the same profile nor exactly the same action design as the PT 92 variants.

Generally speaking, the PT 908 appears to be a type of hybrid between the basic 92 design and the Star Firestar model. It has a 3.8-inch barrel and weighs 30 ounces. Grips are black composition, and the three-dot sighting system is standard. The pistol is double-action/single-action and features a manual ambidextrous hammer drop, as well as a loaded chamber indicator.

This is a nice little pistol. In the author's hands, it produced groups of three to four inches at 25 yards, and it seemed not to matter which loading was being fired — all groups were about the same size and shape. However, the holes in the target were located roughly six inches below the point of aim. This phenomenon was assumed to be the result of my sight picture; no doubt, with some practice the bullets would go where they were supposed to.

This little gun likes the hotter loads better and cycles the

The Taurus Model PT 908 differs from the PT 92 family in that it has an eight-round, single-column magazine, is compact in size and is a bit of a hybrid gun.

more potent offerings with much more enthusiasm. It points surprisingly naturally for such a small pistol. Again, best results were achieved with the Sure Fire ammunition. Both the Black Talon and Starfire loads shot well through this pistol.

For a small, convenient-to-carry handgun it represents an interesting option. Also, it would be a handy handgun for anyone with smaller hands.

Overall, the Taurus 9mmP pistols are in a similar class as that company's other handguns. They are solid designs and made well. Both double- and single-action trigger pulls were smooth and consistent, making the pistol slick and quick to shoot.

Disassembly of any of the Taurus 9mmP pistols is similar. First, remove the magazine and make certain the pistol is not loaded. Then, with the left forefinger, press the disassembling latch release (a button on the right side of the frame just above the trigger housing) and at the same time, with the left thumb, rotate the disassembling latch release clockwise until it stops.

Then pull the slide/barrel assembly forward and off the frame. Next, turn the slide/barrel assembly upside down and remove the recoil spring and guide. The barrel then can be lifted up and out of the slide. That is as far as the pistol normally needs to be disassembled for routine cleaning and maintenance Reassembly is the reverse process, and there are no unwanted surprises in the process. The pistols go back together easily and simply.

Taurus handguns are extremely competitive in the marketplace and the 9mmP models are a large part of the reason why. These pistols are both functional and affordable — a nice combination.

The PT 908 is double-action/single-action, has a 3.8-inch barrel and weighs 30 ounces. Author found in his testing that the little gun likes hot loads!

CHAPTER
Ninteen

CARTRIDGE OF THE CENTURY

The 9mm Parabellum Has Seen More Action Than Any Other Caliber!

IT IS IRONIC THAT American police departments only discovered the 9mm in the 1980s. This rimless 9x19mm round has been common in Europe since its development in 1902. It has killed more men in combat than any other pistol caliber — though mostly when fired from submachine guns," declares David E. Steele, a long-time law enforcement practitioner.

"Probably the most significant change came when the U.S. military adopted a 9mm sidearm to replace its aged, mostly World War II-purchased .45 Colts."

There were several advantages to the adoption of the 9mmP: (1) Ammunition weighs about half as much as .45 ACP with less bulk — important logistic concerns; (2) more rounds could be carried in magazines without excessive thickness in the grip; (3) 9mm ammunition is available in most foreign countries, whether friend or foe; in some nations it is the only common round for military, police or civilians; (4) lighter recoil makes the 9mm easier for inexperienced shooters, including female recruits, to shoot accurately; and (5) the 9mm provides greater penetration than the .45, a significant military consideration where metal helmets and anti-fragmentation (flak) vests have been common for generations. Its only drawback, compared to the .45 ACP, is lower per-round stopping power when used with hardball ammunition.

The list of 9mm handguns reads like a litany of the finest service pistols of the 20th Century: the P-08 (Luger), P35

Steele demonstrates shooting stance using Browning Hi-Power. It has seen duty as a service pistol since 1935.

The Swedish M45 Carl Gustav model has been built for the 9mm Parabellum like most European submachine guns.

(Browning Hi-Power), P38 (Walther), SIG P210, Beretta M1951 (Brigadier), Beretta M92, SIG-Sauer P226, Glock 17, and Heckler & Koch P7. Smith & Wesson is currently making a name for its line of police pistols, beginning with the M39 first developed for the U.S. Army test in 1954, later adopted by the Illinois State Police in 1967. Police use increased with the development of better hollow-point ammunition, and the "competing firepower" carried by the opposition — primarily drug dealers and armed robbers.

There has been a gradual "militarization" of American police departments, starting with the race and anti-war riots of the 1960s. SWAT teams set the model for black or cammie-clad storm troops, copied later by narcotics teams for raids in the "war on drugs." While giving lip service to the British concept of a lightly armed "citizen constabulary," large U.S. departments are becoming more and more paramilitary units

Both 9mm submachine guns, top is the Walther MPK, the MPL below. The MPK was used by Munich police response teams during the 1972 Olympic hostage crisis.

The Australian Owen Mk 1/42 (top) and the Austen Mk 1 fire the standard European 9mm Parabellum cartridge.

like the French gendarmerie, Italian carabinieri or German GSG border police. Instead of being part of the population, many policemen now think of themselves as part of an elite group paid to control unruly segments of the society. Of course, this "us verses them" feeling is mutual, with teenage gang members and narcotics traffickers no longer hesitating to shoot at policemen, unthinkable just 30 years ago.

Until recently, U.S. policemen were armed in much the same fashion as the civilian population, with revolvers, shotguns and deer rifles being the normal deadly force, with the wooden night-stick being used for the vast majority of confrontations.

The H&K MP5K "Personal Defense Weapon" (top) and the Beretta U.S. M9 pistol use the 9mm Parabellum.

The Italian Spectre M4 9mm submachine gun features double handles, high-capacity magazine and a folding stock.

While heavy firepower might have been necessary against mobsters in Chicago in the 1920s, Midwestern bank robbers in the 1930s, or border smugglers during Prohibition, most policemen could expect to serve their entire career without shooting anyone or even drawing their sidearm.

This is still true in many departments, but there is increasing concern, perhaps fostered by the media, about highly mobile, well-armed, dope-dealing gangs. Whatever the reality, the perception is that policemen need more individual firepower.

Since the public is not yet willing to accept uniformed officers with submachine guns slung on their backs, like in Italy or South Korea, the apparent answer is a sidearm with stopping power equivalent to the traditional .38 Special but with greater capacity. While most American cops still carry revolvers, quite a few now carry 9mm Beretta 92s, Glock 17s, SIG-Sauer P226s or Smith & Wesson 5906s, as well as their compact versions.

Police departments and federal agencies are also considering 9mm carbines to replace their shotguns. The caliber overlap with sidearms is a logistics plus, just as it was for European armies in World War II with the adoption of Sten

The H&K MP5 SF 9mm carbine is used by the FBI. Full-auto does not increase effective for agents greatly.

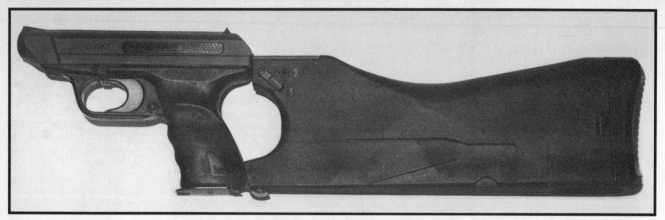

The H&K VP70 9mm machine pistol with holster/stock attached will fire three-round bursts as well as single shots.

and Schmeisser submachine guns. Also, the 9mm carbine provides pinpoint accuracy, unlike the shotgun loaded with buckshot, especially important in hostage situations. Further, it has almost no recoil, unlike the shotgun which kicks like a .375 Magnum elephant rifle, a particularly significant consideration for female and small-statured male officers. At present, the Drug Enforcement Administration issues the 9mm version of the Colt Commando, usually blocked for semi-automatic fire. The FBI is issuing a semi-auto edition of the Heckler & Koch MP5 SMG. Metropolitan Police in London also issue a semi-auto MP5 to officers guarding Heathrow Airport from terrorists. Special weapons teams like L.A. Sheriffs SEB, British Special Air Service, German SEK and GSG-9 use the MP5 in its selective-fire form. When the MP5 was first imported to the U.S. in 1970, I tested it in the course of writing an IACP tech manual called *Submachine Guns in Police Work.* In that book, I rated the HK MP5 number one as a police SMG, compared to the Ingram MAC-10, S&W M76, Uzi and Walther MPK, mainly for its closed-bolt, semi-automatic accuracy, the primary criteria for a law enforcement gun. This was all new at the time, and it wasn't until the SAS used MP5s in 1980, during their assault on terrorists holed up in London's Iranian Embassy, that police sales, mainly for SWAT teams, took off. Some departments and individual officers are now carrying the Marlin 9mm Camp Carbine in patrol cars. This gun has none of the "assault weapon" appearance that some of the (uninformed) public might object to. Hopefully, they will make a lighter weight, plastic stock version in the future.

Most of the other 9mm carbines on the market have tried to emulate submachine gun styling, like those made by Sterling, Uzi or HK, sometimes based on their already popular SMGs. One of the first 9mm carbines on the U.S. scene was the J&R M68, now out of production. I had mine fitted with a Thompson SMG rear sight and an Uzi sling I got from a Druse guard in Israel. I had the sling attached to the left side of the gun in European fashion; it worked very well.

Speaking of Israel, which has been a leader in small arms design, the 9mm has been common there since the British Mandate period. When an independent state was formed in 1948, pistols were in short supply and there was no standardization. Eventually, the M1951 Beretta Brigadier became semi-issue, but the 9mm cartridge was used primarily in submachine guns, mainly Uzis and captured Port Saids (Egyptian version of Swedish M45 Carl Gustav). When I stayed on

a border *kibbutz* in 1969, I rarely saw anyone carrying pistols, but Uzis were everywhere. The military was well aware that SMGs account for far more enemy casualties than pistols. Since those days, however, with an increase in Jewish settlements in the Occupied Territories (captured in '67), and the increase in Arab unrest (the *Intifadeh*), Israeli civilians are now carrying pistols in profusion. After the terrorist takeover of a school at Ma'alot, even schoolteachers started packing pistols.

Israeli combat carry and shooting techniques are standardized for military, police and civilian users. The 9mm semi-auto is the most common weapon, revolvers being considered antiquated. The pistol is carried chamber-empty, whether it is single-action or double-action style, which has drastically lowered the incidence of accidental discharges. It is cocked by gripping the slide with the left hand, then pushing through with the right, on the way up to a two-hand shooting stance. Weapons are often worn unconcealed as a warning to terrorists and local Arabs, just as hitchhiking soldiers carry their issue assault rifles and submachine guns. Street crime is not a significant factor in Israel, so weapons and carrying styles are not chosen with that in mind. The preferred holster is the inside waistband, worn behind the right hip in uniform or plainclothes. Ammunition tends to be issue hardball or Winchester Silvertips. The most common weapons are the Czech CZ-75 and the Italian TZ-75, mainly because they combine quality with lower cost than comparable German or American weapons. Inflation is rampant in Israeli's war economy, and there is high duty on most imports.

Israeli counter-terrorist teams favor the Browning P35 Hi-Power, no doubt influenced by the British SAS. Other teams which use the Hi-Power are the FBI's Hostage Rescue Team (HRT), and commandos from Jordan, Oman, Colombia, Thailand, Portugal and a half-dozen other nations. The 50-year headstart as an issue sidearm for a host of countries gave it entre to special units.

Police departments used to the revolver have often chosen the Glock for special units, which simplifies retraining, as the Glock has no thumb safety or decocking lever. Such units include NYPD's ESU (Emergency Services Unit), London's Metropolitan Police PT17 and the Hong Kong Police Special Duties Unit.

Outside the Communist bloc the 9mm Parabellum is standard for pistols and submachine guns in most of the world's armies. With the U.S. adoption of the Beretta Model 92, the choice is now almost universal, and this will continue well into the next century. Some of the finest centerfire combat pistols in the world are made in this caliber, such as the SIG P210, SIG-Sauer P226, P225, and P228, the Heckler & Koch P7M8 and P7M13, the Glock 17 and 19, Beretta M1951 and M92F, Walther P5 and the Czech CZ75. Even vintage pistols like the P'08 Luger, the Walther P38 (Pl) and Mauser 1896 are still perking along, showing the longevity of this cartridge and the quality of pistols made for it. While the service pistol/9mm cartridge combination was never admired by target shooters, the SIG P210, the HK P9S and some Third Generation Smiths show what this round is capable of, if a pistol is built for competition rather than infantry combat. New designs are entering the market all the time, such as those by Ruger, Star, S&W, Glock and Browning.

New 9mm carbines are coming on the market as well. Those made in the U.S. will probably follow the Marlin Camp Carbine model to avoid the current wave of legislation against "assault"-style guns. New 9mm submachine guns are also being developed, although they tend to be geared toward the commando or counter-terrorist role, since the assault rifle has taken over as infantry equipment in U.S. and Chinese-style armies. Such SMGs are getting more compact and are often equipped with suppressors for ambush, assassination or fighting in closed spaces.

Compact sub guns include the Mini-Uzi, Beretta M12 and M93R, the HK MPSK, Walther MPK and the out-of-production Ingram M10. The M10 was usually equipped with the MAC suppressor; other suppressed guns, occasionally seen in special operations, are the Swedish M45, the British Sterling L34Al and the German HK MP5SD. Custom suppressors are supplied by Wilson Arms of Brunswick, Georgia, among others. These suppressors work best with subsonic 9mm ammunition like the 147-grain hollow point developed for Navy SEAL teams in Vietnam. SEALs used S&W M39s with "Hush Puppy" silencers to take out sentry dogs prior to assaults on VC camps.

While it might lack tack-driving accuracy or optimum per-round stopping power, the 9mm Parabellum has shown itself to be the best all-around pistol cartridge of the 20th Century. Some of the finest pistols, submachine guns and carbines have been made for it, and new bullet designs are made in this caliber every year. The policeman, soldier and civilian now have the widest range of effective proven designs offered in modern history. While far from perfect for every conceivable police or self-defense need, the 9mm has shown itself to be better than most. In fact, "9 millimeter" is is virtually synonymous with "pistol" in some European countries. It has shown itself to be the most universal round of this century, and probably most of the next.

There are several variations of the 9mm cartridges and case dimensions do not make them interchangeable for use.

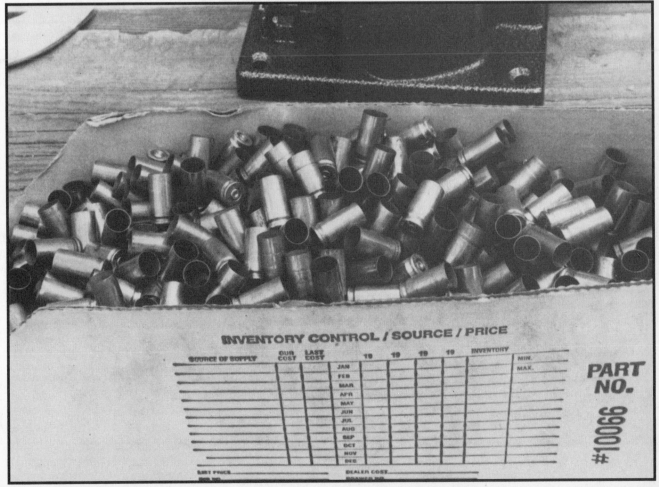

CHAPTER *Twenty*

PROPER FEEDING FOR THE 9mm

Today's High-tech Handgun Bullets Offer A Big Boost In Performance.

This modified 9mm TZ 75 88 Series with a 4.75-inch barrel is a full-size service handgun. The author discovered that the longer barrel did tend to alter the performance — primarily the velocities — of some of the rounds tested.

I N TODAY'S high-tech world of fiber optics, satellite communications and space shuttles, the 9mmP cartridge is somewhat of an anomaly.

Despite the fact that it was introduced in 1902 — making it roughly nine years older than the .45 ACP, and one of the first successful cartridges created expressly for smokeless powder — it remains the most popular military handgun and submachine gun round in use today.

Indeed, during the last decade it even made considerable inroads into the civilian law enforcement community, where it was hailed as the ideal "new police load."

According to Chris Christain, one-time Navy pistol team member, current competitive shooter and hunting guide, "There are a number of reasons for the continued popularity of the 9mmP. Foremost is the fact that some of the most finely engineered handguns in the world were designed expressly for this round. Such guns as the Browning Hi-Power, CZ-75 (and it's Tanfoglio clones) the SIG Sauer P226 and 225 and others are highly reliable, amply accurate and easy to shoot."

To that, you can add increased magazine capacity. Even a compact gun like the SIG Sauer P225 will tote nine rounds. The larger "service-size" guns provide 15 to 18 rounds. When that runs dry, it takes but a second to slap in a new magazine and start all over. Among those who have lived through such an experience, the general consensus is that you can't have too much ammo in a gunfight!

Combine both the above with the fact that the 9mmP is a low-recoiling cartridge that is inherently easy to shoot anyway, and it's not hard to see why it finds favor with both military and civilian law enforcement folks.

"When you get right down to it, the average police officer is, at best, a semi-trained shooter, while the average military individual isn't even up to that standard," Christian contends. "Any gun that makes it easier for them to hit their target with marginal training is viewed as an asset."

We realize Christian's "semi-trained shooter remark will ruffle some feathers, but it won't among police and military firearms instructors, training officers or those savvy, old veterans who have devoted the time required to master the handgun. They know the harsh realities that Christian learned during 10 years as a military and civilian handgun instructor:

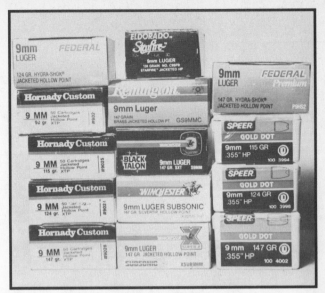

The author gathered an impressive stack of 9mm rounds for his test. The ammunition represents the latest offerings in the high-tech hollow-point race.

Training time and training budgets simply aren't sufficient to take young, mostly urban recruits with little previous shooting experience and turn them into deadly combat shooters.

What kind of training is required to produce that goal? By way of example, when SEAL Team 6 was created in 1980 to become one of premier counterterrorist units in the world, their handgun training schedule called for 2500 full-power rounds per week, per man! And, every member of Team 6 already was a qualified, experienced SEAL who thought he was a great shot!

For the average police officer, that 2500 round weekly allowance would equal his full academy training and five or more years of requalification.

"That's why the 9mmP always will remain popular; a semi-trained shooter can handle it," Christian declares.

That's also why the 9mmP is a subject of controversy among many self-defense-oriented handgunners.

Many big-bore enthusiasts question the stopping power of

Federal Hydra-Shok had explosive expansion at velocities over 1000 fps with only a small core producing penetration.

The SIG Sauer P225 used in author's tests represents the current breed of compact, concealable 9mms that are becoming a popular choice among plainclothes police officers and civilians. Its performance was flawless.

the mild-mannered 9mmP. One wag even opineed that they call them "Wondernines," because you always wonder if the bad guy will go down when you hit him with one.

Other evidence, however — including actual police shooting reports — shows that, with the proper bullet, the 9mmP can be highly effective. The key term, obviously, is "proper bullet," something that has plagued the 9mmP since its introduction.

Originally loaded with a round-nose, full metal-jacketed (FMJ) bullet, the early 9mmP loads were no great shakes at ending an unpleasant confrontation. The tough little slugs would drill a neat .36 caliber hole through the subject of your attention — who then would continue to do pretty much what he wanted for a considerable period of time before assuming room temperature.

Lee Jurras, of Super Vel Fame, attempted to alter that by producing lightweight expanding bullets that did, in fact, offer a measure of improvement — but not quite enough. Bullet-making technology wasn't quite up to the task at the time.

Today, however, that has changed. Within the last six years, each of the major U.S. ammo makers has taken a long, hard look at 9mmP hollow-point loads and undertaken serious steps to improve them. The end result is that, as of this writing, Federal, Winchester, Hornady, Speer, PMC/Eldorado and Remington all have settled on their own version of a 9mmP "high-tech" hollow-point for law enforcement and self-defense.

Each has taken a somewhat different approach in construc-

tion, design and intended performance parameters of their bullets. This gives the shooter an interesting selection from which to choose. To aid in your making that choice, we decided to have Chris Christian put them all through comprehensive performance tests. Here's how he went about it:

THE LOADS

Hornady was one of the first to introduce a revamped hollow-point design in the wake of the FBI tests that resulted

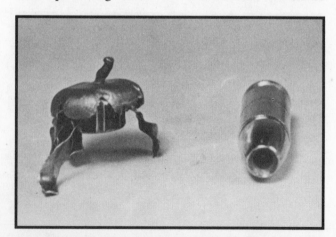

Remington's Golden Saber showed expansion of more than .62-inch from both of the test handguns. It also produced what was an almost ideal level of penetration.

Winchester's new Black Talon was one of the better performers, expanding to .65-inch-plus. The bullet maintained full weight retention from both test guns. The sharp jacket petals undoubtedly contribute to additional tissue damage.

from the infamous "FBI Miami Massacre." Available as loaded rounds in weights of 90, 115, 124, and 147 grains, their XTP bullet is designed to expand to a consistent diameter of approximately 1.67 times caliber — retaining maximum bullet weight — and offer adequate penetration through intervening obstacles. This is what the FBI tests determined to be proper law enforcement bullet performance.

These bullets also are available as components, and the 115-grain version has earned a reputation among competitive shooters as one of the most accurate 9mm bullets available.

Winchester offers three different rounds. Their venerable and effective Silvertip has been slightly re-designed to improve penetration. Their new Subsonic Deep Penetrator is intended to perform similarly to the Hornady XTP. Their newest offering, the Black Talon SXT, is the most radical.

The bullet jacket can contribute to tissue damage in a conventional hollow-point, but it is not normally designed to do so. The Black Talon changes that by incorporating six sharply curved jacket petals designed to rip and tear tissue as they open up to allow the lead core to expand.

Each of the Winchester bullets was available in the 147-grain weight for our tests.

Federal's premier bullet is the Hydra-Shok in 124 and 147 grains. This load utilizes an integal center post within the hollow-point cavity to direct matter contacted by the bullet in an outward manner that forces it against the interior walls of the cavity and promotes quick bullet expansion. PMC/Eldorado's new Starfire 124-grain JHP was designed by the same man, Tom Burczynski, who developed the original Hydra-Shok bullet. This round uses internal ribs within the hollow-point cavity to accomplish the redirection of matter to aid in bullet expansion.

Remington also uses a radical jacket to increase tissue damage. This jacket is of brass instead of the traditional copper alloy. Upon impact, six thick jacket petals expand outward to increase initial bullet diameter prior to the actual lead core expansion. The new Golden Saber round is available in a weight of 147 grains.

Speer's Gold Dot bullet is another controlled-expansion/assured-penetration design. It is intended to expand to a consistent diameter while retaining maximum weight for penetration. Available in weights of 115, 124 and 147 grains, this bullet presented somewhat of a quandry.

It is the intention of this chapter to test only factory-loaded

The PMC/Eldorado Starfire expanded quickly and gave a big mushroom. However, its penetration was less than the other ammunition tested.

TABEL #1
SIG Sauer P225 3.65-inch barrel

LOAD	VELOCITY	ACCURACY	PENETRATION	EXPANSION	RETAINED WEIGHT
Hornady XTP JHP					
90 gr. #9020	1245	1.45	24	.55	89 grains
115 gr. #9025	1095	1.60	28/core-22/jacket	.55	96
124 gr. #9024	1032	3.5	29	.63	121
147 gr. #9028	892	2.1	32	.63	140
Winchester					
147 gr. Deep Penetrator #XSUB9MM	909	2.5	29	.61	147
147 gr. Silvertip #X9MMST147	911	2.4	26	.61	147
147 gr. Black Talon SXT S9MM	943	2.7	27	.65	147
Federal					
124 gr. Hydra-Shok P9HS1	1063	1.7	20/core-13/jacket (A)	.81	82
147 gr. Hydra-Shok P9HS2	946	2.8	23	.70	142
Remington Golden Saber					
147 gr. GS9MMC	970	2.5	29	.65	146
Speer Gold Dot					
115 gr. #3994	1089	NA	34	.54	113
124 gr. #3998	1041	NA	34	.58	124
147 gr. #4002	930	NA	34	.58	147
PMC/Eldorado Starfire					
124 gr. #C9SFB	1037	1.9	22 (B)	.68	117

(A) Jacket fragments in first and second bags
(B) Core and jacket separated — found in same bag.

ammunition, and the Gold Dot bullet will be available as such. Unfortunately, at test time, it was available only as a component.

Christian made the decision to load the bullets to the same average velocity as the other factory loads in the same weights for penetration and expansion tests. He did not test the bullets for accuracy, since he made no attempt to produce accurate loads — just those that produced the right velocity. Comparing the accuracy of hastily assembled reloads to factory fodder is not a fair or valid test.

TEST PROCEDURE

In the real world of the streets, the 9mmP is fired routinely through either full-size service guns or compact, easily concealable models. Differing barrel lengths, however, will affect velocity and, possibly, terminal performance. To reflect that, we chose two different test guns.

"The first is my personal TZ 75 88 Series Tanfoglio that was imported originally by the now-defunct F.I.E. Corp. and currently by European American Armory as their Witness model. A full-size, steel frame, 15-shot piece with a 4.75-inch barrel, it adequately represents the standard uniformed holster gun," Christian reports.

The second gun is the legendary SIG Sauer P225. This compact DA auto has a 3.65-inch barrel and is found routinely in the hands of knowledgeable law enforcement officers (and civilians) who demand a compact, accurate and reliable piece for concealed carry.

"Accuracy testing was conducted from a benchrest at 25 yards. I do not use a mechanical rest, because I have discovered they can produce inaccurate results with some guns.

"Instead, using a two-piece rest, I fired three five-round groups with each gun and load. The largest and smallest groups were discarded, the mid-size group being recorded."

TABLE #2
TZ 75 88 Series 4.75-inch barrel

LOAD	VELOCITY	ACCURACY	PENETRATION	EXPANSION	RETAINED WEIGHT
Hornady XTP JHP					
90 gr. #9020	1359	1.60	24	.60	80 grains
115 gr. #9025	1173	1.45	25	.56	109
124 gr. #9024	1120	2.25	35	.61	120
147 gr. #9028	969	2.35	35	.62	147
Winchester					
147 gr. Deep Penetrator #XSUB9MM	987	2.25	29	.59	145
147 gr. Silvertip #X9MMST147	993	3.5	30	.63	130
147 gr. Black Talon SXT S9MM	991	1.9	28	.66	147
Federal					
124 gr. Hydra-Shok P9HS1	1134	1.45	40	.37 (C)	62
147 gr. Hydra-Shok P9HS2	1021	2.30	44	.38 (C)	70
Remington Golden Saber					
147 gr. GS9MMC	1064	2.0	34	.62	140
Speer Gold Dot					
115 gr. #3994	1160	NA	30	.55	113
124 gr. #3998	1130	NA	34	.56	124
147 gr. #4002	990	NA	34	.58	147
PMC/Eldorado Starfire					
124 gr. #C9FSB	1135	1.75	19	.71	115

(C) Core and jacket separation. Jacket fragments scattered along entire bullet path. Expansion figure denotes recovered core only.

Christian feels this procedure offers a better feel for the gun's real world capabilities, although, in actual practice, all the group sizes with the same load were quite close in size. Groups were reported via a center-to-center measurement. Velocities were recorded by an Oehler 35P chronograph with the start screen ten feet from the muzzle.

PENETRATION & EXPANSION

No artificial test medium will accurately duplicate the passage of every bullet through the living tissue of a mammal. None. Period. The reason for that is simple.

For any artificial test medium to be valid, it must be consistent. Each and every bullet passing through it must encounter the exact same substance and degree of resistance. If not, you can throw your test results out.

Yet, the body of any mammal is anything but consistent. The support structure consists of numerous bones of varying size and density that encapsulate organs and muscles that vary quite a bit in their consistency, as well. A bullet that strikes heavy bone will behave quite a bit differently than one impacting soft, fluid-filled tissues. The difference between those two impacts may be as little as one inch of bullet placement!

Given that, the choice of an artificial test medium needs only be one that can be applied consistently, and bears a relationship to how a bullet may perform in the soft tissue comprising the greater part of the body and its vital organs. The three most commonly accepted are 10 percent ballistic gelatin, wet paper and pure water.

Gelatin is the preferred choice, but must be used under strict temperature controls. If one varies too much from a gelatin block temperature of 39 degrees F., the consistency of the medium changes and so does the validity of the results. "I ruled this out since the 85 to 95F heat of a Florida summer

Author's water box allowed an accurate determination of bullet penetration, weight retention, expansion and recovery of bullet fragments.

made gelatin impractical," Christian reports. "Also ruled out, for the same reason, was wet newsprint. This must be used in a uniformly-soaked condition, which could not be guaranteed in that kind of heat. So, I used pure well water."

Some may criticize that choice, but Evan Marshall and Ed Sanow, authors of *Handgun Stopping Power: The Definitive Study*, relied primarily on ballistic gelatin for their results. On page 169 of their book, the authors make their feelings on water, as a bullet test medium, known.

"Expansion in water gives excellent correlation with expansion in living soft tissue...," they write. In simple and direct terms, if a bullet expands in water, it will expand to some degree no matter what living tissue is involved. If the bullet does not expand in water, the bullet will need to strike bone to expand to any significant degree."

The authors conclude: "Overall, water as a test medium, gives excellent results on the probability and degree of expansion."

To facilitate Christian's use of water, a wooden box — more precisely, a trough open at one end — was constructed and sized to hold one gallon Baggie-type storage bags full of water.

In use, the trough was packed with filled bags, a bullet fired through the open end, and when the spray settled, it was a simple matter for Christain to work his way through the punctured bags until he arrived at the one holding the bullet. The interior of the trough was spray-painted red. This would show whether a bullet had hit the wood at any point in its travels. It didn't happen, but had it been the case the round would have been invalidated and retested.

A distance scale (in inches) was marked on the surface of the trough that showed how far the bullet had penetrated.

"One advantage of using multiple bags is that I was able to

clearly determine if any fragments came off the bullet — and precisely where it happened. They would be in one of the punctured bags. That is important, because a bullet that fragments in the first one or two bags obviously expanded quickly, while one that shed fragments along the entire bullet path was merely coming apart."

The penetration figure achieved must be viewed as comparative only; the degree of penetration achieved by one bullet as compared to another in the same test medium.

It is logical to assume, however, that the relationship between the various penetration depths of the different bullets would remain relatively constant in other mediums.

For those not satisfied with that, Marshall and Sanow note in their book that the Federal 9mm Nyclad 124-grain RNJHP consistently penetrated to a depth of 12.5 inches in 10 percent ballistic gelatin.

Prior to his own test, Christian ran five penetration tests through the water box using this round from the TZ75. All five rounds penetrated to a depth of 29 to 30 inches.

Table #1 shows all pertinent performance data from the SIG Sauer 225, while TZ75 data is shown in Table #2. Results are quite interesting. And, while it is not the intent of this piece to find the "magic bullet," some observations are inescapable.

Some bullets showed a marked difference in performance from the two different barrel lengths. The Federal Hydra-Shok was noticeable in this respect. From the TZ, both bullet weights showed instant, almost explosive, expansion that fragmented the bullet. When the 147-grain version was reduced to subsonic velocity by the SIG, however, it expanded to .70 caliber and retained virtually all its weight while providing excellent penetration . It's something to think about if you tote a short-barreled 9mm.

Some bullets showed little change. The Speer Gold Dot

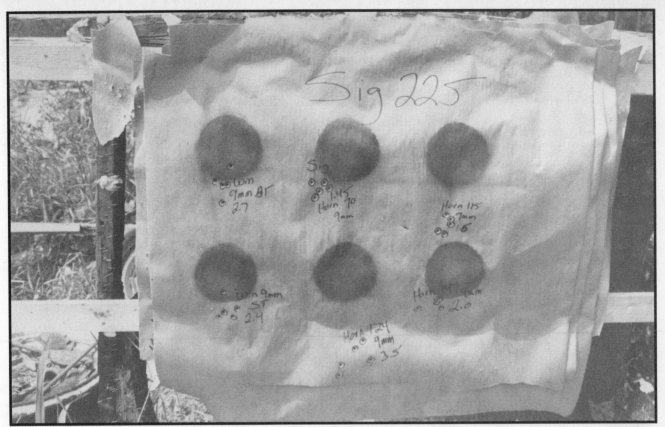

According to the author's findings, the SIG Sauer P225 proved comfortable with most of the ammunition he tested.

was remarkably consistent from both guns, as was the Winchester Black Talon. In fact, its performance was most impressive. Penetration and expansion were consistent with both guns. And. when Winchester talks about sharp jacket talons, they aren't kidding. Christian pricked my fingers several times while handling expanded bullets, until it dawned on me that I had to handle them carefully. They are sharp! Imagine the damage they are doing to the target!

Another interesting factor was the penetration and expansion of most of the 147-grain loads, especially the Winchester and Federal products. This bullet weight has been critized by some for offering too much penetration and too little expansion. In fact, some of the lighter weights penetrated more.

Performance of the new Remington Golden Saber was good, but there was a slight problem.

"It is my habit to examine fired cases, and those from the Golden Saber showed a definite primer wipe — a proper primer indentation with a slashing edge. This happened with both guns and indicates a condition called premature unlocking — the gun moving out of battery before the firing pin has retracted from contact with the primer," Christian reports.

"The cause could be the wrong burning speed powder, too much powder or a characteristic of the brass jacket. Regardless, it needs correction, because premature unlocking can (and at some point, probably will) damage or break a firing pin. Since these rounds are intended for law enforcement and self-defense, that is simply an unacceptable risk. Remington needs to consider this condition.

If you worry about excess penetration, note the performance of the PMC Starfire. If your scenario requires assured penetration, you'll find the Gold Dot and Hornady XTP

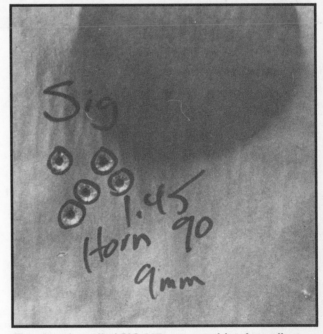

The short-barrelled SIG 225 was capable of excellent accuracy. The 90-grain Hornady JHP was its favorite.

among the best in that category. Each of these high-tech 9mmP rounds offers its own performance characteristics.

"All you have to do to boost the performance of your gun is decide what characteristics you require, then feed your 9mm properly," Christian insists.

CHAPTER
Twenty-One

RELOADING THE 9X19mm

It's A Project Not Unfraught With Complexities, But There Are Shortcuts Around Most Of Them!

SINCE SOME point in 1957 or so, Dean Grennell has been serving as what we might term a reloader's Ann Landers, and a great many readers have inquired as to a good choice in calibers for the launching of their reloading careers. Grennell's usual response has been the .38 Special, with the .357 magnum as a fairly close second. Other handgun calibers with cases having sides that are straight and parallel serve almost as well, including the .41 magnum, .44 Special, .44 magnum and .45 Auto Rim or Colt.

"Personally, I cut my reloader's teeth on the .45 ACP, back in the early Fifties. A friend and I used a Lyman No. 310 tong tool and I recall we were heavily perplexed upon encountering some Frankford Arsenal cases that had primer pockets smaller in diameter, for use with FA's own primer. Normal large pistol primers are .210-inch in diameter and there was just no way you could cajole them into the FA case primer pockets.

"Much as I've come to respect and admire the .45 ACP, it's not a round I'd suggest as the reloader's first project. Much the same in cards, spades and Big Casino can be said of the 9x19mm Luger/Parabellum/whatever. The 9mmP—as we'll term it henceforth — has a straight-sided case with a slight amount of taper and, as the Genie remarked to Aladdin, that's where the rub comes in."

The 9mmP has a nominal case length of .754-inch. The rim diameter is given as .394-inch. It's .391-inch just ahead of the extractor groove and the outside diameter at the case mouth is .380-inch. The .38 ACP and .38 Colt Super have nominally identical case dimensions, with a case length of .900-inch and a uniform diameter of .384-inch from just ahead of the groove to the case mouth, with a rim diameter of .406-inch. The dimensions are quoted from the current Hornady Handbook and may vary slightly in other sources.

A reloaded cartridge needs to end up with its bullet base held in a fairly secure and tenacious grasp by the case neck. As most 9mmP ammo ends up getting used in autoloaders, the stresses of getting stripped from the top of the magazine and slammed up the feed ramp and into the chamber tend to seat the bullet a bit deeper into the case, and you don't want that to happen. It can boost the peak chamber pressures and the 9mmP operates at a high level, even under the best of conditions.

It's obvious you're not going to be able to obtain much of a press-fit of case mouth against bullet base with a tapered case. With some manual/handbook loads for the 9mmP, you start out with the case about level-full and compress the charge to seat the bullet, and such loads provide a reasonable amount of support against deeper seating.

One possible approach consists of resizing your spent 9mmP cases in a 9mmP resizing die, then going on to pass about the front one-third of the case up into a .38 ACP/.38 Super die to iron the mouth down a bit farther. Dillon Precision Products, Inc., 7442 East Butherus Drive, Scottsdale, AZ

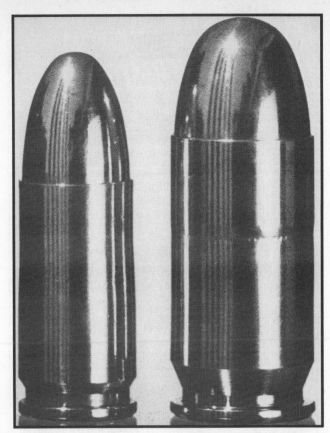

The 9x19mm (left) and the .45 ACP are two of the most widely used military and police cartridges of all time.

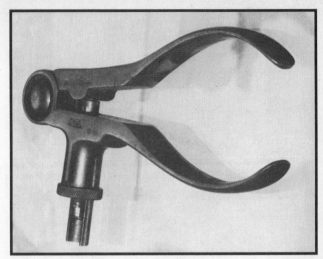

This is an old Lyman tong tool like one author used in getting started reloading the .45 ACP in the early Fifties.

85260, can furnish a carbide 9mmP resizing die that puts a short area of parallel-sided brass at the case mouth, giving the effect of a faint amount of bottleneck. Reportedly, that works quite well.

"I have become quite partial to the Lyman M-die for expanding case mouths," Grennell tells us. The lower end of the expanding punch has a diameter about .003-inch smaller than bullet diameter, fairing into an upper portion about .002- to .003-inch larger than bullet diameter. By careful adjustment of the M-die in the loading press, you can flare the mouth just enough to accept about the first .020-inch or so of the bullet base. That lets you seat the bullet without cocking or scraping, but provides a useful length of case neck that is slightly less than bullet diameter to provide the badly needed friction-fit."

If you don't happen to have a set of .38 ACP/.38 Super dies on hand, you might have a sizing die for the .380 ACP/9mm Kurz/Corto/Short, which has a mouth outside diameter of .373-inch and that can be used for the same purpose.

The effect we've been trying to achieve by all this effort is to provide the 9mmP case with an inside diameter at the neck that is some few thousandths smaller than the bullet base over a reasonable distance for the sake of a secure grip to prevent bullet migration during the feeding cycle.

The 9mmP is one of those cartridges that benefits considerably from intent and careful sorting of the spent cases, prior to reloading. The first and foremost thing to do is to cull out all the Berdan-primed cases, readily identifiable by the presence of two small, off-center flash holes.

Once you've pulled them out of the main herd, it's not a bad

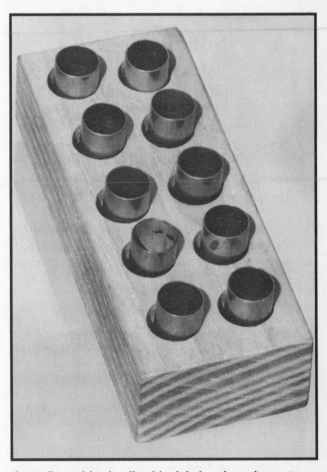

A small cartridge loading block is handy and easy to make. After charging, powder levels can be checked.

idea to mash their mouths with a pair of Vise-Grip pliers to make sure they'll not find their way back into the chain of production again. If present in quantity, recycle by selling them to the scrap dealer.

Once you've gotten your supply of cases down to nothing but the Boxer-primed variety, with the single, centrally lo-

RCBS shell holder No. 16 is used for the 9x19mm.

The free Winchester Reloading Components Catalog contains load data on handgun, rifle and shotgun ammo.

cated flash holes, it's still an excellent idea to sort them by headstamps. A considerable amount of dimensional variation can be expected from one producer to the next. The situation is not as bad as it used to be, but it's still bad enough. I can recall when I had to stock three different shell holders to handle all the Boxer-primed 9mmP empties and it was nearly that bad for the .45 Colt brass," Grennell admits.

"If you've yet to purchase your set of 9mmP reloading dies, I'd recommend you get the kind with a tungsten carbide insert in the resizing die. Redding uses a titanium carbide insert in their dies. Either kind does not require application of lubricant before sizing, nor removal of the lube after doing so. That can save you an enormously useful amount of fuss, work, time and bother. The tapered case of the 9mmP, like that of the .30 GI Carbine, means that carbide dies will cost substantially more than dies for parallel-sided cases such as the .38 Special, but it's still a bargain if you attach any significant value to your person hours."

If your empty cases are from military loads, some or most may have the primers stamp-crimped into place for the sake of better performance in full-auto weaponry. You need to remove the stamp-crimp for the sake of easy seating of fresh primers. That can be done in any of several approaches. The one Grennell prefers is to use one of the inside/outside case neck deburring tools, held in a crank-operated base, as available from Forster Products. Three or four turns of the crank

will remove the stamp-crimp for easy seating of the new primer.

The 9mmP uses small pistol primers and, due to the limited amount of available powder space, Grennell usually uses the standard, rather than magnum-type small primers, regardless of the powder he's using.

The primers need to be seated firmly for the sake of lightly pre-stressing the wafer of priming compound, but without excessive force that might crack the wafer and result in a misfire or hangfire. It's a simple matter of educating your wrist muscles and maintaining a uniform seating pressure, according to the old pro.

Reloading presses are to be had in a great many designs and formats. There are single-station presses in which you install one die at a time to perform one or perhaps two operations. There are turret presses with three or more stations that can handle the given number of operations and there are progressive presses, either manually or automatically indexed, to

Another resource available on request is Scot's manual.

Berdan-primed cases such as CCI's Blazer have two off-center flash holes which can break decapping pins.

Carbide resizing dies, like this one from RCBS, have a tungsten carbide insert and don't require case lube.

Here is a look at the tungsten carbide insert in the die.

perform all the needed operations with each stroke of the operating handle.

If you have a hard need for producing many thousands of rounds per day, there are fully automatic presses that only need to be fed with primers, powder and bullets as production goes along. If one of these catches your fancy, be soberly advised the price tags run to five digits and a bit.

"Quite candidly, I am what a contemporary once termed an Experimental Ballistician, because they didn't care to mention the publication that employs me. I make up a few rounds of these, a few more rounds of those and take them to the range for testing," Grennell explains.

"I don't indulge in practice because I've not fired a round in competition since some point back in the mid-Seventies. It's not for a lack of interest but due to a sharp shortage of time.

"For that basic reason, much of my reloading can be handled quite nicely on a single-station press. I produce a batch of load-ready cases, consult my data sources, adjust

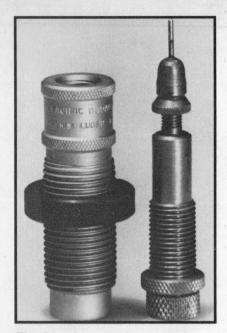

The decaping stem is removed from this resizing die from Pacific.

Midway Arms, Inc. supplies numerous needs for serious handloaders. These gummed labels are convenient for identifying different loads quickly, easily. Such labels were used in developing the loads reported on in this chapter.

measures to dispense suitable powder charges, drop them into load-ready cases, scan the powder levels with a keen eye under good light and go on to put bullets into the slightly flared case mouths. Then I seat the bullets and take them out for testing."

It is not too early to note the extreme importance of maintaining a comprehensive set of records of all the reloads you make up. You need to specify the case headstamp, make and type of primers, type and charge weight of powder, make/weight/type of bullet and its seating depth or cartridge overall length (COL) and, after test-firing, you need to add the performance data.

"Various suppliers offer excellent books for controlling such records. Personally, I just use an informal system of spiral-bound notebooks, due to my innate birth defect. You see, I was born without the soul of a bookkeeper or the soul of a filing clerk. My system works well enough for my personal needs, provided I don't lose track of the blasted notebooks, as sometimes happens," Grennell explains.

It is a good idea to put the reloads in some manner of package and label the package as to the makeup of the loads. Several manufacturers offer ammo boxes or you may be able to use the boxes in which the factory loads were packed. Some suppliers—Midway, for one—can furnish printed, self-adhesive labels for such purposes.

"In my own informal system, using the spiral-bound notebooks, I number the pages and the lines down the page. When a notebook gets filled, I buy the next one with a different color of cover. I've gone through notebooks with red, yellow and green covers and am working with a blue-covered one at the moment.

"That makes identification of the given reload a conveniently simple matter. For example, I could use a grease pencil to label a box, "B-27-14" and, if needed, could turn to page 27 in the blue-covered notebook, scan down to line 14 and learn all the pertinent particulars. When the reloads are used up, a bit

The seating die is used in the final step of reloading.

With non-carbide dies, lube is applied before resizing and removed after the job is done. It's time-consuming.

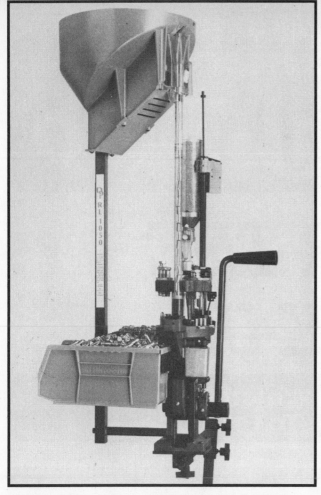

For those who need a lot of reloads, progressive presses like the Dillon Precison RL 1050 save time.

Speer's 124-grain JSP bullets offer excellent expansion.

of lighter fluid on a facial tissue removes the grease pencil markings. A problem with using paper labels is the build-up in the course of time and the difficulty of removing them."

Choosing the best powder will depend somewhat upon the length of the barrel through which the reloads will be fired. The faster-burning powders usually give best results in the shorter barrels while longer barrels develop their best ballistics with powders that are somewhat slower in burning rates.

With the IMR powders, as tested in a four-inch barrel, their SR 4756 powder delivers the highest velocities; 1175 fps with a 115-grain bullet and 1160 with a 124-grain bullet. The charge is the same in both examples: 6.3 grains of SR 4756, a compressed charge. The chamber pressures, respectively, are 30,600 and 32,400 cup.

The Sporting Arms and Ammunition Manufacturers Institute — SAAMI— decrees a maximum industry working pressure of 35,700 copper units of pressure (cup) for the 9mmP and most commercial loads are somewhat below that figure. SAAMI also specifies 1.169 inches as the maximum cartridge overall length.

The eleventh edition of Speer's load data book shows Hercules Blue Dot as the powder that delivers the highest velocity with the 88-grain Speer JHP bullet —1486 fps out of a 4.9-inch barrel on 10.9 grains, which is a maximum load to

be approached with appropriate caution. The same source lists IMR's SR 4756 as giving the highest velocity with the 95-grain Speer bullet; 1309 fps. For the 100-grain Speer JHP, they top out with Winchester 231 powder at 1295. Hodgdon HS-6 hits the peak of 1315 fps for 115-grain bullets. For 124-grain bullets, Blue Dot beats Accurate Arms No. 7 by a narrow nose: 1226 against 1225 fps.

For dope on the heavier bullets, we consulted the data booklet from Accurate Arms and find their No. 7 powder rated for the highest velocities with bullets weights of 130, 132/135 and 147 grains. AA-7 powder was developed expressly for use in the 9mmP cartridge, so that's hardly surprising.

As we get into longer barrels, such as the Colt or Marlin's Camp Carbine, Hodgdon H-110 becomes a remarkably good performer. With 10.8 grains of H-110 behind the 115-grain Hornady No. 3554 JHP bullet, ballistics were a modest 1162/345, but five rounds at 25 yards went into a group with a center-spread of only 0.25-inch; good for .954 minute of angle.

Hensley & Gibbs currently lists 18 mould designs for use in the 9mmP and Grennell is inclined to include a nineteenth: their No. 333, which is a little wadcutter only 0.25-inch from front to back, weighing 66.5 grains in typical casting alloys. As you'd suppose, the wadcutter design rarely feeds well in semi-auto pistols, but it can be used effectively in revolvers, single-shots or hand-chambered in autos. Out of the Marlin Camp Carbine, with 10.3 grains of Accurate Arms No. 7 behind it, the little 333 H&G wadcutter averaged 1874/519; hand-chambered, of course.

When Lee Jurras was running Super Vel out of Shelbyville, Indiana, he worked up a 9mm JHP bullet weighing only 80 grains. The lightest currently available is Speer's No. 4000 JHP at 88 grains. Weights of jacketed bullets range upward from there to 147 grains, but H&G can furnish mould blocks for two cast bullets at 150 grains. Mindful of the short 9mmP case and the restriction to an overall length of 1.169 inches, it's obvious that's about the end of the line.

CHAPTER
Twenty-Two

AFTER THE WORK-UP

When You've Found Which 9mm Load Is Best, It's Time To Produce!

Lyman offers a four carbide die set for reloading straight-walled 9mm cases. Shown with the dies is a S&W auto.

WHEN IT comes to reloading for the 9mmP, there are a number of theories extant in Gundom. Some say it is among the world's most difficult and frustrating cartridges to load correctly and consistently. Others say it is more or less like a lot of other cartridges. Relatively few preach that it is easy to reload — few except for the author, who feels it is among the easiest ever encountered.

Although such a supposition might be tantamount to blasphemy in some circles, it happens to have been the way it worked out for me. But before going too far into the particulars, some explanation is necessary.

Making consistent home-brewed handgun ammunition *is* tricky. It requires total attention to a number of details, and those details are not necessarily so critical when loading centerfire rifle ammo. Perhaps that is one point where others have assumed the 9mmP is a tough nut to crack when stationed at the loading bench.

Because of a host of dynamics, handgun ammunition generally is in a totally different league than rifle ammunition. Among the easiest explained of these dynamics is the burning characteristic of the powder. Pistol powder is generally much faster burning, and has a totally different power "curve" and pressure "curve" than does rifle powder.

Some shooters have imagined that this dynamic is inexplicably tied to the shorter barrel lengths. This supposition may not be entirely wrong, but it really isn't always correct in every way, either. Frankly, more arguments centered around firearms related topics are tied to matters that aren't totally correct than those which are actually wrong.

There will be no effort here to engage in a dissertation about the various dynamics of rifle and handgun cartridges, because that could be the subject of an entire book by itself. However, there are some dynamics which can make the difference between consistent loads and inconsistent ones — dynamics over which the handloader himself or herself has much control.

In all handloading, uniformity is a paramount requirement if the loads are to be as good as they can be. The difference is that a little bit of non-uniformity makes a bigger discernible difference in handgun ammo than it does in most rifle ammo.

As much as this is true for handgun ammunition, it becomes even more critical when the ammunition happens to possess two of the features of the 9mmP. This cartridge is relatively small with relatively little internal case capacity, and it is designed to operate at relatively high pressures (high intensity). To a degree, these two factors work at odds with each other when it comes to cooking up some really consistent loads.

But there is more. Since everything about 9mmP ammo and handguns is manufactured routinely at all manner of places all over the world, there can be and is a tremendous range of actual sizes and dimensions involved. This phenomenon is predictable whenever an item is truly a high volume proposition, and since the 9mmP is the world's single highest volume centerfire handgun reality, it naturally takes top honors for having available the most widely diverse combination of actual dimensions of anything involved with it.

To load really consistent 9mmP ammunition, the person

The Redding powder measure accurately dispenses propellant while speeding the reloading of 9mm cases.

doing the loading must pay total attention to every detail. First, let's discuss some of the considerations which are applicable to loading in general, handgun cartridge loading itself, and finally, 9mmP loading specifically.

Since the brass case is the first component a handloader deals with when preparing loads, it is the logical place to begin. General advice holds that all of the brass used in a particular batch of handloads should be from the same manufacturer, and from the same manufacturing lot, when possible. It is true for the 9mmP, as well as for any cartridge.

But there is more. Not all manufacturing facilities which crank out 9mmP brass are guilty of good quality control. When selecting brass, first segregate it by maker, then get out the calipers. I have experienced cases from the same production run of 9mmP which have varied as much as .005-inch in length. That may not sound like a lot of variance, but remember that pluses and minuses are relative.

The 9mmP case is supposed to be .754-inch long (that's ever so slightly more than three forths-inch). Or, put another way, it doesn't take much imagination to turn a few thousandths of an inch into another cartridge. There are a number of cartridges which are quite close to the 9mmP, and much slop in the dimensions department can make one more like the other than to other loadings in its own designation.

But more to the point, a .005-inch difference among cases in a single production run says quite a bit about the kinds of variances one can encounter from one production run to another at a given factory, or among various production runs at numerous factories. And anyone who thinks relative dimensions in the Land of the 9mmP don't make a whole lot of difference might note a statement which has appeared in the Speer reloading manuals for a number of years: "But more important, loads that produced 28,000 cup went to 62,000 cup when bullets were purposely seated .030-inch deeper!"

This points up the need to stress another reality in reloading. Although any handload is no better than its weakest or worst component, every handload is the composite of all of its components, working in concert with the firearm through which it is fired. The operative term here is "composite."

If pressures can more than double when a bullet is seated 30 thousandths of an inch deeper, it doesn't take much of a dimensional difference here and there to add up to a similar sum. There is no suggestion here that unsafe loads necessarily will happen every time, if everything isn't within a thousandth of an inch of what it is supposed to be every single time. However, there is no room for sloppiness in reloading the 9mmP, either.

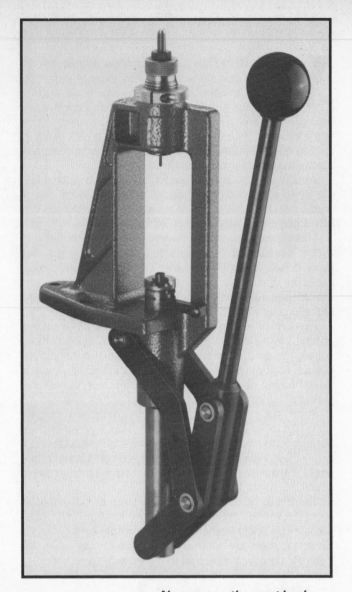

Above, even the most basic single-stage press will work well for reloading 9mmP. Left, RCBS's Accessory Kit provides the needed gadgets for the reloader.

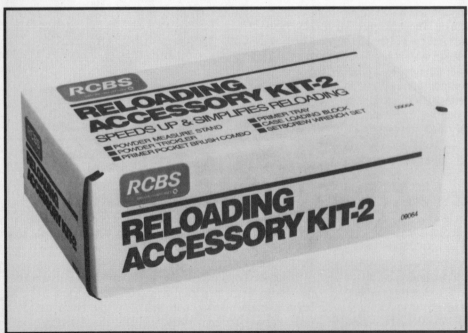

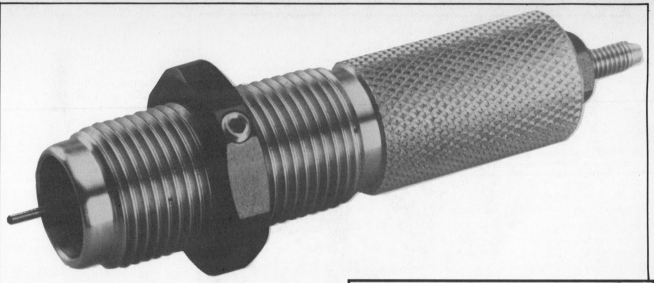

In the instance cited by Speer, it was shown that by seating the bullet deeper, the pressures skyrocketed. This is the product of powder charge relative to interior case capacity. The deeper the bullet is seated, the less working capacity there is. That is why many reloading manuals stress that there is a "minimum" suggested overall length when assembling specific components. If those same components which make a safe and effective loading at one length are assembled into a cartridge which is shorter overall, then the pressures will go up, and they can go up dramatically. Not only is this potentially unsafe, but it makes for inconsistent performance of the ammunition.

Although the interior dimensions of most cases from a particular manufacturer are generally consistent, there is no necessary consistency from one manufacturer to another. For example, the cases from Company A may have thicker walls near the base than those from Company B. That means that cases from Company A have less internal volume, assuming equal lengths with cases from Company B.

Those differences may not be much, but they are both measurable and important. They become even more important when one considers that not all cases are the same length — even from the same production run at the same factory. By now, some picture about the interrelationships of various dimensions should be taking form. It doesn't take much imagination to suggest that there could be, and indeed there are, situations in which several of the components in a particular cartridge, when assembled together, could represent a significant difference in the final case capacity, which makes a significant difference in the pressures at the moment the cartridge is fired.

Although most of these plus and minus production differences aren't generally enough, even in combination, to make an otherwise safe loading unsafe in a particular pistol, they absolutely are enough to make individual cartridges in a batch

Author used the multi-stage Ponsness-Warren Metal-Matic for reloading all the cartridges used in the development of this book. With the press are the RCBS powder measure and Lee carbide reloading dies.

Primer trays, like this one from RCBS, are useful for keeping primers handy and their right sides facing up.

inconsistent in performance. Again, it is important to stress that the 9mmP is a high intensity cartridge with relatively little capacity. This means a relatively slight difference in components can make a decided difference in how the load performs.

Anyone who wants to be fanatic about the matter could take case segregation still another step. Each case could be filled with a uniform substance to determine its exact capacity. Then, only cases with precisely the same capacity could be included in a particular batch of reloads. Some truly serious target shooters (generally of rifles) do exactly that. They use water, and measure each case. This is really not practical for most 9mmP applications, but it would work.

Within reason, variations in case length can be remedied by the handloader via the use of a case trimming device. For example, all cases in a particular batch can be trimmed to precisely the same length, so long as the length is neither too long to work in the pistol, nor too short. In 9mmP terms, it is generally held that maximum case length should be .754-inch, and that minimum case length should be .751-inch. Unlike many centerfire rifle cartridges, 9mmP cases do not stretch significantly from one firing to another, although they do stretch a little each time.

Assuming the cases to be loaded are all of like and proper length, the sizing operation comes next. There is no real secret here, except to note that the sizing die needs to be adjusted properly, and that the sizing stroke should be the same for every case in a lot. One other note about sizing dies: When considering the purchase of any at this date, it makes sense to opt for a carbide die. The reason is simple. Carbide dies preclude the need for case lube, and that eliminates a number of potential problems, as well as the time needed to lube the cases before sizing, and then removing the lube following

Author had a wide variety of spent cases to use in the 9mmP load development.

The author believes in taking as many short-cuts as possible in turning out shootable ammo. As a result, he found the RCBS Rifle/Pistol Ammo-Crafter-2 a great aid in giving him the loads he wanted.

sizing. It is simply quicker and cleaner with carbide dies.

Depending upon the design of the equipment and dies being used and the ways they might be adjusted, the next steps of the reloading procedure become increasingly important if consistent ammunition is to be achieved.

Logically, the cases need to have been cleaned somewhere during the process. And, it is assumed here that they will have been cleaned before they are re-primed. Some handloaders prefer to deprime old cases before doing anything else, then cleaning them. Others clean the cases with the old primers in place, then deprime them with the sizing die and follow up by cleaning the primer pocket separately. Whatever technique is employed, it is important that the cases be clean when the new components are being assembled.

Priming a case may appear to be so simple and inert as to be a "given." For consistent loads, it is important that all of the primers be seated uniformly. There are gauges available for those who want to be able to measure such things as primer seating depth. However, so long as the primers are seated deeply enough to preclude slam-fires or pistol malfunction, it is more important to make certain that they are all seated to the same depth than it is to determine a specific depth. We are talking about some very small potential variations here, but they are measurable and can make a difference.

Assuming the cases have been primed properly, it is time to charge the case with powder. For many years, I scaled every single powder charge of every single cartridge I handloaded. And, for some cartridges, I still do. But for most 9mmP loads,

A little reloading every day provided author with the 9mmP ammo needed for his extensive evaluations.

selection of powder can result in a situation in which the powder will meter through a measure consistently enough to work well. For example, it is not uncommon for me to load 500 9mmP cartridges and have the variation from any one to another anywhere in the batch be noticeably less than one-tenth-grain. In performance matters, there can be more difference between manufacturing lots of a specific type of cannister powder than would be noticed in such a small powder weight difference. It may sound strange, but when the differences are so small, the powder charge has less overall effect on consistency and accuracy than do several of the other considerations.

The next step is to prepare the case to receive the bullet. This is one of the absolutely critical stages in the entire process if consistency is to be achieved. This is when the expander plug determines exactly how much and how deeply the case mouth area will be expanded. Remember, when the case is sized initially, it is sized to less than its final diameter in the area of the case mouth. The expander die, then, works the brass back out to the proper dimension.

Die sets come with expanders which will work. However, not all expanders are the best choices for all bullet designs, nor for all bullet compositions. At the very least, the expander will form a slight belling at the mouth of the case so the base of the bullet can be guided into the case when it is time for the seating process to be performed. This works fine with jacketed bullets, but effective loading of cast bullets calls for a different type of expander.

Lyman is famous in the industry for its "M" die which features an expander that, rather than belling the mouth, expands it slightly and to a determinable depth. This aids in the loading of cast bullets, because it does not deform the outside of the bullet, and contributes to uniform and straight seating of the comparatively soft bullets. Such a die should be considered mandatory for the effective loading of cast bullets for the 9mmP.

The next step often is referred to as the crimping step. There is need for some discussion about both the terminology and actual function of this step when it comes to loading 9mmP ammunition.

One of the single most critical factors in loading consistent 9mmP ammunition involves a concept called "bullet pull." This is the amount of force needed to pull a bullet from a loaded cartridge. In the industry, it is used to measure crimp amount and consistency. The idea is that the more consistent the pull amount is from one cartridge to another, the more consistently the cartridges will perform.

Although this concept is important in any kind of cartridge, it is more important in handgun cartridges than in many rifle cartridges, and it is even more important among the high intensity, small volume cartridges — like the 9mmP.

As was pointed out above, pistol powder is "fast" when compared to rifle powder. And, since the 9mmP has relatively little case capacity, it uses some of the faster of the pistol powders for most loadings. What this means is that by the time the bullet is beginning to go down the barrel, peak pressures

The RCBS Rock Chucker Master Kit is a major league reloading set up for everything from handguns to big-bore riles.

either have been achieved or are at the verge of being achieved. This also means that every micro-second from the time the primer ignites until the bullet is going down the barrel is critical, and that the exact way each case releases each bullet can and does make a noticeable difference in performance. Hence, how snugly each case holds the bullet makes a difference in how the powder actually burns, and how that bullet will be propelled down and out the barrel.

Back to crimping. There is crimping, then there is crimping. When it comes to 9mmP ammunition, the subject of crimping becomes critical, since supposedly the case headspaces on its mouth, which means very much crimping can cause added headspace concerns.

Granted, in theory the 9mmP headspaces on the mouth of the case. However, in reality there are situations in which the case either doesn't "headspace" at all, or in which anything that approaches headspacing happens with respect to the base area of the cartridge rather than the mouth.

This all relates to the wide range of plus and minus dimensions mentioned earlier. For example, there may be industry standards which are quite precise, but when one considers the enormous number of places where 9mmP guns and ammunition are made, and the vast disparity in the conditions under which they are made, it is not difficult to find examples of guns and ammunition which are significantly "out of specification." And, it is not odd to find a situation in which ammunition that is on the minus end of acceptable dimension is shot in a chamber which is on the plus end of

acceptable dimension. Yet, most 9mmP ammunition will function and shoot through most 9mmP firearms. How does this happen?

In many instances, the extractor in the firearm is strong enough to hold the cartridge in place for the firing pin to dent the primer and set off the cartridge. This reality is demonstrated sufficiently whenever someone accidentally fires a .380 ACP cartridge in a 9mmP firearm. There is no effort here to suggest that anyone purposely try it — indeed, I strongly suggest that it not be done.

However, on occasion shooters have put .380 ACP ammo in 9mmP handguns, pulled the trigger and the gun goes "bang." The bullet goes out the barrel (the bullets, by the way are the same .355-inch diameter for both cartridges). However, when the .380 case is inspected following such a firing, it is bulged out, because it is thinner than the 9mmP. The base diameter of the .380 is .374-inch, while the base diameter of the 9mmP is .394-inch. And, the .380 case is .680-inch long, compared to the .754-inch length of the 9mmP.

What this means then is that the .380 ACP could not possibly headspace on its mouth in the 9mmP, because there is a difference of .074-inch in length. And even if the lengths were similar, the diameter of the .380 at the mouth is .373-inch, compared to the 9mmP at .380-inch at the same place. That would be enough, in theory, to preclude practical headspacing on the mouth. But even more noticeable is the difference at the base. It is .020-inch. Yet, the extractor of the 9mmP obviously held the thinner .380 case securely enough

The author's reloading set up includes (from right) empty cases, CCI primers, Ponsness-Warren Metal-Matic press, Hercules Unique powder and finished cartridges. The primers and powder contributed to extremely consistent loads.

to set it off. If such a huge degree of slop can allow an entirely different cartridge to fire in a 9mmP, then there obviously is a lot of room for "error" from one 9mmP cartridge to another, yet still have it function.

But back to the consistent loading of the 9mmP. Since crimping is suggested to be kept to a minimum, because the case headspaces on the mouth, then some form of taper crimp is better than the more radical bending crimp used on other cartridges like the .44 Magnum. Crimps which actually bend the mouth of the case inward only work well when a bullet with a cannelure is used, and such bullets are the exception rather than the rule when it comes to the 9mmP.

In practice, the 9mmP is probably handloaded best when no crimp as such is used at all. Rather, it is important merely to adjust the die so the bullet is squeezed quite snugly by the case. It can take a degree of experimentation when using specific combinations of brass and powder to come up with the best adjustment, but time spent focusing on this part of the reloading procedure is extremely well spent. Major advances in consistency generally can be experienced more quickly here than at any other single step of the entire reloading procedure when it comes to 9mmP ammunition.

Face it, the manufacturer of the dies determines when the dies are made just how much a case will be sized (when they are adjusted properly). And, the manufacturers of the various components determine the specific dimensions and characteristics of them. The only real control the handloader has over such things is in the initial selection process.

But the handloader does have control over the adjustment of the dies, and that includes both the depth to which a bullet will be seated and the degree to which it will be crimped in place. So, those are the two factors which should warrant critical focus when handloading. Consistency in those two areas will go a long way toward the making of consistent loads.

Back to the discussion about what cartridges are hard to load and which ones are easier. I didn't reload 9mmP cartridges until fairly late in my handloading career. This meant that I already understood the various dynamics and was careful to focus attention in the proper areas right from the start. This meant that many of the kinds of consistency errors one makes early in a handloading career were precluded, and that meant that the loads tended to be more consistent.

Handloads developed to create data for this book generally were acceptably consistent. It was not uncommon for the Oehler 35P chronograph to record standard deviations within five-shot strings of less than 10, with standard deviations of three to five achieved on numerous occasions.

Although gun writers routinely try all kinds of different combinations of components when working up loads for specific firearms, loads prepared for this book were limited severely. The reasons for such limitations might also have merit for many 9mmP shooters should they decide to load their own ammo.

When comparing relative performance characteristics of many different firearms, it is generally a good idea to establish certain benchmark, or baseline, loads. To that end, specific factory loads and specific handloads were chosen.

However, given the tremendous number of powders which will work in 9mmP cartridges, as well as the number of different primers, cases and bullets, there literally are thousands of different combinations possible. Compound that with the large number of different guns, and the matter could get totally unmanageable in a hurry.

As a result, for most data-gathering chores, my loads used only a few different bullet weights and designs, a couple of different kinds of primers, not many different kinds of cases and only one kind of powder: Hercules Unique.

With respect to the choice of powder, I confess to being arbitrary. There are many in the handloading fraternity who argue — and justifiably so — that there are "better" powders for any number of the loads. They are probably not wrong.

However, Unique is one of the powders which is credible for just about any 9mmP loading, and it is a powder which, in my experience, has been incredibly consistent from one lot to another over the years.

There is no effort here to suggest I used Unique from a number of different lots. For this book, I used powder from

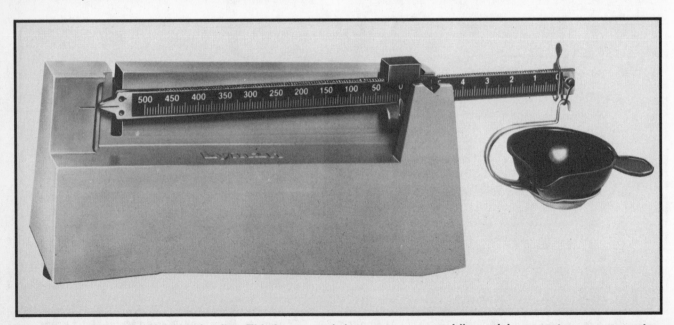

A powder scale is essential for reloading. This Lyman scale is easy to use, providing quick, accurate measurements.

only two separate lots. However, readers likely will be using powder from many different lots, and if the results are to be similar, it seemed logical to use a powder which is probably very close to the same Unique powder that any reader might be using. Keep in mind, though, that the difference between lots in some powders can be more than the differences between two closely related powders.

There is one more area of concern when it comes to loading consistent 9mmP ammunition. It is the press itself. Trying to decide what kind of press is right can be frustrating. However, it need not be terribly difficult to determine just what is needed, if logic rather than passion dictates action.

It is never a bad idea to have a good, solid single-stage reloading press. Such equipment lasts virtually forever, and it is good for all kinds of loading and loading-related functions. For shooters who plan to load a lot of different kinds of cartridges, a big, solid single-stage press should be considered mandatory.

Some of the better single-stage presses on the market are the Hornady 00-7, Lyman Orange Crusher, RCBS Rock Chucker and Redding Model 721 "The Boss."

Multi-station, single-stage presses which are credible include the Lyman T-Mag Turret, Ponsness-Warren Metal-Matic, RCBS 4x4, and Redding Metallic Turret.

Most of the major manufacturers also market some form of full-progressive press. They include the Hornady Pro-Jector and RCBS Ammomaster Auto.

However, if the only cartridge to be loaded is the 9mmP, then there might be some other options which make better sense. A multi-station single-stage press might be the answer, or the better bet might be a full-progressive. A note of caution here, however. Full-progressive reloading presses are right only for those who load a whole lot of ammunition in a given cartridge.

They are complicated, and can take a while to learn to use effectively. But, once they are set up properly they can really help crank out the ammo — hundreds of rounds per hour.

For this book, I opted for one of the many multi-station single-stage presses for a number of reasons. First, such

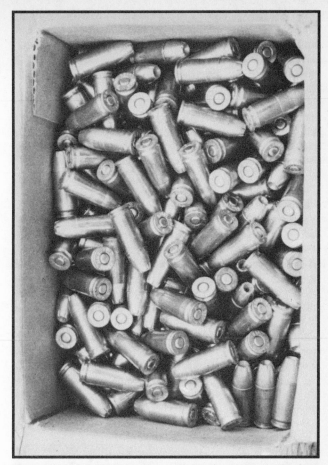

The goal in handloading any ammo is to be certain that the finished cartridges are uniform — inside and out!

presses are capable of producing a lot of ammunition efficiently. But more important, they are not the challenge to the concentration that the full-progressives are.

Whether the press is a multi-station or a full-progressive, there is one advantage over time that simply does not exist

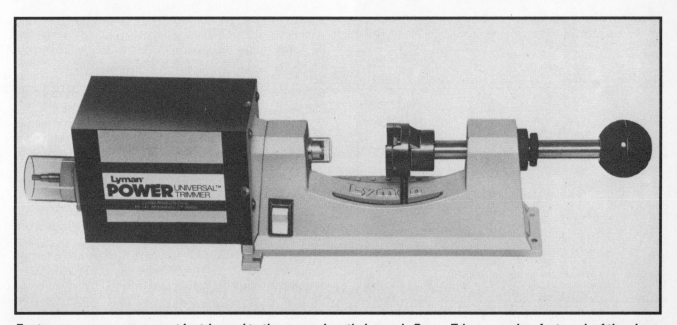

For top accuracy, cases must be trimmed to the proper length. Lyman's Power Trimmer makes fast work of the chore.

with a single-stage press. It has to do with die adjustment. Once the desired load has been worked up and the dies on a multi-station press (and full-progressives are also multi-station propositions) are adjusted and set, the same load can be created in large numbers then or any time in the future. It is the epitome of repeatability.

It is important to stress, however, that when working up particular loads, it is often handier to do such work on a single-station press. This is because subtle adjustments are easier and quicker on such a piece of machinery. But, once the load is determined, and it is time to crank out large supplies of ammo, then the multi-stations and full-progressives come into play.

For the handloads used in this book, I opted for the Ponsness-Warren Metal-Matic multi-station press. Ponsness-Warren is perhaps best known for its shotshell loading presses, but the company also markets two highly effective multi-station models for metallic cartridges. One is the Metal-Matic, which is both compact and heavy duty, and the other is a somewhat larger model called Metallic II. The Metallic II is excellent for handgun cartridges, and is somewhat better suited for some of the rifle cartridges than is the Metal-Matic.

Although there are enough threaded stations on the top turret of the Metal-Matic to handle two complete sets of dies (for two different cartridges), I used only the one side and devoted the press entirely to the 9mmP. Dies were Lee's carbide offerings. Although the expander die (second in the series used, with the resizing/depriming die being the first) is equipped to accept Lee's own version of a powder measure, I

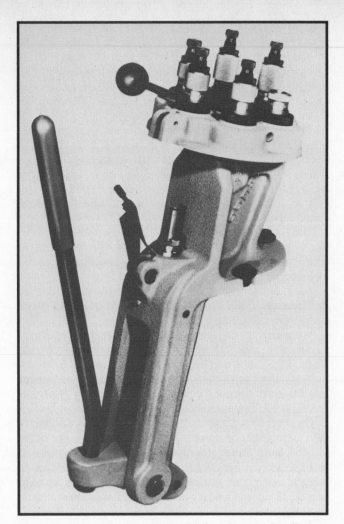

The Lyman turret is handy for high volume reloading.

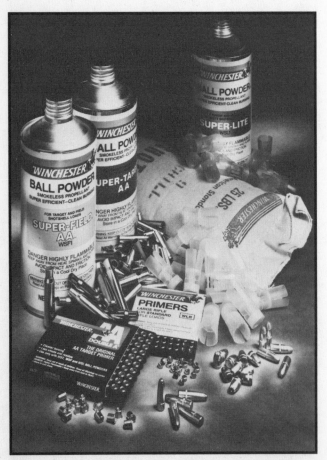

Major manufacturers like Winchester offer shooters a wide variety of high quality reloading components.

opted to mount an RCBS Uniflow powder measure by itself at the third station. On the fourth station, I mounted a Lyman M die (for cast bullets), followed by the seating die in the fifth station. The seating die was adjusted not only so it would seat the bullets to the proper depth, but also so it would barely begin any kind of crimp. I didn't want to crimp the bullets heavily, since I would be loading both jacketed and cast bullets interchangeably, and wanted to bypass the need for fine tuning adjustments each time I wanted to load.

For example, with the press so configured, I can put the empty case into the shell holder, resize it (and deprime it simultaneously if I have not done the depriming procedure independently before when getting the brass ready for cleaning), then move the shell holder with deprimed and sized case to the next station where it is re-primed.

At that point, I have a choice. If I am loading jacketed bullets, I can run the case directly up and into the standard Lee expander die, then move it to the next station to drop a powder charge into it, followed by still another move to the seating station where the bullet is put into the case and seated. Presto, a completed round! If loading cast bullets, I merely re-prime the case at the second station and then bypass the third (powder measure) station — stopping instead at the fourth station where the case is pushed up and into the Lyman M die

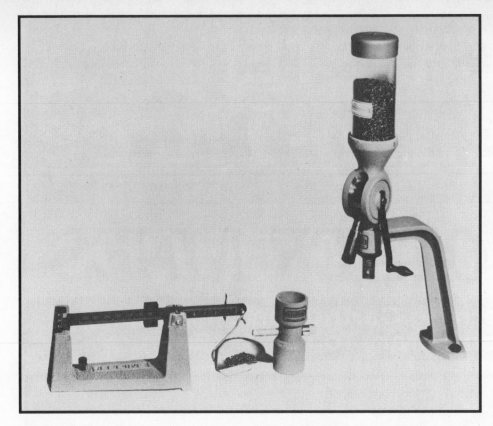

Redding is one of the makers that turns out a line of tools that can be used to custom-build the cartridges you want.

for the proper expansion for such bullets. Next, I move it back from the fourth to the third station, drop the powder charge, then move directly to the seating station to complete the load.

This way, with a minimum of movement, I can load either jacketed or cast bullets any time I want, without ever having to readjust any of the dies. Something interesting happens when equipment remains set-up in this manner. It is quick and easy to get started, which means that the loading procedure happens, rather than procrastination.

Here is another place where a powder like Hercules Unique becomes very handy. I could use the same 6.0-grain Unique powder charge for 115-grain jacketed, 124-grain cast (hardcast) and 124-grain jacketed bullets and still have totally credible loads in each weight class — loads which were within industry standards and which would function well in a wide variety of handguns.

During some of the loading sessions, however, I did change the powder charge a little for certain shooting. For example, I dropped back to 5.0 grains of Unique for entire runs of cast bullets, and used the same powder charge for some of the 115- and 124-grain jacketed bullets. These loads were used in some of the handguns when the faster loads did not perform well. Sometimes the lighter loadings improved accuracy, sometimes they didn't.

Also, to keep things simple and consistent, I used CCI No. 500 Small Pistol primers for all handloads. Jacketed bullets were Winchester 115-grain jacketed hollow-points, Winchester 124-grain metal jackets, Winchester 147-grain jacketed hollow-points and 124-grain hardcast round-nose bullets. Granted, these are arbitrary choices, but for standardization certain things have to be dictated.

That is not to say that there weren't other loads used.

Indeed, in other chapters, some of them are discussed. However, as working standards to be shot through every kind of 9mmP used, those were the handloads. Incidentally, they happen to be very good loads for most 9mmP handguns.

Brass used was somewhat more varied. However, the loads used for any specific handgun always used brass from the same manufacturer. Brass used included Federal, Hansen, PMC, Remington and Winchester. One note here, however. Very few of the 9mmP handguns fired delivered the level of accuracy it took to notice any significant difference in performance of loads which were similar, except for the type of brass.

When it comes to what I call "shootin," ammo for semiautos like 9mmP handguns where informal target work or flat-out plinking is the order of the day, mixing and matching brass from different manufacturers while keeping all other components consistent usually will deliver acceptably consistent accuracy. However, for those who want to squeeze out more performance, segregate the brass and keep it set apart by specific manufacture.

Since I knew I would be shooting a huge amount of ammo and had copious supplies of brass from all of the manufacturers mentioned above, and since the other components were all the same, I merely loaded the thousands of cases from a single hopper, and then sorted them out by maker of brass later. It accomplishes the same thing, and can simplify life.

So, there are ways to be totally consistent, and there are ways to crank out large volumes of ammunition. If care is taken, both qualities can be accomplished simultaneously. The point is that when it comes to loading for the 9mmP, it is probably a good idea to plan on loading a lot. After all, 9mmP handguns tend to have voracious appetites.

CHAPTER
Twenty-Three

THE OTHER NINES

Concerning Cartridges That Are Contemporary To The 9x19mm.

From left are the 9mm Win. mag. .38-45 Clerke, .38 Super, 9x19mm, 9mm Federal, 9x18mm Ultra and .380 ACP.

SEVERAL OTHER cartridges are designed for use with bullets of .355-inch diameter, if jacketed, .356-inch if cast, the same as the 9x19mm Parabellum. The .38 Special, .357 Magnum and .357 Remington Maximum use jacketed bullets of .357-inch diameter, .358-inch for cast. Rifle cartridges such as the .35 Remington, .350 Remington Magnum and .358 Norma use jacketed bullets of

.358-inch diameter, .359-inch, if cast.

Two nominal 9mm cartridges, the 9x18mm Ultra and the 9x18mm Makarov, utilize bullets of .364- or .365-inch diameter. Both of these are spinoffs of a treaty stipulation that the given country was not allowed to use guns and cartridges of military persuasion. Let us discuss the more significant of these examples, under suitable subheadings.

THE GUN DIGEST BOOK of 9mm HANDGUNS

L.A.R. Grizzly is one of the autos that has been made in 9mm Winchester magnum as well as other calibers.

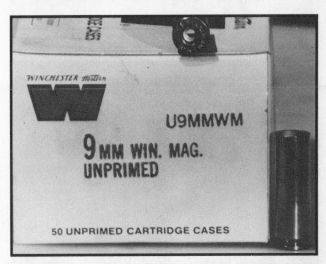

IAI, now known as AMT, manufactured 9mm Win. mag, 147-grain jacketed hollow-point ammunition.

Winchester currently only offers unprimed empty brass in 50-count boxes, for the 9mm Winchester mag.

THE OTHER LUGER

This is known variously as the .30 Luger, 7.65mm Luger or 7.65mm Parabellum, and the nominal case length is .850-inch, compared to the .754-inch length of the 9mmP. Winchester loads at least one factory round for it, their No. X30LP, with a 93-grain FMJ bullet. Various bullet makers offer .308-inch bullets in the 90- to 93-grain weights for reloading it.

It is possible to pass a 9mmP case up into the .30 Luger full-length resizing die to produce a case with a vestigial neck that may function after a fashion in various guns chambered for the .30 Luger. RCBS (601 Oro Dam Boulevard, Oroville, CA 95965) can supply dies for making true-scale .30 Luger cases from .223 Remington brass.

Load data listings for the .30 Luger are few and far between. It's covered on page 366 of the 47th edition of the *Lyman Reloading Handbook* for a 93-grain FMJ bullet and an 84-grain cast bullet from the Lyman No. 313249 mould blocks. The 25th edition of the *Hodgdon Manual* lists a small block of data on page 380. The 26th edition has considerably more, with listings for Hodgdon, IMR, Winchester and Hercules powders on pages 612 to 614.

The latest data booklet from Winchester has one load listing: 4.2 grains of their No. 231 powder behind a 93-grain FMJ bullet for 1085/243 at a pressure of 25,500 cup. The Vihtavuori booklet has one listing: 5.4 grains of their No. N340 powder behind a 93-grain bullet for 1001/207 at a pressure of 260 megapascals. One megapascal (MPa) equals 145.0376 pounds per square inch (PSI), so that works out to 37,710 PSI. One PSI, incidentally, is not precisely equal to one copper unit of pressure (CUP). One may be greater than the other, or both may be identical. It is one of the more confusing aspects of ballistics.

Apart from the foregoing, there is little information on reloading the .30 Luger. That may change soon because, for the first time, a domestic gunmaker is tooling to produce pistols to handle the cartridge. Sturm, Ruger & Company recently announced they'll be making the P93, a revised version of their P89 to be supplied with an auxiliary barrel and recoil spring to handle the .30 Luger.

THE .38-45 CLERKE

This is the .45 ACP case, necked down to accept bullets of .355-inch diameter. It was conceived by John A. "Bo" Clerke — pronounced "Clark"— to offer owners of .45 autos a cartridge with pleasantly modest recoil they could use for practice purposes.

The popular AMT Automag III is still in production.

Sierra now makes .363-inch bullets for the Makarov.

From left, 9x18mm Ultra, 9x18mm Makarov, 9x19mm.

Unfortunately, the vast majority of the shooting public seemed to regard it as a cartridge to be hotrodded to the firewall. Being based upon the .45 ACP, with its SAAMI-specified pressure limit at 19,900 CUP, the upper limits of safe performance are depressingly low. It is possible to make up cases from .45 Winchester Magnum parent brass that will withstand somewhat higher pressures.

Bar-Sto Precision (Box 1838, Twentynine Palms, CA 92277) can supply barrels in .38-45 Clerke for M1911-type pistols and fit the barrels to the owner's frame. RCBS can supply case-forming and reloading dies. You will not find suggested load data for the cartridge anywhere. It is a number for those who have reason to feel convinced they know what they are doing.

THE 9x21mm

This is a wildcat, like the .38-45 Clerke, meaning commercial loads for it are not generally available. Load data listings for it are about as commonly encountered as Genghis Khan at a Tupperware party. Its ostensible mystique is that it may be at least theoretically possible to concoct loads that will make major power factor (MPF). MPF is obtained by multiplying muzzle velocity in feet-per-second times bullet weight in grains and dividing by 1000. Most competitive events that hinge upon MPF require a minimum figure of 175, which is difficult to achieve safely with the 9x19mmP. It is not all that easy and simple to achieve with the 9x21mm.

THE .38 ACP/.38 SUPER

The .38 ACP was developed by John M. Browning early in the present century, and the .38 Super was introduced in the latter Twenties. Load data for the .38 Super is given in most, if not all, data sources. Data for the lower-pressure .38 ACP is all but impossible to locate. Old Western Scrounger (12924 Highway A-12, Montague, CA 96064) manufactures and markets loaded ammunition for the .38 ACP that does not exceed its pressure limitations. Most makers of ammunition offer one or more loads in .38 Super, sometimes terming them .38 ACP +P.

From left are the .30 Luger, 9x19mm, 9mm Action Express, .40 S&W necked to .355-inch and the .38-45 Clerke.

By following listed .38 Super load data, is it reasonably simple and possible to put together loads that will meet and slightly exceed the 175 MPF figure.

THE 9mm ACTION EXPRESS (AE)

This is a spin-off of the .41 Action Express (AE), a cartridge with the head dimensions of the 9x19mmP, scaled to accept bullets of .410-inch diameter. It was introduced by Action Arms Ltd. (P.O. Box 9573, Philadelphia, PA 19124) some while before the appearance of the .40 Smith & Wesson with its .400-inch bullet diameter. The two cartridges are virtually identical in case capacity and some sources say data for the two are interchangeable.

After the .41 AE made its debut, Evan Whildin and Bob Olsen collaborated to work up a cartridge that remains a wildcat to the present. It is the .41 AE necked down to accept a bullet of .355-inch diameter and known as the 9mm Action Express.

Bar-Sto Precision can supply barrels in 9mm AE for M1911-pattern pistols, possibly others, as well. RCBS can supply reloading dies for the 9mm AE. The good news is that no case-forming dies are required. It is simply a matter of running a .41 AE case up into the full-length resizing die of the 9mm AE, followed by a pass into the neck-expanding die and it's ready to reload.

The .41 AE case, unlike the .45 ACP case, is not tethered to a limited pressure level. Thus, the 9mm AE can exceed performance levels of the .38-45 Clerke by a useful margin. The exact peak of performance has yet to be established. To the best of our knowledge, there are no data listings whatever

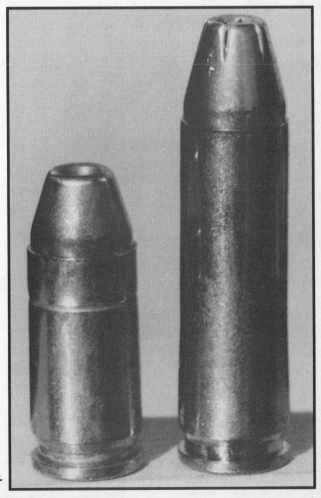

A 9x19mm is dwarfed by the 9mm Winchester magnum.

for the 9mm AE. It is unlikely that any will ever be published.

If you have a solid basis for believing you know what you're doing, the 9mm AE is a remarkably intriguing avenue to explore. It is not a cartridge for the beginning reloader. Dean Grennell confides he has gotten 88-grain Speer No. 4000 JHP bullets out of the five-inch barrel of my Colt at 1920/721 and he regards that as respectable. The ejected cases showed no symptoms for concerned alarm, but we prefer not to specify the actual powder charge.

THE 9mm WINCHESTER MAGNUM

Like the .45 Winchester magnum, the 9mm Winchester magnum was designed for use in a gas-operated autoloading pistol designed by Wildey — pronounced "Wil-dee" — Moore several years ago. There has been no more than limited production of the Wildey pistols, in either caliber.

L.A.R. Manufacturing (4133 West Farm Road, West Jordan, UT 84084) has produced a few of their Grizzly autoloading pistols in 9mm Winchester magnum, along with a larger number in .45 Winchester magnum.

Arcadia Machine & Tool (6226 Santos Diaz, Irwindale, CA 91702) has produced some of their Automag III autoloading pistols in 9mm Winchester magnum with 6.5-inch barrels, as well as loaded ammunition with a 147-grain JHP bullet. To the present, Winchester only supplies empty, unprimed cases in the caliber.

The AMT load puts 15.0 grains of Winchester 296 powder behind the 147-grain JHP bullet at a COL of 1.552 inches. Case length of the 9mm Winchester magnum is 1.155 inches, the same as the .38 Special. In the 6.5-inch barrel, the AMT load averages 1275/531.

Vihtavuori quotes its load pressures in megapascal and provides a conversion example to aid reloaders.

$$1 \text{ MEGAPASCAL} = 145.0376 \text{ PSI}$$

$$\text{EXAMPLE:} \quad 350 \text{ Pa} =$$

$$350 \times 145.037 \underline{\text{ OR }} 50{,}763.16 \text{ PSI}$$

THE 9mm FEDERAL

This was a rimmed look-alike of the 9x19mmP, introduced and produced for a short time by Federal Cartridge Company of Anoka, Minnesota. It was intended for use in revolvers, and it delivered ballistic performance approximately on the same level as the regular 9x19mmP. It was discontinued after a short while, perhaps because it could be chambered and fired in revolvers drilled for the .38 S&W, few, if any, of which can cope with pressures generated by the 9mm Federal.

THE .380 ACP

This cartridge, widely used all over the world, sometimes is termed the 9mm Browning Short, 9mm Corto or 9mm Kurz. It has a case length of .680-inch and an overall length of about .984 or less. The industry maximum chamber pressured is 18,900 cup and most loads develop somewhat less. Typical

Thankfully, Vihtavuori's Reloading Guide is in English.

Vihtavuori's N 330 powder works favorably in 9x19mm.

performance for factory loads is 955 for a 95-grain bullet for 190 foot-pounds. Jacketed bullets larger than .355-inch diameter may cause bulged case walls when seated, leading to stoppages.

THE 9x18mm MAKAROV

Unlike most so-called 9mm cartridges, the 9x18mm uses jacketed bullets of about .363-inch diameter, with cast bullet sized to .365-inch; diameters equal to slightly more than 9.2mm. The cartridge has a case length of about .695- to .697-inch and its head dimensions are virtually identical to those of the 9x19mm, enabling the reloader to use the same shell holder for both rounds. Cartridge overall length is about .967-inch and any load much longer than that may not fit into the magazine. Load data given for the .380 ACP seems to function well in the 9x18mm Makarov and typical factory loads develop about 929 fps and 182 fpe.

CHAPTER
Twenty-Four

GLOCK ARMORER'S SCHOOL

This Course Is Specific To The Breed, But In Some Respects, Relates To All 9mmP Autos!

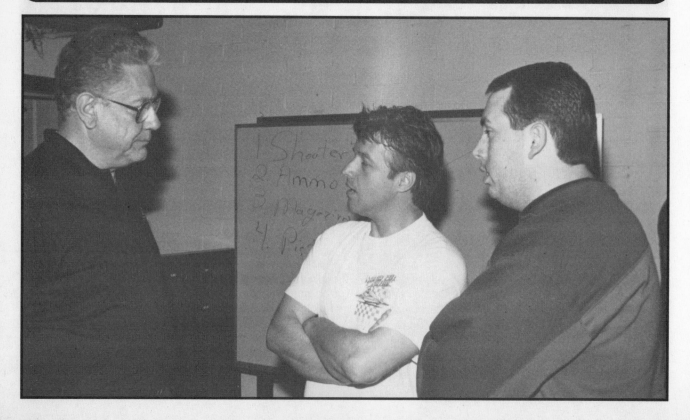

THE GUN DIGEST BOOK of 9mm HANDGUNS

At left and above, Bob McCracken, an instructor with Glock's armorer's school, answers questions, points out major components and operation of the Glock 17.

GLOCK PISTOLS LITERALLY, have taken over the American law enforcement community, to say nothing of making major inroads into military and civilian shooting fraternities around the globe. What is there about the Glock 9mmP which has triggered such an unprecedented phenomenon? To answer some of the questions, the author attended one of Glock's armorer schools to get an up-close and personal view of the gun and what makes it tick. It was as necessary to comprehend the "ethic of Glock" as it was to understand the mechanical workings of the design.

The Glock pistol is the brainchild of Austrian engineer Gaston Glock, whose company also makes a number of other basic military items like knives and entrenching tools. In fact, Glock never had been involved in the firearms industry when he came up with one of the winningest pistol designs of the era.

Although Gaston Glock himself is a bona fide genius, close examination of the Glock pistol reveals that if Glock wasn't part of the firearms business before he designed the gun, he did his homework and researched the situation well before firing up the production line. In fact, the Glock pistol is a variant of John M. Browning's basic recoil design. It is really a sophisticated combination of Hi-Power/SIG features with the firing characteristics of a trigger-actuated zip gun.

This is far from a condemnation of the design or the gun. Hardly. It is merely recognition that Gaston Glock had the insight to incorporate the simplest and most efficient systems the gun industry has ever known into a space age package which works, and works, and works. In fact, these guns are so

incredibly efficient that wearing one out could take a lifetime, or more, of deliberate effort.

It is difficult to be around Gundom very long without accepting the fact that there are mystic forces involved in the ultimate success or failure of designs and models of firearms. Some seem to be conceived under a friendly star, while others are apparently snake-bitten right from the get-go. In the case of the Glock, it was sweetness right from the start — a start which brought worldwide attention to the gun for reasons other than those which later put it into the law enforcement driver's seat.

The Glock is the original "plastic pistol" which, when introduced, was condemned by many social architects as a terrorist special which could defeat airport security systems. Although such a rap was totally unjustified (85 percent of a Glock handgun is metal, and 15 percent is plastic), it put the pistol on the map, so to speak. It was Gundom's equivalent of a book being banned in Boston. The attacks upon the gun spotlighted it, and gave it an identity which might have taken years to achieve, if ever, under the normal processes.

Identity may be enough to put a particular gun into the collective consciousness of shooters, but it is not sufficient to catapult the design into world prominence. Having the right stuff is important, but so is timing. And, the Glock came onto the scene at precisely the right time to make it such a successful phenomenon. Frankly, the same design a decade earlier well may have been relegated to relative obscurity. The fact that the Glock pistol became a reality at precisely the moment

McCracken reviews the finer details of the Glock 17.

During the one-day course, McCracken explains how to get the most from the Glock.

in time when law enforcement agencies were switching from something else to 9mm P high capacity pistols meant there was a gigantic market potential — one which did not exist before, and likely will not happen on the same one-time grand scale ever again.

To understand the gun and the popularity among law enforcement circles, it is first necessary to understand that Gaston Glock did not set out to make the world's most popular cop gun when he designed his pistol. Rather, he was challenged to come up with a gun for the Austrian military.

Anyone who has spent more than a few days in any of the world's military organizations understands well that the best equipment for soldiers is the simplest and easiest to use gear — items which are literally "idiot proof." The more widely accepted term is: "soldier proof."

The Germanic countries have a centuries-old tradition when it comes to military matters. Soldiers there, it is always assumed, have no prior civilian background in the handling of weaponry. It is assumed that literally everything they know about shooting is taught to them when they go through their various levels of training after joining the military.

Such has been the case with most militaries of the world, and is a fact of life even in the United States now. There was a time in the U.S. when it was somewhat different — a time when the Second Amendment to the Constitution was real and citizens practiced their responsibilities to keep and bear arms. Granted, the military in the U.S. always has had to conduct specialized instruction to bring everyone into a state of uniform competence, but there was a time when the military was an organization of experienced riflemen.

When the basic assumption is that equipment has to be soldier proof, and that all the soldier ever knows about weaponry will have been taught in the military, the simplest design is the best. So it was with the Glock pistol in Austria.

The same ethic holds true for law enforcement agencies around the world. Most police officers are not gun people. They may carry firearms as part of their duties, but as a group they view them merely as basic gear in the same way they view a flashlight as a piece of standard equipment.

Concurrently with the emergence of the Glock pistol upon the world scene was a new phenomenon involving law enforcement agencies in the United States. It was a matter of accountability and liability. Accidental shootings were never popular, but the price tag for such unplanned shootings skyrocketed significantly as the nation became one of litigation first. At the same time, American law enforcement agencies were changing their handgunnery, going from the time-despised revolver to the semi-auto.

Law enforcement officers found themselves facing a new breed of bad guy — a bad guy who was much more heavily armed than his counterparts before, and bad guys who were less reluctant to shoot at those who wore the badge of authority.

Double-action revolvers, which had been used for years in law enforcement, inherently were rather "safe" when in the hands of officers who generally didn't know much about guns. But semi-auto handguns, in the traditional sense, are a different proposition. They can be dangerous in the hands of careless or inattentive officers.

Enter the double-action, semi-auto handgun. This type of pistol, many argued, was the best of both worlds. It could hold a lot of ammo in a double-column magazine, yet offer the relative safety of the double-action revolver. Gun companies quickly jumped on the bandwagon and offered variants of their designs which were double-action for the first shot, and then single-action for successive rounds. Then came the double-action-only design which meant that every shot was accomplished in a double-action mode.

As all of this was happening, Glock was there in the background with an action which already offered precisely what law enforcement administrators wanted in an age of liability litigation.

Glock terms the system "safe action," and it truly is different from the traditional double-action designs. Although the author was aware of the phenomenon, it became obvious that a broader understanding of the internal workings of the Glock was needed to be able to relay meaningful information about it.

To accomplish this, it was off to Glock's one-day armorer's school — an intense instructional program designed to show law enforcement armorers and gunsmiths how the Glock works, how to work on those pistols, and how to keep the guns which go over their benches in action.

Perhaps the most impressive aspect of the Glock Armorer's School is the fact that armorers can keep these handguns in action without a lot of "gunsmithing." It means that for law enforcement purposes, it is a parts replacement proposition. When something goes wrong with any part of the firearm, pop out the bad part and replace it with a new one. Evidence of this is the fact that there are only three tools required for the maintenance of Glock pistols: a 3/32-inch pin punch, a 1/8-inch blade screwdriver and a pair of long nose pliers. Most of the maintenance can be performed with only the punch. In fact, for the armorer's school, the punch was the only tool used.

It wasn't until this fact of life about Glocks was pointed out most clearly during the school that an unresolved question deep in the recesses of my mind became answered. There is a major trend in handgun manufacture now which truly separates many of the current products from those that came before. It has to do with the concept of "disposable" products and parts.

This phenomenon has been a factor in other industries for years, and has been creeping into the gun industry so slowly and quietly that it is all but undetected in many quarters.

As computerized manufacturing processes evolve into an age of advanced robotics, the making of precision products without the hassles of human involvement has become reality. Likewise, the design of parts and products which are never intended to be "repaired" has grown as a logical offshoot of such mind boggling mechanization.

Although a number of recent firearms design changes have begun to incorporate this philosophy, nowhere in the gun industry is it more apparent than with the various Glock handguns.

For example, the complex trigger and trigger bar are considered to be a single item, and should anything go wrong with any part of that assembly, the entire assembly is replaced by the armorer. This theme is consistent with regard to any of the parts for Glock pistols. They simply are not designed to be altered, and, in fact, altering some of the parts on Glocks can really harm them.

For example, the major steel parts of the handgun — slide and barrel, feature a finish which is more than simply a matte black. It happens to make the surface almost diamond hard. That is nice when it comes to things like eliminating wear or inadvertent scratches, but it spells potential problems for those who would want to change things a bit.

As much as the outer surfaces are totally hard, the steel just under those surfaces is on the soft side. That means that if someone meddles with the part and in doing so gets below the extremely hard surface, there is a good chance the gun could literally wear itself out in quick order. Most shooters never need to worry about such an occurrence, because in order to get through the tough surface, a person really has to want to do it and use some exotic means to accomplish it.

From top are the Glock 19, Glock 17 and Glock 17L. They are the basic Glock 9mms. Sharing the same basic design, many of their parts are totally interchangeable.

As much as this parts replacement approach to keeping handguns in service may very well be great news for most law enforcement agencies from a number of perspectives, there is no free lunch. Keeping Glock handguns functioning is fairly simple — so long as all one wants to do is keep standard Glock handguns functioning. Anyone who might want to do some creative "slicking" up of the gun likely is going to be discouraged.

That is what was meant earlier when it was suggested that Glock handguns do not lend themselves to "gunsmithing." In

EXPLODED DRAWING AND PARTS LIST FOR GLOCK 17

NATO Stock. No. 1005/25/133/6775

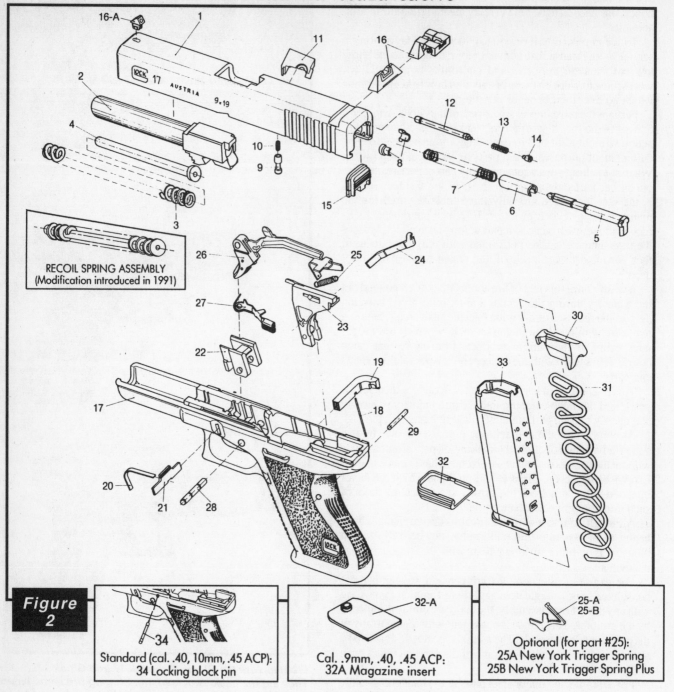

RECOIL SPRING ASSEMBLY
(Modification introduced in 1991)

Figure 2

Standard (cal. .40, 10mm, .45 ACP):
34 Locking block pin

Cal. .9mm, .40, .45 ACP:
32A Magazine insert

Optional (for part #25):
25A New York Trigger Spring
25B New York Trigger Spring Plus

1	Slide	14	Spring-loaded bearing	25	Trigger spring
2	Barrel	15	Slide cover plate	25-A	New York Trigger Spring
3	Recoil spring	16	Rear sight	25-B	New York Trigger Spring Plus
4	Recoil spring tube	16-A	Front sight	26	Trigger with trigger bar
5	Firing pin	17	Receiver	27	Slide stop lever
6	Spacer sleeve	18	Magazine catch spring	28	Trigger pin
7	Firing pin spring	19	Magazine catch	29	Trigger mechanism housing pin
8	Spring cups	20	Slide lock spring	30	Follower
9	Firing pin safety	21	Slide lock	31	Magazine spring
10	Firing pin safety spring	22	Locking block	32	Magazine floor plate
11	Extractor	23	Trigger mechanism housing	32-A	Magazine insert
12	Extractor depressor plunger		with ejector	33	Magazine tube
13	Extractor depressor plunger spring	24	Connector	34	Locking block pin

other words, it is highly unlikely that any Glock handgun ever will have anything that approaches its own personality. To a most measurable degree, then, a Glock is a Glock is a Glock.

If the Glock phenomenon was genius on the manufacturing front, it was nothing short of fine art in the law enforcement marketing arena. After all, Glock pistols are three things: Functional, safe and relatively inexpensive.

When any agency looks at potential firearms to be used for standard issue, there are actually relatively few major points which determine winners and losers. To understand the phenomenon completely, consider that most of those who decide upon what model or models will be used by the agencies are not shooters or firearms enthusiasts themselves. It means that non-gun people make the call.

What does a non-gun bureaucrat look for in an issue handgun? First, the price has to be within budget constraints or there is no need to pursue anything further. For example, the world's absolute best firearms are never standard issue at any agency. They simply cost too much for any public agency to afford.

There are always, however, a number of competing models of handguns which fall into the affordability parameters. It is from among those that the issue model will be chosen.

What this means from the Glock perspective is that the use of polymers and automated manufacturing techniques made it possible to market the pistols in the line at very competitive prices, while maintaining an acceptable institutional level of quality and a favorable profit line. But that alone would account for only a small share of the market.

Function is perceived to be all-important to gun people, and it is somewhat important to the bureaucrats who ultimately make the decisions. Without question, Glock handguns were used in a number of tests and demonstrations which showed they will work. However, here is where there needs to be a little of bit of an explanation. They work fine, so long as exactly the right ammunition is used.

Again, from an institutional standpoint, whether a firearm will handle a wide range of types of ammunition is somewhat moot. It only matters that it be able to handle the kind of ammo that agency uses, and it is relatively simple for an agency to opt for whatever firearm/ammo combination happens to go well together. Couple that with the fact that such agencies almost universally use factory-loaded ammunition, and it becomes an easy choice.

However, from a gun person's viewpoint, the ability of a particular kind of handgun to handle a variety of different loads interchangeably may be very important. But not at the agency level.

Since the original Glocks were 9mmP and designed to be used with NATO (North Atlantic Treaty Organization) specification ammunition, they generally work best with some of the more potent loadings. Minimum (lower limit) specifications for 9mmP ammunition in Glocks are a 115-grain bullet at 1180 feet per second. Maximum pressures should not exceed 43,500 pounds per square inch (3000 BAR). What this means is that the Glocks function well with factory loads, including the +P+ and 147-grain subsonic ammunition currently being marketed by major manufacturers in the United States. However, Glock goes beyond discouraging the use of reloads in its firearms. Not only is such practice not suggested, it voids the factory warranty on the gun itself.

From the agency level, then, it would appear that on the price and performance front, Glock handguns should be able to pass the tests. Still, those two features alone have not been responsible for the extremely widespread switch by law enforcement agencies to Glock pistols. There is a third factor which serves as a trump card, all other factors being even remotely equal. It is the "S" word — SAFETY.

Bureaucratic administrators almost never actually see a street shooting of any kind. While officers within their departments are taking care of business in the real world, they are snuggled behind a desk in some headquarters building, justifying their existence by juggling paperwork and crunching numbers. It is in the numbers game that Glocks come to the fore.

Administrators will always opt for equipment which will reduce, if not totally eliminate, accidental discharges and any related injuries. To address that sort of concern, the Glock pistols are designed so whoever is holding one really has to want to shoot it, or it won't go off.

Again, the features which make this possible are the same things which cause consternation for firearms enthusiasts. But the fact is that most law enforcement officers are not gun fanciers. They carry a handgun on the job in the same way they carry a flashlight and a notebook. So the object of those deciding upon firearms hardware is to end up with equipment which will preclude as many accidents as possible.

Glock pistols have three safety devices built into them. First is the trigger safety, which is built into the trigger itself. It is the small lever in the middle of the trigger which, in its untouched state, blocks the trigger from being moved backward.

"To fire the pistol, both the trigger safety and the trigger must be depressed at the same time," Glock notes in its literature. "If the trigger safety is not depressed, then the trigger will not move to the rear and the pistol will not fire. This is designed to prevent the trigger from going to the rear when dropped."

The second safety system on the Glock is the firing pin safety. It is a spring-loaded pin which projects into the firing pin cutout and blocks it. It is released only when the trigger is pulled.

Third is the safety function of the trigger mechanism housing, which might also be described as a drop safety. With this system, the trigger bar is pushed onto the safety ramp by the firing pin. Although the safeties are designed to keep the handgun from accidentally discharging when dropped from a distance of 6.5 feet, which exceeds NATO standards, the pistols are not known for going off unintentionally when dropped from all kinds of distances. Perhaps some of this is due to the fact that there is not just one type of safety system, but three operating both independently and in tandem.

Another factor which helps preclude accidental discharges is the way the entire firing system works. The action is not cocked until the trigger is pulled. This also makes a big difference when it comes to the gun not going off when it is not intended to do so.

So, there were a number of factors which helped put Glock handguns into the big-time, and there are several factors which have enabled that line of pistols to stay there. Without question, the combined safety devices, functional reliability and price point are the big three items that have been responsible for this design to take over much of the law enforcement interest, and a lot of the civilian attention, as well.

CHAPTER
Twenty-Five

FIELD HUNTING WITH THE 9mmP

It Doesn't Down Elephants, But It Does Have It's Proper Uses!

Steve Comus took this 250-pound ram with a single round of Winchester's Black Talon 9mmP ammo with the 147-grain bullet. The handgun used was his own Browning Hi-Power.

The Browning Hi-Power autoloader was the original model to feature a high-capacity staggered magazine. The author has found it and other 9mmP handguns to be more than adequate for hunting small game, varmints at short ranges.

The 9mmP can be the best hunting cartridge in the world. And I can prove it.

Yes, 9mmP handguns show up in the darndest places! When one considers the millions of 9mmP handguns and billions of rounds of ammunition extant in the world, it is logical to imagine where all they may be used, and for what purposes.

Obvious applications include military and police. Also a "given" are uses like self-defense, business defense and home defense. Some scribes have even gone so far as to suggest that the 9mmP might be credible for small game. Actually, legitimate uses for the 9mmP go far beyond those few listed above. I know. I've done it.

My first personal exposure to the 9mmP came in the 1950s and constituted one of my first gun deals. It was a P-35 (wartime production Browning Hi-Power) and a handful of ammo for $10. That was a bargain price even then, but the particular handgun was far from pristine. Sometime in its life, the pistol had been rusted heavily, leaving some serious pits on the slide. In an attempt to remedy the situation, someone had tried to nickel-plate it, but the coating didn't stick well in some spots. To put it mildly, it was (and is) an ugly handgun — but only "skin deep."

Mechanically, the P-35 was in great shape, and it shot well. The handful of cartridges went quickly, forcing me to learn an important lesson about semi-autos: It costs a lot to feed them. I scoured the countryside filling the basket on my bicycle with pop and beer bottles, turning them in for two-cents each and using that money to buy ammo.

Only once did I afford myself the entertainment to fill the high-capacity magazine all the way and pull the trigger as fast as I could until it was empty. It was then that as a young shooter I learned how hot a handgun could get. Subsequent shooting sessions were more reserved, involving the expenditure of one or perhaps a couple of expensive shots at a time. Keep in mind that at that time and in that place (rural Ohio), the 9mmP was a rare cartridge. Ammo had to be special ordered, and at premium prices.

Yet, I put a lot of rounds downrange over time. The P-35 was almost a constant companion. Youngsters in rural areas experience frequent close encounters with a wide variety of critters. The P-35's first "hunting" experience in my hands involved a turtle — a big turtle. I was visiting a friend on his grandfather's farm when we spotted the turtle atop a log in the middle of a creek which cut through the cornfields.

Before embarking on our safari, my buddy had grabbed the little Winchester Model 99 Thumb Trigger rifle from beside the back porch door at the farm house. With it, he had grabbed a partial box of .22 shorts (the rifle was chambered only for shorts, and was used normally for farm pest control). I had the P-35, considered locally to be a semi-useless war souvenir. Almost universally, it was assumed around the community that I had become a hopeless gun nut, and that I had been "taken" in the deal for the P-35. After all, it was made for killing humans and had no credibility for the gathering of game, right? Not only that, but one could buy a whole box of .22 long rifle ammo for the price of three or four 9mmP cartridges at the time.

I'll have to admit that there were times when I wondered if perhaps the others were right. I had little experience with

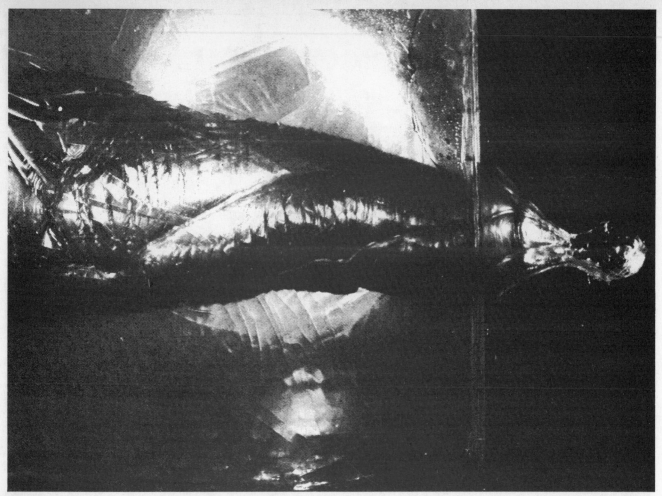

Laboratory shooting tests into ballistic gelatin showed the effectiveness of the Black Talon 9mmP in this medium. Usefulness of this particular round since has been proved in the field for some types of small-game hunting.

handguns by that time in my life, and was far from an accomplished shooter of them. It had taken me many hours just to figure out how to disassemble the pistol (no instruction booklet came with it, and no one else around town knew anything about the pistol). But I was determined to make it work.

But on that hunt, as the two of us slithered along the cut bank of the creek, my buddy drew first "blood" with the .22 rifle. It was a large, black beetle which happened to be slogging up the cliff. Around the next bend, we encountered a blacksnake. It was a magnum-size snake, but it slid into the bushes before either of us could decide whether to cap off a round, or not.

Then we saw it. This huge turtle was sunning itself midstream on a half-submerged log. The situation called for a serious discussion. I argued that my buddy's rifle wouldn't do the trick, because he was not a good enough shot to hit the turtle in the head, and the .22 short would doubtless not penetrate the shell and dispatch the turtle quickly enough to keep it from diving into the water and out of sight. He opined that I probably couldn't hit the turtle with the P-35, and that even if I did, it doubtless would blow the critter apart and ruin any meat that otherwise might be salvaged — and his grandparents truly did enjoy eating turtle meat.

We may have been too young to engage in a meaningful debate about ballistics and bullet performance, but the ab-original concerns about such matters surfaced anyway. Neither of us was sophisticated enough to realize that the ammo I was shooting was military ball, which meant that it wouldn't tear up any meat at all — at least nothing much beyond the .355-inch wound channel.

The turtle, located a full 100 feet or so away, remained unaware that its future might be in jeopardy. The sun glistened off its shell, and its beaked head was profiled in the morning light.

During our debate, it was decided that we would sneak behind the thick creekside foliage to a willow tree near the turtle, use the trunk of the willow for cover and see if the amphibian was still there when it would be time for the shot. If so, I would try to hit it.

To that point, I had been carrying the P-35 unloaded and with its slide locked to the rear. It had seemed the logical way to do things. So, when it came time to launch the stalk, it was the moment to load the firearm — an example of the way tradition does not always keep up with technology. It had never occurred to me to carry the pistol loaded, and, as was the tradition of the era, when it came time to take an animal, the hunter would load a cartridge and go for the kill. So, that's precisely what I did. I slid a single 9mmP cartridge into the chamber, depressed the slide release lever and allowed the slide to slam forward. I then activated the manual safety, and became point man on the stalk, my buddy following in my

The javelina, a native of the Southwest, is the type of game that is ideal game for capabilities of the 9mmP.

footsteps with the Winchester .22, which also remained unloaded and open whenever it was not actually being shot.

We made it to the tree, and as I peered around the side, I could see the turtle was still on the log, and that was no more than 20 or 30 feet away (it seemed farther at the time, but it wasn't).

Using the bark of the tree to help steady the P-35, I took careful aim, aligning the fixed battle sights with the center of the turtle's shell. I took a deep breath, flipped the safety lever to the "fire" position and double-checked the sight alignment. Gnats were swarming around my head, and one went up my nose as I inhaled, but it failed to break my concentration. My blood pressure skyrocketed, and my ears began to ring as I put increasing pressure on the trigger with my right index finger. Just when I thought my head was going to explode, the P-35 went off.

My buddy and I learned another pair of lessons in a heartbeat right then and there. I had not considered the fact that the P-35's slide would shoot to the rear simultaneously with the recoil. I learned all about that as some tiny specks of bark from the tree sprayed into my eyes. And, my buddy learned that semi-autos eject empties with a vengeance. He had been standing just to the right of the handgun, peering through some bushes, and was jolted when the spent cartridge casing bounced off the side of his head.

Neither of us actually saw the hit. But by the time we regained our composure, one thing was certain: the turtle was no longer atop the log. My buddy was convinced that I had missed. I didn't have a clue, but standard procedure was to inspect the impact zone — up-close and personally. He was

bare-footed and I was wearing a pair of canvas tennis shoes with holes in the sides large enough for my small toes to stick out. We did not indulge in ceremony. Rather, we slogged through the water (knee-deep) to the log and took a look. There was a perfectly round hole in the log, right where the turtle had been.

The log was closer to the far shore than it had been to us, and the thick foliage choked all the way to water's edge there. As we visually scoured the area around the log, I spotted the turtle. It was belly-up and motionless in the shallow water at the far edge of the creek, slightly downstream from the log. I lunged to it, and grabbed the huge shell with both hands, dropping the P-35 into the water in the process. Excitement of the moment had made me forget I had the unloaded pistol in my hand. In a fitful moment of panic, I dropped the turtle, scrambled for the pistol in the muddly water and fell face-first into the creek. My hand located the pistol, and as I was shaking the water from it, my buddy retrieved the turtle.

He held the lifeless turtle to the sky, admiring the magnificent trophy. We stood knee-deep in the creek for what seemed an eternity, inspecting the entry and exit holes. I had center-punched the shell, killing the turtle instantly. We opined that the turtle must have bounced from the impact of the bullet and flipped through the air to the spot where I had recovered it initially. Actually, it probably just fell off the log and turned upside down as the slight current of the water carried it to the spot where I found it. But we were hearing nothing of mundane — it *had* to have been spectacular!

I forgot all about being drenched. Two prouder boys could not have been found. Our safari had ended, because we wanted to waste no time taking the turtle back to my buddy's grandmother so she could prepare it for supper. I couldn't stay for the feast, but I heard it was a tasty turtle. In fact, that escapade had made the both of us heroes, of sorts. The grandmother mentined the turtle every time I saw her for several years, recalling how impressed she was that her grandson and I had bagged it with that "strange foreign pistol from The War."

In fact, that was the way almost everyone around the area referred to the P-35. It was a nameless piece of hardware that had been dragged off a battlefield by a GI. And for them, it obviously had little meaning in the world. After all, it had been an implement in someone else's army and was so foreign it didn't even shoot "regular shells." For me, however, it was becoming more of a treasure all the time.

As I peddled my bicycle back home that day, I replayed the shot over and over again. Those flashbacks continued as I took the pistol apart, used one of my mother's best towels to dry it off, and then drenched a rag with oil and wiped down every part. It was bedtime and I continued to admire the P-35. The pistol had proven its worth as a hunting tool.

Over the remainder of that summer, the P-35 continued to show its stuff, taking a ground hog on one outing, a frog on another and a seemingly endless array of bugs and dirt clods. Cottontail rabbit hunting in that part of the country was serious stuff back then, and the accepted practice was to take the bunnies with a shotgun. Also standard operating procedure was to take along a handgun to pop the critters when they decided to sit tight, rather than try to hop away.

The hunting season began in the late fall and continued into the period of cold weather. The first rabbit claimed by the P-35 happened on a November afternoon. I was hunting with another friend on a different farm, and as we walked through

An area such as this stretch of Arizona desert not far from Mexico's border illustrates good javelina-hunting country. For the most part, the terrain is barren except for cactus, requiring the hunter with any handgun to stalk carefully.

the knee-high cut corn, our boots crunched through the crusty snow. It was unseasonably cold that fall, and the rabbits were sitting tightly on most occasions. So it was that day when I spotted the bunny's eye looking at me from under a snow-covered clump next to a cornstalk. He was no more than 10 feet away. I froze in my tracks and waited for a moment to see if the rabbit would break from cover. He remained motionless.

I handed my shotgun to my buddy, reached into the game bag on the back of my tan canvass hunting coat and pulled out the P-35. I pulled the slide to the rear, inserted a single cartridge, released the slide and took careful aim. By then, I had a degree of confidence in the pistol's performance, so when it went off, there was no question that the rabbit would be mine. It was. In fact, the exercise was unceremonious that day. But would it be any other way? Already, the talk around school was that the P-35 was a superb shooting instrument. In fact, it was well enough known that one day I had taken it to class and shown it proudly to the teachers and fellow students. After admiring it, the principal instructed me to put it into my locker and not take it class where it might distract the other students from the lessons of the day. Yes, it was a different time back then. A 9mmP in a school locker now is an entirely different matter. But back to uses for the 9mmP.

For several seasons, the P-35 accompanied me on "hunts" around the area. I tried several times to bag tree squirrels with it, but never connected. It remained home when I went off to college, and waited there during my stint in the Army during the 1960s. I shot it a few times after being discharged, but put it away again when I headed West to get on with my life.

Hunting with a 9mmP was put on hold for a couple of decades or so. My interests changed, and I found myself using other kinds of implements. The thought of returning to the 9mmP for serious hunting didn't recur until I found myself on a rocky mountainside in south-central Arizona. The occasion was one of that state's HAM hunts for javelina. HAM is an acronym for "Handgun, Archery, Muzzleloader," because hunters are limited to those implements on such special hunts.

For the occasion, I was armed with a Thompson/Center Contender with a 14-inch barrel chambered for the .30-30 Winchester cartridge. It was topped with a 4x Bausch & Lomb scope. The rig had been used successfully on Santa Cruz Island off the California coast for rams, on the mainland in the Golden State for wild boar and blacktail deer. What had proven to be so successful on a handful of hunts in California turned out to be less than ideal in the hills of Arizona that time.

The javelina were few and far between, and they were on the move. We either spotted them fairly close and moving through the brush, or running full-out across a canyon after they had been spooked. The problem I had was that the 4x scope was too powerful to allow meaningful use on the close javelina, and too jiggly on the running animals at longer distance. I spent a couple of truly frustrating days on that hunt, and vowed never to be improperly gunned again.

The following year when I showed up in camp, fellow hunters chuckled at first, giggled a bit and then broke into outright laughs. I've never cared much how I look on a hunt, but in retrospect, it probably was a bit of a sight. When it came time to hike out after the javelina, it took me several minutes to "suit-up."

First, I buckled on a Tex Shoemaker tan leather rig containing a Smith & Wesson Model 29 .44 Magnum with 8 3/8-inch barrel. Then, in a Michael's of Oregon nylon web rig, I had a

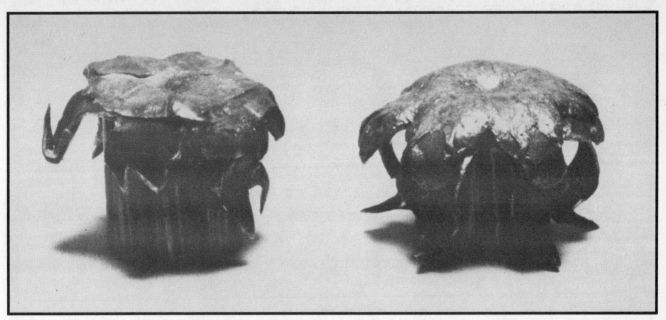

These two Winchester Black Talon bullets were taken from game downed by Comus and Winchester personnel.

Browning Hi-Power (not the original P-35, but a new pistol with adjustable sights) in a cross-draw position. Then, around my neck and hanging in front of my chest was another Uncle Mike's rig containing the scoped Contender in .30-30. Over the huge, camo-colored T/C holster dangled a pair of Steiner 7x50 Military & Marine binoculars.

All of that gear in place, I flipped a backpack/aluminum pack frame rig onto my shoulders. In it were my hunting tag, pair of Bausch & Lomb 20x80 binoculars, tripod, canteen, first aid kit, rope, red marker ribbon, two knives, spare socks, other odds and ends and a couple of candy bars. After adjusting everything properly, I grabbed my pair of shooting sticks and was ready to assault the mountain.

Maybe I looked like a walking sporting goods store, and I'll assure anyone who asks that all of that gear is heavy, but rest easily that I was ready for whatever happened! There simply was no way a pesky javelina was going to show itself and not have lead flying at it!

As much as my technique has since become a standing joke in the industry, it actually made sense then and continues to be logical for me now. The game plan was simple: If I spotted a javelina walking through the brush at close range, I would dispatch it with the Hi-Power. If a javelina occurred from 25 to 50 yards away or so, I'd pop it with the Model 29. And, if the shot was farther, the Contender would be pressed into service.

Further, if I happened to encounter a javelina while sitting and glassing, I could use the shooting sticks to take careful aim and have several options of handguns, depending upon the precise circumstance.

When it comes to firearms taken afield, I have a basic philosophy: If hunting with one gun is fun, then hunting with more guns is more fun. And isn't it supposed to be enjoyable?

Meanwhile, I have found myself on a number of other hunts, carrying a 9mmP — either as the primary firearm, or as a backup/coups de grace implement. One such hunt occurred when I accompanied representatives from Winchester ammo (Olin) on a hunt for exotics shortly after that company introduced its Black Talon handgun loads.

The scene was the Bighorn Canyon Ranch near the community of Moreno Valley, inland in Southern California. Operator Chuck Wagner accompanied Mike Jordan and John Falk from Winchester and me on the expedition which was intended to check out the performance of the then-new bullet design.

Jordan, a superlative shooter with any kind of firearm, carried a scoped Thompson/Center Contender chambered for the .40 S&W cartridge. Falk had a Smith & Wesson semi-auto chambered for the same round, and I carried my trusty Browning Hi-Power in 9mmP.

Candidly, I got the impression that Jordan and Falk wanted to steer away from overt suggestions that the 9mmP might be used seriously for anything that hinted of big game hunting. Given the traditional "wisdom" of gunwriters, such trepidation is understandable. There are "politically correct" cartridges for the different disciplines, and 9mmP has not been known as a big game cartridge. However, I was totally confident.

I had used the Hi-Power on a number of wild boar hunts in California, pressing it into service to finish off hogs which had been wounded and stopped but not killed quickly by fellow rifle hunters. Performance with standard bullets on the several hogs had proven the 9mmP could do the trick if the bullet went into the right spot.

Even so, no one could fault someone representing an ammo company officially for taking care not to raise unneeded controversy.

As the hunt was taking shape, Jordan explained that the .40 S&W Black Talon loading had shown that it definitely had the stuff to take animals at reasonable distances. It wasn't long before he had an opportunity to show what he meant.

There was a billy goat atop a cliff about 100 yards away. The cliff was actually a sharp finger of ground which jutted up between where we were and another, higher cliff just beyond. Jordan took as steady a position as he could on the steep hillside, resting the pistol as much as possible on the thin

Winchester's Mike Jordan was reluctant to consider the 9mmP as a hunting round , as are the custom among ammo makers, who can be conservative. He took this wild boar with scoped Thompson/Center Contender in 10mm Auto.

branch of a bush, the base of which he was using to keep from sliding downhill.

I put my binoculars to my eyes and concentrated on the billy as I waited for Jordan to cap off the round. At the report, the goat shuddered and fell to its right, tumbling from view as it went. Not only had I seen the quake from the impact of the bullet, but the projectile had made that unmistakable "thwap" when it connected with the animal. Judging from the tremors on the animal, I congratulated Jordan for having made a perfect shot — right at the shoulder.

The recoil had precluded Jordan from actually seeing the hit, and he was somewhat uneasy when we couldn't spot the downed animal. I had no doubt, insisting that we would find it just on the far side of the finger, hooves up.

Although the air distance to the goat was only about 100 yards, it took us a full 15 minutes to reach it in the totally rugged terrain. When we got there, the goat lay motionless, just on the far side of the top of the finger. The shot had been perfect and the animal never knew what hit it. A postmortem examination revealed that the performance of the bullet had been classic. And, the mushroomed projectile looked precisely as it was supposed to — almost like it had been shot into ballistic gelatin at the factory test lab.

We were particularly pleased with the size and nature of the lengthy wound channel, as well. The bullet had cut, ripped and torn its way through flesh and bone, leaving a sizeable permanent wound channel. Even if the animal had not died at

the shot, it would have expired quickly due to massive hemorrhaging along the wound channel. But that had not happened. Relatively little blood had leaked out, indicating that death had been extremely fast, and that the animal's heart had not had time to pump more than once or twice following the hit.

Later on the hunt, it was my turn. We spotted a huge ram in a small herd atop another steep cliffy finger on the ranch. With the Hi-Power in hand, I began a stalk. The last many yards were straight uphill, and I used the sparse brush there for cover, eventually getting into position for a shot about 15 yards away from the animal.

The herd was uneasy, and, as is the want of most big rams, he used other animals for cover. It seemed like an eternity as I held the pistol ready, waiting for a clear shot at the ram. The animals began to move away slowly. It was beginning to look like they might disappear over the other side before I could get a shot. But then it happened. The other animals allowed a slight window of opportunity. I could see the ram's shoulder clearly and took the shot.

For those who have never had the opportunity to go along on a genuine "field test" of guns and/or ammo, there is a lot more on the agenda than merely bagging an animal. It is assumed the participants can do that, or they wouldn't be along in the first place. In fact, the real work begins once the animal is down. It is then that the detailed postmortem examination begins, with particular attention to the slightest

There long has been a tendency to compare ballistics of the Browning Hi-Power 9mmP (top) with those of the venerable Goverment Model 1911A1 .45 ACP, but the former's magazine carries a greater number of cartridges.

details of performance.

It is also common on such expeditions for the shooter to place the bullet in a particular spot, because such placement is intended to provide new and meaningful information. So it was with that particular ram.

First off, it was decided that I should take it with the 9mmP because of the kind and size of animal it was. The dirty, oily, thick wool would be a meaningful challenge for the bullet in that it would enable us to see whether the hollow-point cavity would clog up and cause the projectile to fail to open up as it is supposed to do.

Secondly, such rams have dense muscles and hard bones in their shoulder area, again offering a meaningful challenge for the new design of bullet. And, finally, such big rams are noted for their ability to take a heck of a hit and still trot off — even when hit with standard centerfire rifle bullets.

When the shot rang out, the other sheep scampered off, but the big ram stood still. Eventually, he rolled over and down the opposite side of the mountainous finger. The postmortem examination revealed that the 9mmP Black Talon had performed in a manner one would expect of a full-power .357 Magnum with 158-grain hollow-point bullet under the same circumstances.

The 147-grain bullet had splintered the near shoulder, opened up and continued through the chest cavity, leaving a sizeable wound channel on the way. It continued its path through the animal, breaking the far shoulder and cutting through muscle before coming to rest just under the hide on the far side. The performance surprised even Jordan. It made me feel good.

We continued the hunt, and Falk bagged a goat before we concentrated on pigs. In a coups de grace mode, the 9mmP was used for further testing, finishing off animals from the side and front-to-back. Penetration was 12 to 13 inches or so, depending upon what it encountered, in each of the animals shot, and wound channels were uniformly impressive.

Whether one could take that information and justifiably apply it to hunting something else like deer is questionable. However, within effective range, there is little doubt that the 9mmP could work.

There are other normal game animals, however, that can be taken effectively with the 9mmP. I know, because I've done it.

Over the years, I have bagged most of the smaller game species with a 9mmP — like raccoon, opossum and muskrat. But some of the more exciting hunts with a 9mmP have

Jokingly, Steve Comus refers to the Browning Hi-Power Reniassance Model with overall engraving, mother of pearl grips, gold inlays as his "ideal" handgun for smaller game.

involved predators — coyotes for the most part.

Occasionally, when calling coyotes, hunters encounter what are known as "shark dogs." These are the coyotes which come running full-bore, right at the call. When not shot at or spooked in some other fashion, these coyotes literally can end up in a hunter's lap. They are on a beeline, answering the dinner bell.

Hence, it is not uncommon to find coyote hunters arm themselves not only with rifles, but also with shotguns, knowing that the smoothbores will be just the ticket for the shark dogs.

It doesn't take a lot of times in the field after old wily coyote for a person to realize that from time to time there are opportunities to use a regular handgun to bag one of these challenging animals.

So, now when I go out for a coyote shoot, I generally carry some form of regular handgun along — often a Hi-Power or other pistol in 9mmP. My hit percentage is not bad, considering that I don't fire the pistol unless the animal is quite close.

Interestingly, at distances of about 25 yards or less, the 9mmP is quite effective as a coyote killer. It has enough diameter to make a meaningful hole, and has no trouble penetrating enough to get the job done. And, with the right bullets, it doesn't tear up the hide much at all — just an entry and an exit hole.

Of all the places I have encountered the 9mmP on legitimate hunts, even I was surprised when an outfitter in Alaska slipped a Taurus 9mmP into his day pack during a moose and caribou hunt on the Alaska Peninsula one year. Yes, we were also in big bear country, but traditional wisdom suggests that even the .44 Magnum is marginal in such places. Why, then, would the outfitter bother with a high-capacity, 9mmP semi-

auto which happened to be loaded with military ball cartridges?

Later that day, I learned the answer. He used it as a signal gun, because there was no need then to waste any of the more expensive centerfire rifle ammo just to make a little noise.

On such hunts, it is common for participants to use shots in the air to signal others in the party should there be an animal on the ground, or should the hunter get into some kind of trouble. The sound of a shot travels a long way in that open tundra country. The code is simple: two quick shots if an animal is downed, three quick shots if there is a problem. On other hunts in the Rockies, we have used single shots in the air at night when we are trying to close in on the location of a fellow hunter who has been injured and cannot move. Under such situations, we would shoot once in the air, and the other hunter would answer with a single shot. That would allow us to head into the right direction. After travelling for a few minutes in that direction, we would cap off another single shot into the air and listen for the answering shot. By doing this several times, we could reach another hunter, even if he originally had been a long way off.

Meanwhile, with respect to the Alaska system of signalling, if one of us would hear a rifle shot (or more), we would listen intently. If, after a couple or several minutes, we heard two quick shots, it meant the other hunter had an animal down, and we would know to head that way to help out. Consider that processing a downed moose is a big job, and that the hunter who shot it can use all the help he can get from his buddies, both in the carving up of the animal and in the packing out. So, the signalling system works well.

Through the years, I have been involved in a host of handgun hunting experiences. Some have become legends of sorts, like the Arizona javelina expedition when I carried all of the hardware, or the handgun hunt in South Texas one time that involved a now-famous raccoon (but that is another story for another time).

Although not all of these expeditions have involved 9mmP handguns, enough of them have to establish that cartridge/pistol combination as credible in a number of situations. I may never have learned some of things I have about the 9mmP, however, had it not been for a tidbit of wisdom passed on to me by a very old hunter when I was a very young lad.

Following the dictates of corporate caution, John Falk of Winchester did not consider the 9mmP Black Talon round for his own test hunting. He opted for the .40 S&W, fired at 50 yards in S&W Model 4006. However, both he and Jordan were surprised at effectiveness of the 9mmP in Comus' hands.

Each time I encountered that character, it seemed as though he was hefting a different gun. Yet, each time he insisted that he was holding "the best gun in the world."

After a number of such encounters, I mustered the courage to ask: "How can that be the best gun in the world when each of the guns you had the other times were also the best guns in the world? There can't be that many best guns, can there? Doesn't one have to be the best, and the others not quite so good?"

He chuckled, put his leathery palm where my shoulder and neck met, looked toward the sky and sighed, warning me ahead of time that what he was about to reveal what had been told to him sometime in the distant past, and that he reckoned it probably had been passed on from one generation of hunter to another since time began.

"Kid, I'll let you in on a secret," he said as he reached into the back pocket of his bib overalls, retrieving a crumpled bag of Mail Pouch chewing tobacco with one hand as he released his semi-grip on my shoulder with the other. He leaned against an adjacent oak tree, crammed the wad of tobacco strands into his mouth and began to chew, forming the dark brown substance into a cud as he leaned his Marlin 39 against the tree beside him. With the plug properly positioned, and following

the initial spit at a leaf on the ground and the ceremonial wiping off of the side of his mouth with the cuff of his flannel shirt, he continued:

"You see, young fella, for me right now, that Marlin there is the best gun in the world. For you, the best gun in the world is that (Stevens) Favorite you are holding (we were squirrel hunting at the time). What you have to understand is that the best gun in the world is always the one you happen to have with you at the time. No other guns count right then and right there. Do you understand?"

I nodded in the affirmative, but, frankly, I failed total comprehension, perhaps due to my age at the time. Over time, however, I came to understand the concept a lot better. For example, pilots are well aware of the opposite truth: For them, there is nothing more useless on takeoff than the runway behind them.

So, whenever the subject of 9mmP comes up in a discussion around a hunting camp or at the range, and someone suggests everything isn't "the best" thing to use, excuse me if I smile and take on a modified form of the thousand-yard-stare. In my mind I see two boys, a turtle and a P-35. Yes, the 9mmP can be the best hunting gun in the world. It was then and there, at least.

CHAPTER
Twenty-Six

OF AMMO & HANDGUNS

Here's A Trio Of Relatively Unknown 9mmP Launchers That Show Special Talents!

The Thompson/Center Contender has been around for decades, but 9mmP barrels for this single-shot are rare.

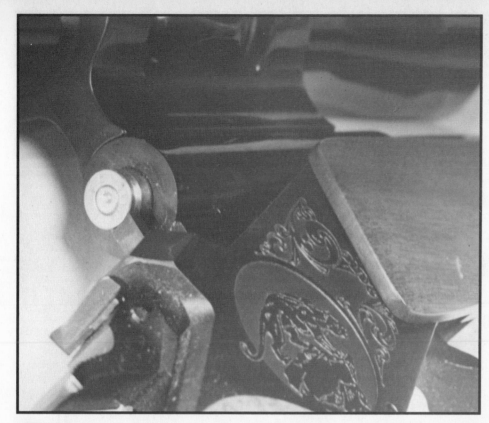

Contender handles the 9mmP well enough in the single-shot barrel. Extraction presented no problems during the tests.

DURING THE course of developing data for this tome, I encountered literally scores of handguns chambered for the 9mmP cartridge. Although specific focus has been put upon the product lines of a number of companies, there were other 9mmP handguns which, for several reasons, did not fall into a stand-alone category. In most instances, it was because they were quite different, or because they were alone in a particular company's line of products.

THOMPSON/CENTER CONTENDER

The Thompson/Center Contender may be one of the most easily identified handguns in the world. This break-open, single-shot pistol is found around the globe, filling roles as a target firearm, a serious hunting instrument or an example of plinking perfection. Even more varied than its uses are its chamberings. I made no attempt to count all of the chamberings, but they total well over 100 if one considers the many wildcats.

Oddly, there are relatively few Contenders shooting the 9mmP cartridge. The reason is simple: Thompson/Center has made relatively few 9mmP barrels, compared to those made for other cartridges. Yes, at one time there was a 9mmP barrel in the T/C lineup, but it was dropped over a decade ago. Since then, almost no 9mmP barrels have been made, and the ones which have been produced were the result of the T/C custom shop operation.

So it was my own 9mmP barrel. When the assignment to write this book was made, I contacted the folks at Thompson/Center, explained the situation and arranged to have a barrel made especially for this work. It is a nine-inch (why not have a barrel of 9 for the 9?) tube sans sights. A T/C 2.5-7x telescopic sight in a T/C mount was attached, putting the entire rig among the world's most accurate 9mmP handguns.

During extensive range sessions, the Contender served as an instrument to establish ammunition benchmarks when it came to consistency, and it helped demonstrate a factor of the 9mmP which is discussed rarely among shooters or gun writers.

This factor is the performance latitude of a cartridge that is so small and compact, yet which delivers one of the most diverse levels of performance in the firearms world. Barrel length determines performance levels for any cartridge, but few in the world are as diverse when it comes to varying barrel lengths than is the 9mmP. For example, the 9mmP establishes high performance levels in handguns with very short (like two or three inches) barrels, achieves normal working performance levels in barrels of four to five inches and keeps getting even more impressive as the tube length grows.

Granted, with judicious handloading, it is possible to make many different cartridges perform thusly. However, with respect to the 9mmP, this latitude is experienced with normal factory loaded ammo. Put another away, the 9mmP — fired through the T/C nine-inch barrel — delivered near .357 Magnum performance with standard factory loadings of the 9mmP cartridge. Talk about efficiency! Yet, with those same factory loadings in a snub-nose revolver, the 9mmP again rivals the performance of the .357 Magnum. Intriguingly, it is only in the realm of "standard" length barrels that the .357 Magnum shows a particular tactical edge.

Hence, it is safe to suppose that the 9mmP cartridge, even in its least comparatively effective role, falls squarely between hot .38 Special loads and the many .357 Magnum loads.

How does this happen? The answer is rather simple, actually. It has to do with standard working pressures. The 9mmP operates at relatively high pressures, and because of the relatively small case volume, it is loaded with powders which develop high working pressures quickly. Yet, when loaded

Stamped as 9mm Luger, this Contender barrel was a special order by the author to conduct tests outlined here.

with anything but the fastest of pistol powders, there is enough gas expansion power to continue to offer more and more boost to velocities as the barrel lengths get longer and longer.

Most 9mmP ammunition offered by the various factories is loaded with powders which are slightly slower than the really fast-burning varieties. For handloaders, this means, for example, that in a general sense it is a better idea to use Hercules Unique powder than it is to use Hercules Bullseye powder, if one is to concentrate on that company's line of cannister powders.

If the concept remains mentally unresolved, take a look at some of the data developed by the author during the various range sessions. All ballistic data was checked by an Oehler 35P chronograph with its three skyscreens located 15 feet from the muzzle. The measurements involved five-shot groups. Results with the various loads through the T/C Contender with nine-inch barrel were:

Winchester's 115-grain Silvertip load delivered a high of 1409 and low of 1382 for a median 1397 feet per second. Extreme spread was 27 and standard deviation was 12.

PMC's 115-grain FMJ load delivered a high of 1334 and low of 1271 for a median 1314 feet per second. Extreme spread was 63 and standard deviation was 25.

Winchester's USA ball loading delivered a high of 1399 and low of 1341 for a median 1378 feet per second. Extreme spread was 58 and standard deviation was 22.

PMC's 115-grain hollow-point loading delivered a high of 1335 and low of 1319 for a median 1326 feet per second. Extreme spread was 16 and standard deviation was 6.

PMC's 115-grain Starfire JHP loading delivered a high of 1324 and low of 1291 for a median 1307 feet per second. Extreme spread was 33 and standard deviation was 12.

CCI's Blazer 115-grain JHP loading delivered a high of 1452 and low of 1424 for a median 1440 feet per second. Extreme spread was 28 and standard deviation was 11.

CCI's Blazer 124-grain JSP loading delivered a high of 1363 and low of 1308 for a median 1350 feet per second. Extreme spread was 55 and standard deviation was 23.

CCI's Blazer 147-grain TMJ loading delivered a high of 1229 and low of 1221 for a median 1221 feet per second. Extreme spread was 15 and standard deviation was 5.

Remington's UMC 115-grain Metal Case load delivered a high of 1410 and low of 1388 for a median 1399 feet per second. Extreme spread was 22 and standard deviation 9.

Yes, those are some pretty impressive ballistics for factory loaded 9mmP ammunition. But how do they compare with the numbers established from other barrel lengths? Using one of the Remington factory loads as an example, the high velocity numbers were:

The Baby Eagle is a compact version of the original and is chambered in 9mmP, .40 Smith & Wesson, .4l AE.

REMINGTON UMC 115-GRAIN METAL CASE

T/C CONTENDER
  9-inch barrel: ....1410 fps.
GLOCK 17L
  6-inch barrel: ....1267 fps.
BROWNING BDM
  4.73-inch barrel: ....1197 fps.
CZ 75
  4.7-inch barrel: ....1193 fps.
SMITH & WESSON 915
  4-inch barrel: ....1077 fps.
SMITH & WESSON 6906
  3.5-inch barrel: ....1045 fps.
SMITH & WESSON 940 *(Revolver)*
  2-inch barrel: ....1051 fps.

A quick look at those numbers reveals what one might be tempted to term a statistical anomaly. As the barrel lengths become shorter, the velocity continues to drop until the shortest barrel length when the trend is reversed. Further, that velocity trend is reversed when the shorter length barrel is in a revolver as compared to an auto, and that means the increased velocity occurs despite any gas bleed-off due to the gap between the cylinder and breech end of the barrel. How does one answer this seemingly contradictory question? It is simple, actually, but before revealing the answer, a quick look

at a number of cartridges fired through those two handguns helps establish a pivotal bit of data.

	S&W 6906	S&W 940
USA 115-grain ball	1075 fps	1083 fps
UMC 115-grain MC	1045 fps	1051 fps
AMERICAN EAGLE		
124-grain MC	1046 fps	1014 fps
PMC 115-grain FMJ	1104 fps	1106 fps

Several factors are at play here. First, the designated barrel length of the revolver is somewhat deceptive. Although the barrel is two inches long, the actual length from the rear of the chamber to the muzzle of the barrel is longer — longer by the length of the cylinder to be precise. After all, the barrel length of the auto is measured from the breech of the barrel to the muzzle, and that includes the entire chamber length. So, in actuality, the effective tube length of the revolver is longer than the tube length of the auto — ending up being almost identical for those two handguns.

But there is a more interesting factor which pops up in the data above: Although the revolver (with its measurably longer length of free-bore) has a tiny edge over the auto with 115-grain loads, when the bullet gets heavier, the auto goes into the lead. This, too, is logical and continues as the weights get heavier — within reason, of course.

The Wilkinson Linda was named for one of the designer's daughters and was built originally as a selective-fire handgun. This 9mmP semi-auto was possibly the most accurate of all the guns checked out in our tests.

However, what the numbers indicate is that if one assumes the "typical" muzzle velocity for a 9mmP 115-grain load is approximately 1100 feet per second (just about exactly the speed of sound), then it is meaningful to discover that velocity does not drop off significantly when the barrel length is shortened: to roughly 1050 feet per second with the 3.5 or 2-inch barrels.

What this means is that the actual performance of virtually any typical 9mmP handgun is more or less the "standard" established in most data bases. The same does not hold true for some of the other cartridges. For example, in a snub-nose revolver, actual velocities achieved by the .357 Magnum are essentially those obtainable from a hot .38 Special and near or even slightly under some 9mmP loadings through the same length barrel. The reason is simple: With really short barrels, the powder charge in the .357 Magnum has not had a chance to develop standard working velocities. Or, considered from another perspective, anyone shooting a .357 Magnum revolver with a very short barrel may be putting .357 Magnum ammo into the chambers, but in effect is shooting nothing more than a .38 Special. This comparative difference doesn't occur with respect to the 9mmP.

This means that when the 9mmP barrel gets longer, the actual ballistic performance approaches that which is achieved with a .357 Magnum when it is shot through a "standard" four-inch barrel. Again, it must be stressed that there is no effort here to suggest that the 9mmP is capable of superior performance when compared to the .357 Magnum, because the .357

Magnum has more room for powder and thus has more ability to be loaded more heavily. However, the point which is being made is that when a shooter uses a 9mmP with a longer barrel, actual performance can approach that of the .357 Magnum — and at much lower degrees of muzzle blast and noise.

For example, Remington's factory data indicates that the muzzle velocity of its various 158-grain bullet loadings is 1235 feet per second through a four-inch-barrel. That is the number many shooters use when comparing one cartridge to another. Yet, through the nine-inch T/C Contender, CCI's Blazer 147-grain 9mmP loading went 1229 feet per second.

Yes, the 9mmP bullet was 11 grains lighter than the .357 Magnum bullet and, yes, the 9mmP barrel was five inches longer. This establishes clearly that when the .357 Magnum is shot through a barrel long enough to make use of its powder charge properly, it has performance superior to the 9mmP. However, as the numbers indicate, the 9mmP does not always trail by much — certainly not by enough to put it into a significantly different league.

Viewed from a different angle, the actual difference is not necessarily as much as it might appear were a person to make comparisons based solely upon data offered by commercial ammo companies. In the case of data from Remington, for example, the 125-grain .357 Magnum loading from a four-inch barrel is listed with a muzzle velocity of 1450 feet per second, compared to the same company's 124-grain 9mmP loading (one grain difference) at 1115 feet per second through a four-inch barrel.

Comus found the Wilkinson Linda a real blast to fire in his desert testing grounds. This particular gun has belonged to Dean A. Grennell for decades.

So what does all this really mean for most 9mmP shooters? Not terribly much, because most 9mmP shooters use handguns with barrel lengths in the four- to five-inch category. Hence, they achieve velocities which are typical.

However, those who use 9mmP handguns with significantly shorter barrels actually are getting ballistics very close to those using standard length barrels. And, those shooting 9mmP handguns with the longer barrels actually are experiencing "Super 9" performance.

There is no effort here to allege that the 9mmP is anything it is not. However, the discussion above might help establish that the 9mmP is far more versatile than most shooters know.

Frankly, this is one of the reasons why the 9mmP, when fired through submachine guns, seems to take on a whole new personality. The answer, as was shown here with the longer T/C barrel, is that when put through such lengths of tubes, the 9mmP is truly a different cartridge!

It always has been a mystery to the author why more shooters who invest in custom barrels for 9mmP handguns haven't opted for significantly longer tubes.

BABY EAGLE

In 1992, Magnum Research introduced the Baby Eagle semi-auto pistol which, among other cartridges, is chambered for the 9mmP. This is a full-size, high-capacity service-grade 9mmP handgun similar to the Jericho 941 pistol.

The Baby Eagle has a 4.37-inch barrel, weighs 33 ounces and is 8.12 inches long overall. Sights are blade front and notched rear (drift adjustable for windage). It is a double-action/single-action pistol, meaning the first shot is double-action, followed by successive shots in single-action, or single-action for all shots, depending upon whether the hammer is cocked before the first round is shot. Like other handguns in the Magnum Research line, rifling in the Baby Eagle is polygonal.

It was the author's feeling that the Baby Eagle is among the world's finest service-grade 9mmP semi-auto handguns. Following hundreds of rounds of every imaginable kind of 9mmP ammo, the Baby Eagle was found to be flawless in operation, while offering superior tactical accuracy.

To put it bluntly, whenever I pointed the pistol at a target from five feet to 25 yards, the target was hit (six-inch diameter plates). Accuracy off the bench at 25 yards was equally impressive. Groups routinely ranged from slightly over an inch to 2-1/2 inches, depending upon the loading. That approaches target-grade accuracy from a service-grade handgun. And, the pistol shot all bullet weights, including the 147-grainers, with equal aplomb.

Yes, the Baby Eagle is an impressive handgun.

WILKINSON LINDA

Dean Grennell provided one of the more intriguing 9mmP firearms used during my quest for the limits for the cartridge and firearms to shoot it. The handgun in question is called the Wilkinson Linda, a semi-auto that looks more like a mega-capacity submachine gun than a "normal" 9mmP pistol. That's not surprising, because the Linda appears strikingly close in configuration to the Wilkinson M-9-S full-auto firearm.

The Linda is 12-1/4 inches long overall, and that includes the 7-5/8-inch barrel. Magazine capacity is 31 rounds. That's a bunch.

On a trip to the range, the Linda showed its stuff in fine form, delivering groups of one-half- to three-fourths-inch with a variety of 9mmP factory loads. For the session, a Bushnell 2.5x scope was mounted, and shooting was done off the bench at 25 yards.

The scary part of the range session was that I came away convinced that pilot error had resulted in the groups being so large! This was without question the most accurate 9mmP firearm I had ever fired — and the author has fired a whole gaggle of 9mmP firearms!

CHAPTER
Twenty-Seven

TOOLS OF <u>THIS</u> TRADE

Three Handloads, 27 Different Factory 9mm Rounds And A Batch Of Accessories Went Into This Volume!

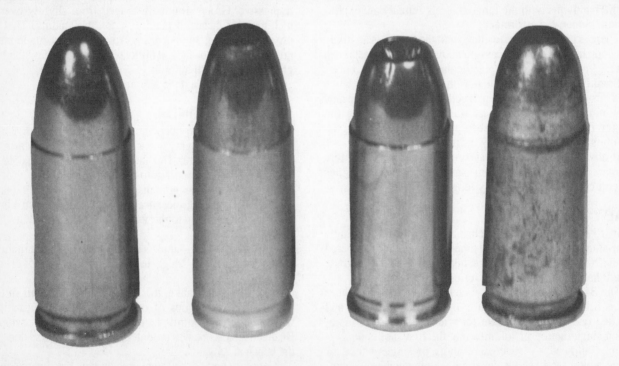

Various bullet configurations were used during the test series. From left are: round-nose full metal jacket , the traditional flat-point , a jacketed hollow-point and a round with a cast lead bullet. All these 9mms shot well.

The author cleaned out his ammunition locker for various brands, weights of 9mm for his test firing.

COMPILING THE mounds of data necessary to complete a book about the 9mmP requires a lot more than just time. It demands the firing of thousands of rounds of ammunition through scores of different firearms. And, it requires a number of specialized fixtures, jigs and technical equipment — all of this to arrive at the numbers, statistics and other data necessary to put the items of discussion into some meaningful form.

AMMO

For this book, the author used 27 different kinds of factory 9mmP loads and three different handloads, bringing the total number of loadings to 30. Not every loading was fired through every firearm. However, virtually all pistols shot during the compilation of data for this book saw several hundred rounds of ammo go through their barrels.

In all those thousands of rounds, there were only three failures to function with respect to ammo. All three of those involved the author's handloads, and these were deemed as suspect before firing. They were shot just to see if rounds so out of form might still work. They did not.

The remainder of the track record speaks highly of the ammunition and the firearms used. Not only did all of the factory ammunition fire and function the pistols, but readings over the Oehler 35P chronograph indicated that most loadings were extremely consistent. Granted, some loads shot better through some individual guns than others, and some pistols were more accurate. But, from an ammunition standpoint, I could not be more pleased.

It is reasonable that factory ammunition for the 9mmP would be good overall. This is a high volume production proposition for any company which chooses to load the cartridge.

The Ransom Rest, discussed at length in text, was used to test accuracy of this Baby Eagle, all the others. This particular mechanism is able to maintain the same hold from shot to shot, if the gun has been mounted properly.

By company, the types of factory ammunition used included:

CCI/BLOUNT

Blazer 115-grain jacketed hollow-point.
Blazer 124-grain jacketed soft-point.
Blazer 147-grain total metal-jacket (TMJ).

All of the CCI ammunition used was from the Blazer line, which features casings made of aluminum with Berdan primers. This means they are not meant to be reloaded. Function was superlative with all of the loadings.

The 115-grain JHP is a good choice for self-defense, because it features an expanding bullet. This particular loading also lends itself well to informal shooting. It is a good all-around offering.

The 124-grain JSP loading is one of the "sleepers" in the industry. This is a snappy loading with a flat-nose, soft-point bullet that is great for self defense.

The 147-grain TMJ loading proved to be extremely interesting. It offered high speed for such a heavy bullet, and accuracy was superior. It could be considered a good all-around bet for just about any 9mmP use, except perhaps for hunting of medium-size animals where an expanding bullet might be preferable.

FEDERAL

Premium 124-grain Hydra-Shok jacketed hollow point.
Classic 115-grain Hi-Shok jacketed hollow point.
Match 124-grain Metal Case SWC.
American Eagle 124-grain Metal Case.

Blaine Huling indicates some of the thousands of holes punched by 9mm ammunition in preparation of tech data for this volume. The frame was lightweight but stable and was built so damaged wood parts could be replaced quite easily.

Of the Federal ammo used, the highest quantity involved the rather generic American Eagle loads. These were among the most consistent performers encountered, and should be considered superlative loads for general use. The bullet, being a round-nose metal case proposition, does not expand when it penetrates a target.

The Federal Match loads worked well, but, frankly, were not noticeably more accurate than were the American Eagle loadings. Perhaps, in specific target grade pistols, the match loads would give an edge, but not a lot. This is not a negative comment on the match ammo, however. Rather, it is a glowing comment on the generic offering which delivers match or near match-grade performance at an affordable price.

The Classic 115-grain JHP loading was another winner. It was not only consistent, but the bullets opened up well in test media. This might be considered a most viable self-defense loading for those who want to combine the higher velocities

of the 115-grain bullet with the expansion characteristics of a jacketed hollow-point bullet.

For self-defense among the Federal lineup used, there is no question that the Premium 124-grain Hydra-Shok JHP loading is the "premium" choice. It offers a mid-weight expanding bullet which has been designed specifically for defensive purposes. This is one of the several "wonder bullet" loads being marketed by the several major manufacturers, and is totally workable as a 9mmP defense proposition. Accuracy also was as good overall with this loading as it was with any of the other Federal offerings.

HANSEN

COMBAT 9 115-grain full metal jacket.
NATO MILITARY 123-grain full metal jacket.

This handgun benchrest was built by Comus' co-worker, Dean A. Grennell, for tests. It is simple, exceedingly strong.

Both of the Hansen loadings are military-type round-nose offerings, with bullet weight being the most noticeable difference. This is solidly good general purpose ammunition and is loaded to full potency, which means that in some cases it is "hotter" than some of the domestic civilian offerings. This means that for pistols which have excessively strong recoil springs, or for military surplus pistols which tend not to cycle the less potent loads, this ammo might be considered for trial. For example, some of the surplus Walther P-38 pistols extant in the world function better with loads like these.

PMC/ELDORADO

No. 9A 115-grain full metal jacket.
No. 9B 115-grain jacketed hollow-point.
Starfire 115-grain jacketed hollow-point.
Starfire 124-grain jacketed hollow-point.

The most frequently fired loading from this source was the generic 115-grain FMJ offering. I refer to it as "camo ammo,"

because the box is camo-patterned. This is good, basic ammunition for the 9mmP. It is snappy, and functions very cleanly.

The No. 9B loading with its 115-grain jacketed hollow-point bullet is PMC's main line expanding bullet loading for the 9mmP. It performs similarly to the No. 9A FMJ loading, except it offers the added performance of an expanding bullet. It is a good, overall choice for informal shooting or for serious self-defense.

Speaking of self-defense, the two Starfire loadings from PMC/Eldorado are among the best on the market for such purposes. The jacketed hollow-point bullet is specifically designed for such purposes, and is one of the "super" bullets on the market from the major manufacturers. Both loadings performed admirably. About the only question the shooter 'might have is which bullet weight he or she prefers. Certainly, if a particular pistol likes one of the loadings better than the other, then the gun has spoken. However, assuming similar accuracy and function reliability experienced during my many range sessions, it is merely a matter of personal preference. Either would get the job done.

Assisting Comus, Blaine Huling attaches a steel leg to shooting table the two devised especially for the 9mm hand-gun tests. The table weighed a lot when completed, but didn't move during the data-gathering sessions.

PROLOAD

124-grain jacketed hollow-point +P.

This is a really good loading for general use, as well as for specific self-defense applications. The bullet used is Hornady's XTP, which has established itself as a superb performer, both in the accuracy department and in target media.

REMINGTON

UMC 115-grain metal case.
115-grain metal case.
115-grain jacketed hollow-point.
Subsonic 147-grain jacketed hollow-point.
Golden Saber 147-grain brass jacketed hollow-point.

The UMC loading is Remington's generic full metal jacket offering, and it is credible overall loading for general 9mmP purposes. The same can be said of the main line 115-grain metal case offering. The author found little, if any, difference in performance between the two. And, the 115-grain jacketed hollow-point falls squarely into the same performance category, but with the added offering of an expanding bullet. For a general-purpose expanding bullet, this one is a good bet.

Remington's 147-grain subsonic jacketed hollow-point offering is aimed primarily at the law enforcement market, which means it also makes a good choice for civilian self-defense purposes. This loading shot well in the various tests, and could be considered a good all-around proposition.

The Golden Saber loading is the company's entry into the "wonder" bullet arena. This brass-jacketed hollow-point offering is designed as a top-notch self-defense loading. Although introduced after much of my testing had been completed, when it was used it performed well and, as might be expected, is a top level product.

SAMSON

Match Grade Carbine full metal jacket loads.

These were used only in the "carbine" type of firearm, because this ammunition is designed for use in submachine guns and not in normal pistols. For example, it was used in the Wilkinson Linda pistol. Yes, this is powerful stuff, but it would not be advisable to shoot it in most pistols.

SURE FIRE

115-grain round-nose full metal jacket.
115-grain jacketed hollow-point.

This is a line of commercially loaded ammunition being marketed by a relatively new firm in the Los Angeles area. Essentially, this company uses a number of generally available components to make the ammo — like Remington cases in the lot used by the author.

Overall, Sure Fire ammunition performed superbly. The only noticeable difference between the two loadings used was that one featured a hollow-point bullet, and the other had full metal jacket bullets.

These are full-potency offerings, which means they function well even in firearms that might have problems with some of the more sedate loads.

WINCHESTER

USA 115-grain ball.
Super-X 115-grain Silvertip hollow-point.
Subsonic 147-grain jacketed hollow-point.
Supreme Black Talon 147-grain SXT.

It is difficult to imagine a better generic loading than Winchester's USA 115-grain ball offering. These loads worked great in any and all of the pistols which were shot. For general purpose applications, this is a great bet.

The Super-X 115-grain Silvertip is an interesting loading. Some pistols really liked it, others did not. Accuracy was never really bad, and in some specific pistols, it was outstanding. This is a high performance loading meant for self-defense, and the author feels it is a great choice for such purposes.

Winchester's 147-grain subsonic loading is used by many law enforcement agencies across the country, and its performance has been rated good to outstanding by officers who have been involved in actual shootings.

The Black Talon loading offered by Winchester is among the best in the industry for self defense. It was one of the first of the "wonder" bullet offerings, and continues to be as good as it can be.

CHRONOGRAPH

It is impossible to write seriously about firearms performance without the services of a reliable chronograph. It is necessary to determine precisely how fast bullets are going. Fortunately, chronographs have benefitted tremendously from the technological explosion of the past few decades, and even the most accurate equipment is within the economic reach of serious shooters.

For gathering 9mmP data, I used an Oehler 35P chronograph. One of the major reasons this particular model makes sense to anyone who does a lot of chronographing is that it uses three rather than two sensors (sky screens) which, when connected to the computerized unit, act like two separate chronographs — one checking the other to make certain everything is as it should be. And, that is what the "P" stands for in the unit's designation —"proof."

It is not uncommon for a chronograph to register a grossly false reading. All kinds of things can cause the problem, including birds flying overhead. Radically angled lighting is another culprit — and the list goes on. What the Oehler 35P does is measure velocities between two sets of sensors, then it automatically alerts the user if one of the readings is significantly different from the other. This feature alone saves a lot of time and effort on the range, because it is easy for a shooter to miss one errant reading in a string, and not be aware of the problem until the session is over or until it is too late to re-shoot the string.

Another handy feature on the 35P is the printout it provides. This makes tallying the information much easier later. In addition to each individual set of readings, when the operator hits a button, the machine automatically computes the fastest and slowest velocities in the string, then computes the median velocity (this would take a rather long time to do separately). It also automatically computes the extreme spread in velocities within the string, as well as the standard deviation. Again, this saves a whole lot of time and trouble.

Further, the 35P operates on a standard 9-volt dry cell battery, each battery good for several hours of continuous use. In real world terms, this means each battery is good for many trips to the range, because the chronograph is turned on only when actual chronographing is being done.

RANSOM REST

Regardless how good or bad a particular shooter is when it comes to shooting for group, no human is as repeatably accurate as a machine. The Ransom Rest is a machine rest which allows the shooter to return the pistol precisely to the same spot, shot after shot.

This means a particular pistol's precise accuracy potential can be determined by using the machine rest. Although the author did not use the Ransom Rest for each and every pistol shot during the research period for this book, many of the handguns were clamped into the device and given a thorough wringing out.

The most necessary times to call upon the Ransom Rest were when a particular pistol was behaving extremely well, or extremely badly, when fired from a more common bench rest setup.

If the pistol showed extreme accuracy promise, the author would clamp it into the Ransom Rest to see just what that potential really was. If a pistol seemed to be shooting badly, the Ransom Rest was called upon to help rule out problems caused by the shooter rather than those inherent with the gun itself.

For example, it can be terribly difficult to achieve meaningful accuracy at 25 yards with a handgun that has a hard, gritty trigger pull. Those factors do not affect performance when the firearm is clamped into the Ransom Rest, thereby allowing the inherent accuracy of the pistol to be known.

For pistols which were behaving well when shot off the normal benchrest, groups improved little when the gun was clamped into the rest. This is because the pilot error with them was not so significant. However, rest assured that no human is capable of the same level of repeatable objectivity that machine rests like the one from Ransom puts right at hand.

There is need to develop proper technique when using a Ransom Rest. First, it has to be mounted solidly, and the operator has to develop a repeatable routine when putting the pistol back into battery if the results are not to be affected adversely. It takes only a little practice to get the feel for using the rest. Once that is accomplished, it is consistent.

TARGET STAND

Due to the huge numbers of shots that would have to be fired over the course of the research for this book, I constructed a wooden target stand that was "modular" in design — any and all parts of it could be replaced quickly and easily without the use of sophisticated tools.

I did not want to have to cut short a range session just because the target stand took a blitzing. And, when the shooting involves scores of handguns fresh out of the box and 30 different ammo loadings, not all bullets are going to go right into the 10-ring. Fortunately, the stand never was shot down, but it did suffer a number of hits.

The stand was made from 2x3-inch pine (it was the cheapest such wood available). The base is 4x4 feet, and the uprights are six feet tall with a cross-bar on top.

Holes were drilled every foot throughout the center stretch of each upright, and bolts with metal "L" pieces were used to hold a 2x4-foot piece of Masonite which served as the target holder. A staple gun was used to attach the target paper to the Masonite. Target paper included everything from official NRA targets to paper plates to computer paper.

In fact, the computer paper was used extensively when taking pistols to the range for the first time. Two rows of three sheets of the paper (still connected on each row) were stapled to the backboard, then one-inch orange target pasters were placed in the center of each sheet. That way, if a particular pistol was shooting way off target, the holes still would register on paper, and as long as the author maintained the same aiming point, the group would form — regardless of precisely where it happened to be on the paper itself. This saved a lot of time during initial shooting sessions.

Handguns that either showed great promise or were causing problems then were returned for other sessions at the range as I attempted to put everything in order. Usually, things worked out fine.

SHOOTING BENCH

With the help of fellow shooter Blaine Huling, the author made an industrial-strength shooting table that served many purposes, depending upon the order of the day.

We started out with two three quarter-inch plywood sheets (4x8 feet) and glued them together, making a table top which was almost 4x8 feet on the sides and more than a full inch thick. Before the glue could dry, we also used several dozen wood screws to clamp the two sheets of plywood together, eliminating any future warpage.

The massive table top then was bolted with half-inch bolts to four heavy legs which were made from one-eighth-inch-thick steel angle iron that was four inches on a side. An eighth-inch-thick square plate of steel six inches on a side then was welded to the top of each of the four legs — but not before the proper size holes were drilled near each corner for the half-inch bolts which would hold the legs to the top.

On the bottom of each leg, an eighth-inch-thick triangle of steel was welded to form a false "foot." There was a five-eighths-inch hole drilled in the middle of the false foot and a foot-long section of half-inch threaded rod was inserted with double-nuts above and below the false foot. Already welded to the bottom of the rod was another eighth-inch-thick steel plate that was six inches on a side. Before being welded to the rod, the plate had a half-inch hole drilled near each corner.

This design — brainstormed by Huling — allowed for fine adjustment of each leg to match the ground where it was set up. After all, we knew we would be using the equipment in a number of different places, including the open desert. By using a two-way level, the table top could be made perfectly level on any terrain by merely adjusting the massive steel feet. Once they were adjusted, foot-long spikes could be used to anchor the individual feet into the ground. What resulted was a table that simply would not budge — not even a little bit. It weighed over 100 pounds total, but that was okay. It worked.

This table was used to anchor the Ransom Rest and to hold the massive piles of equipment needed during the full-on range sessions. It also held reloading presses and scales and all of the gear needed to make handloaded ammo right on the spot.

At times, it was handy to have still another "bench" which could be more mobile or which could be used by one shooter while another was using the main table. This was accomplished with a three-legged portable shooting bench made for the author by Tucson gunmaker David Miller. Although the initial purpose was for lengthy prairie dog shooting sessions, this portable bench proved valuable during the research session for this book, as well.

No portable chairs were used — empty plastic five-gallon buckets and empty plastic cases which once held four gallon jugs of milk are much more productive. Not only could we sit on them when wringing out the guns and ammo, but we could carry the mounds of gear to and from the bench in them.

To extend effective time in the field on hot summer days, we created a 12-foot-square tarp awning that was held up by a modular frame of lightweight plastic PVC pipe. Once up, the entire rig was guy-roped to stakes in the ground, withstanding some fairly stiff breezes in good order.

Experiences gained during the research period offered some handy tips for others who want to get more serious about their shooting, and who have access to places other than established ranges.

First, create an entirely separate tool chest with everything needed for every piece of equipment to be used. Unless there is a dedicated, self-contained tool box, the shooter *will* forget something sometime — or several things — often.

Also, never forget to take a cooler with water, sodas or something else to drink. Shooting sessions get long and thirsty. Sunglasses are a must, as is a good hat. Sunscreen doesn't hurt, either.

CHAPTER
Twenty-Eight

"NINES TO THE LINE!"

After Years Of Neglect, The 9mm Is Getting Competitive Attention!

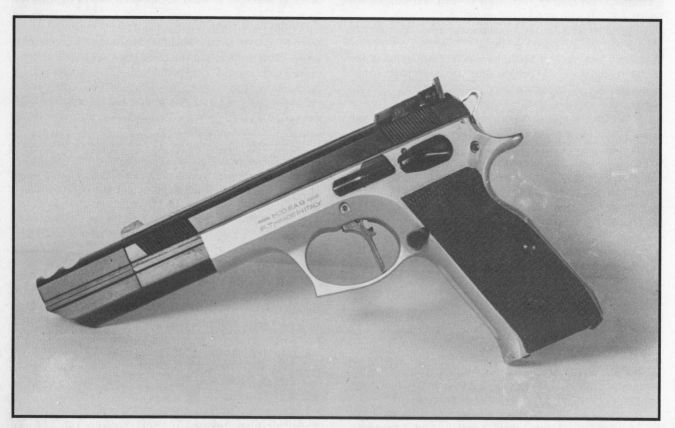

Most 9x19mm guns can be converted to the more potent 9x21 with nothing more than rechambering. This E.A.A. Witness in 9x21 meets Major caliber requirements and is becoming the choice of many discerning shooters.

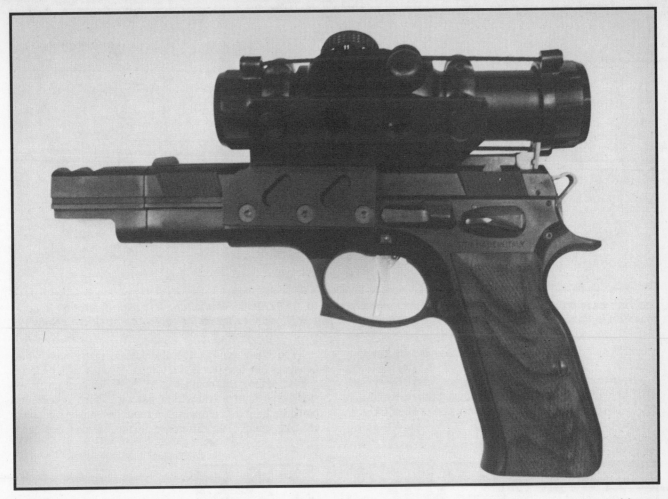

The 9mmP is the preferred tool for Steel Challenge-type matches. This full-blown E.A.A. Witness race gun combines excellent accuracy, light recoil, lots of rounds in the magazine. Christian has found this an excellent handgun.

IN WHAT can only be considered one of those paradoxical twists of gundom, one of the hottest selling handguns extant is the 9mm semi-auto. Yet, when it comes to that bastion of recreational shooting — competitive events — the 9mm has been conspicuous by its absence.

In some cases there are good reasons. The relatively slow-paced, but precise NRA bullseye shooting is a good example. In this game, competitors attempt to punch out X-rings with three different required calibers: rimfire, centerfire and .45. The latter category is nothing more than a holdover from the days when the .45 ACP was the service caliber of our armed forces. On the surface, that would seem to indicate that each competitor would require three handguns to compete, but that's not the case.

"The 9mm certainly has the accuracy to be a competitive cartridge in the centerfire class. It is not, however, any more inherently accurate than a properly built .45 ACP wadcutter gun. Since the .45 is also a centerfire — and quite legal to use in that class — many of the top competitors avoid the expense and logistics of a third gun and shoot centerfire with their existing .45," reports Chris Christian, a long-time competitive competitive marksman.

"Circumstances doom the 9mm here, and while it is certainly a viable choice, it is one that is not likely to see any serious use unless the NRA establishes a specific 9mm category. Most observers feel that is not likely in the foreseeable future."

Another case of "circumstantial doom" occurs in the exciting game of NRA action shooting (a la the Bianchi Cup). In this contest, the 9mm has a lot going for it due to more than adequate accuracy and soft recoil. Some competitors use it with some success.

Unfortunately, the top competitors have discovered that, due to the time limits involved in the various stages of the contests, a revolver offers an advantage over a semi-auto.

"A smooth double-action revolver trigger offers an easier 'surprise break' under the quick but still generous time limits than does a crisp single-action semi-auto trigger," Christian contends.

With the long, smooth pull you are less likely to break the shot while your sights are off the critical X-ring of the target.

Among top shooters, the .38 Special revolver has become the tool of choice — and shooters tend to follow the leader when it comes to equipment use. In this case, it is not the cartridge that is wanting — just the launching pad.

One area where the 9mm cartridge — and the guns that shoot it — becomes the perfect choice is in IPSC-style action shooting. When faced with an array of targets at varying distances, and your score becomes a combination of how

The 9x21 case (at right) is nothing more than a longer version of the 9x19mm Parabellum. It is slightly stouter in construction to handle the higher pressures at which it works. The 9x21 qualifies for Major caliber competition easily.

quickly you can deliver accurate hits, the 9mm may have no peers.

Given the round's velocity, its trajectory is relatively flat. Your hold on a 60-yard target isn't much different than for a 10-yard target. That's not the case with a slower round like the .45 ACP.

"The lighter 9mm bullets also have less bore mass, which translates into less recoil and torque. You get back on target quicker. If the gun is compensated, the higher pressure generated by the 9mm provides more gas with which to work. In a properly designed compensator, more gas makes for a more efficient comp. The difference in muzzle rise between a

THE SPORTSMAN'S
TEAM CHALLENGE

HANDGUN EVENT

Sponsored By:

Accurate Arms Co., Inc.

Smith & Wesson

Taurus International

1:67.84

In such competitions as The Sportsman's Team Challenge, meticulous records are kept by means of electronic equipment. This registers times, accuracy and effectiveness of the various cartridges used in the series of shooting events held annually.

This 9mm Thompson/Center Contender offers performance that almost equals that of popular NRA Hunter Pistol round guns such as the .270 Ren and the .32-20, yet the 9mm is often overlooked when choosing a gun for this particular competitive event.

comped 9mm and a comped .45 ACP is noticeable."

Last, but certainly not least, is magazine capacity. The 9mm is the hands down winner in this respect. The more rounds you have in the gun the fewer times you have to reload. Even if you can swap mags in just one second that's still a second you save on your score.

Yes, the 9mm is the perfect action gun. Unfortunately, the IPSC has recognized that and deliberately adopted a rule that penalizes its use. To understand that, you need to understand Power Factor.

The Power Factor is a simple mathematical formula that takes bullet weight, in grains (mass), and multiplies it by velocity, in feet per second (speed), to come up with a final figure that gives us, in essence, a measurement of momentum. To keep things simple, the product is divided by a constant of 1,000.

The lone 9x19 (extreme left) will not qualify for Major caliber competition. All of the varous 9x21 loads shown will do so easily and are short enough to work through most 9x19 guns. A rechambering job is the only requirement.

Although the 9mmP has the accuracy to compete in NRA Bullseye Matches, the venerable .45 ACP is favored for the centerfire classes. The author is among those who sees no change in this trend in the foreseeable shooting future.

If the resulting figure — bullet weight multiplied by velocity divided by 1,000 — equals or exceeds 175, you have a Major caliber. If the figure falls between 174.9 and 125, you have a Minor caliber. Some matches use 120 as the Minor caliber lower end. If the figure falls below 125 (or 120) you have *no* caliber! The round is not considered powerful enough to be legal in that match.

Notice that nothing has been mentioned about bullet shape, caliber (frontal diameter) or bullet construction (FMJ, hollow-point, SWC, et al).

This is strictly a measurement of mass multiplied by speed equaling momentum. As such, it is right out of the rather outdated Hatcher theories. But, even then, it is not complete, because even Hatcher recognized that certain bullet shapes were more — or less — efficient at transmitting their energy and he assigned modifier values to bullet shapes.

"Major caliber cartridges are rewarded by a higher score for rounds that impact outside of the A zone on the standard IPSC target, than are the Minor caliber rounds. In effect, Minor caliber shooters are penalized for anything less than a perfect hit," Christian explains.

The theory behind that — at least, according to the founding father of practical pistol craft — is that it takes a big bullet to do "man's work," and anything less is "wimpy" and should be punished.

No 9x19 load can make Major caliber at safe pressures. So, the 9x19 remains a Minor caliber. Nobody has won a major IPSC match with a Minor caliber in recent memory; the point drop for rounds outside the A zone is just too severe. This has caused a lot of misconception about the Power Factor.

Among naive gunwriters, the term has come to mean "good round" versus "poor round." There is a tendency to divide all handgun rounds into "Major" or "Minor" calibers. It's trendy, and it makes some individuals sound like they actually know what they are talking about. "If I need a self-defense gun, I'll pick a Major caliber. I wouldn't bet my life on a Minor caliber." Such a train of thought has no bearing on the real world.

Consider this: Let's suppose you are sitting on the front porch sipping one of those marvelous chilled beverages that made Milwaukee famous and you happen to see Jeffrey Dahmer charging up the driveway with a meat cleaver in one

There is plenty of discussion, pro and con, about the contesting capabilities of the 9mmP in action shooting circles.

hand a bottle of catsup in the other. Would anybody in his right mind pick up a six-inch barreled .44 Special revolver loaded with the standard 246-grain RN lead slug at 770 fps...in preference to a 15-shot 9mm stuffed with one of the proven law enforcement loads like the Federal 9mm 115 JHP+P #9BP-LE? In actual shooting, the latter load had been proven significantly more effective than the old round-nose .44.

"I'd grab the 9mm in a heartbeat. Yet, a look at the power factor for the two loads would show I was wrong!" Christian admits. The .44 Special load (246 multiplied by 770 divided by 1000) has a power factor of 189.4. The "Minor caliber" 9mm comes out at 115 multiplied by 1300 divided by 1000 — only 149.5!

"That's the problem with the IPSC Power Factor — bullet technology has rendered it as obsolete as the dinosaur. Yet, those who refuse to believe that the 20th Century actually does exist continue to cling to it. And that's the reason the 9x19 has not made greater inroads into the one area of popular competition where it is not only ideal, but eminently practical.

Fortunately, that is changing. The advantages of increased magazine capacity, more efficient compensator performance and lighter bore mass — reduced recoil, again — have made the .38 Super the winning gun in IPSC competition. Using specially built guns, bullets in the 135- to 160-grain range can be driven fast enough to make Major. This still does not offer the increased magazine capacity of a basic, double-column mag 9mm. Even with the high-capacity 1911 frames, the cartridge rim can cause feeding problems.

The .38 Super does offer advantages over the .45 ACP, but not nearly the advantage a 9mm does. So, in a move intended

solely to beat the Power Factor, two new 9mm cartridges have come into being — the 9x21 and the .356 TSW (Team Smith & Wesson).

The 9x21 already is well-established in Europe where it was created to beat government bans on civilians shooting military calibers. By lengthening the 9x19 case by two millimeters, the new round becomes "not a military cartridge." Yet, it is short enough to function perfectly in standard 9x19 guns and magazines. Virtually any full-size and some compact 9x19s can be adapted to the 9x21 with nothing more than a quick rechambering job.

Additional case length easily allows 9mm bullets in the 150-grain weight range to be driven to velocities that will make Major caliber.

Brass, as well as chambering reamers, loading data and even drop-in barrels (for Colt 1911 and CZ-75 clones) are readily available. RCBS and Lee also offer dies. One source for 9x21 components and information is CP Bullets, 1814 Mearns Rd., Warminster, PA 18974.

Although the round is relatively new, in this country it is already supplanting the .38 Super as the IPSC caliber of choice.

The .356 TSW is even newer. In essence, it is a 9x21-1/2. Developed for the Smith & Wesson shooting team, it is not nearly as established as the 9x21, and its future is less certain. Although it is too new to truly gauge its potential, it would appear this cartridge will not be incorporated as easily into existing 9mm guns as is the 9x21. The round is being loaded by Federal Cartridge Company with an initial match load using a 147-grain FMJ bullet at approximately 1230 feet per

The action shooting sports have made accuracy with heavier bullets a requirement the 9mmP meets only partially.

second from a five-inch barrel, easily making Major. Guns for the new round will be available from Smith & Wesson.

But what of the lowly 9x19? It, too, is alive and well. Pure speed shooting, a la Steel Challenge, is one of the fastest-growing competitive handgun matches in the country, and the sponsors here decided to drop the outdated Power Factor.

In this relatively new game, the 9x19 is the tool of choice. In fact, some of the most popular loads are much lighter than standard factory loads!

In speed shooting, it is important to actually hear the bullet strike the plate in order to confirm a hit, since the plates are not always designed to fall on impact.

That is accomplished most easily by driving the bullet at subsonic velocities. The crack of the bullet breaking the sound barrier interferes with hearing it strike the plate. As a result, most competitors load bullets in the 115-grain range to velocities of about 950-990 fps. This is noticeably less than the standard 1150 fps with the 115-grain bullet offered in factory 9x19 rounds. Quick-burning powders like Winchester 231 will accomplish this with charges as light as 3.6 grains, and recoil is virtually nil.

Two popular bullets are the Hornady 115-grain XTP hollow-point and the new 115-grain Speer Gold Dot. These are proving to be some of the most accurate 9mm bullets made and rival the best match loads in virtually any other centerfire pistol caliber.

Interestingly, the 9x21 can be loaded down easily to velocities in the 950 to 1050 range with these same bullets. Those who have rechambered their 9x19 to 9x21 will find they have essentially the same versatility as those who shoot the .357 magnum revolver — the ability to create a wide variety of power levels in their loads.

Another area where the 9mm is seeing increased competitive use is in bowling pin matches. On the surface, this seems quite illogical, because bowling pin matches — in which the pins must be driven completely off the table — are one of the few scenarios where the old Hatcher/Momentum/Power Factor theory actually works. A big, heavy bullet does a much better job of driving pins to the ground than does a lightweight, high-speed hollow-point.

Yet, due entirely to the popularity of high-capacity 9mms and the desire of their owners to shoot them, special 9mm Pin matches are held frequently. Generally, there will be nine bowling pins — but sometimes eight — that the shooter must clear. This often requires the full services of an overstuffed magazine!

One of the best loads for this is one of the 147-grain hard cast flat point bullets driven to a velocity of over 1000 fps. In my TZ-75, 4.4 grains of Unique will produce 1050 fps with no pressure signs whatsoever. It's one of the best 9mm loads for clearing pins I've found.

Another competition where the 9x19 truly shines is, surprisingly, one in which it often is ignored completely — NRA Hunter Pistol Silhouette.

The 9mmP has plenty of power for the lighter metal silhouette targets, such as the chicken, which are shot at closer ranges. A plus for the 9mmP cartridge for this segment of silhouettes is the high degree of accuracy it offers.

In this game, half-sized silhouettes — ram, turkey, pig and chicken — are engaged from an offhand position at ranges of 40 yards (chicken), 50 yards (pig), 75 yards (turkey) and 100 yards (ram). Like any silhouette event, targets must be knocked completely off their stands to score a hit. These silhouettes, unlike some others, don't take much knocking over.

The game is shot as a rimfire and centerfire event and the silhouettes are lightly constructed. A .22 rimfire magnum will drop the centerfire ram at 100 yards! Because of that, competitors are restricted to modestly powered, straight-walled cartridges. Not surprisingly, the game is dominated by the accurate, moderately-priced Thompson/Center Contender handguns, with scope.

Top cartridges in NRA Hunter Pistol are the .270 Ren, a wildcat made by fireforming a .22 Hornet case to straight-walled configuration. It launches a .277 caliber 100-grain grain jacketed slug at about 1400 fps. The .32-20, with a 100-grain slug travels at 1500 fps. Both sets of velocity figures are average for a 10-inch Contender barrel, and both calibers are capable of between two-and three-inch groups at 100 yards. That's more than enough for the rams.

From a nine-inch Contender barrel, the 9x19 will spit out a 90-grain Hornady XTP at 1500 fps, making 1250-1300 fps with cast or jacketed bullets in the 115- to 124-grain range.

Christian's Contender will hold five rounds into three to four inches at 100 yards with many different loads.

"Performance differences are slight, yet 9x19 brass is considerably less expensive than the other two rounds and is made more stoutly. That means more loads per case," Christian has found. Brass, as well as a wide selection of bullets, is also easier to find. If a shooter already owned a 9mm, and was loading for it, entering the NRA Hunter Pistol game would be as simple as obtaining a scoped Contender in 9x19.

Compare that to what the shooter opting for the .270 Ren. goes through: obtain dies, shell holders, et cetera, then pay through the nose for expensive .22 Hornet brass. Expending a bullet, primer and powder charge is required just to make the case, which will have about half the reloading life of the 9x19. And, all for a very marginal performance edge!

In reality, the 9mm makes a lot of sense for a lot of competitive games. One reason it has been held back is what can only be called reluctance on the part of some rule makers to abandon the venerable .45 ACP as a required round (NRA bullseye) or to abandon rules that favor the .45 (IPSC).

As the 9mm becomes even more popular among American shooters, however, chances are good that will change.

CHAPTER
Twenty-Nine

THE BIG SWITCH

Training Trauma Has Been Reduced With Ultimate Acceptance Of The 9mmP For Law Enforcement

The Smith & Wesson Model 15 revolver was replaced by the Beretta 92F. Both of the handguns are roughly the same in overall dimensions.

CONTROVERSY IS one issue that always remains constant in law enforcement circles, especially when dealing with firearms and ammunition. Along with controversy, 'not being very receptive to change' is another trait that runs consistent. No matter what the department says, no matter what data they show you, there always will be those individual officers and deputies who have their personal preferences.

"When dealing with the Los Angeles County Sheriff's Department, any decision for change of any type is costly. Supplying approximately 8,600 sworn members with any piece of equipment costs plenty, especially if specialized training is necessary to facilitate the change. With a department of this size, changes don't come easy.

"Scheduling alone is a major obstacle to ensuring everyone gets the proper training. Unlike some businesses in which things can stop for a day or two while a change-over takes place, law enforcement service never stops. It keeps on ticking, 24 hours a day, seven days a week."

Having been a member of the law enforcement community for over twenty years — primarily with the Los Angeles County Sheriff's Department — Pete Fosselman has witnessed many changes first hand. Fortunately, most of them have been for the better, he feels.

The crux of this chapter on revolvers being replaced with 9mmP semi-autos — is based on personal points of view and information gathered from various department members. The text should be considered Fosselman's personal points of view based on experiences, observations and conversations with fellow deputies, but not policy of the Los Angeles County Sheriff's Department.

According to FBI statistics, violence toward police officers continued to rise during the 1970s. In fact, in the United States, there were over 1,100 law enforcement officers killed in line of duty during one 10-year span. That averages to over 100 per year; about double the number, 54, killed in all of 1992. With this increased aggression, police officer survival finally began to get some attention. One of the areas that generated controversy back then and remains a subject of debate today is the officer's sidearm.

The criminal element was reportedly armed with large-capacity firearms while most of law enforcement still was using the six-shot wheel-gun.

Many agencies began to look at semi-autos with large capacities as a replacement for the revolver. Smith & Wesson made early inroads with their Model 39. It was followed shortly thereafter with the somewhat similar Model 59 with nearly twice the capacity as its predecessor.

These two semi-autos were adopted eventually by the Los Angeles Sheriff's Department for off-duty use only. Personnel who opted to carry one off-duty had to attend an eight-hour department training, familiarization and qualification course on their own time. The S&W Model 59 became the standard-issue sidearm for many municipal agencies, even though it, like the Model 39, had a sporadic history of problems.

As the Los Angeles County Sheriff's Department approached the 1980s, still mandating a revolver for on-duty use, many law enforcement agencies across the United States had made the switch from revolvers to semi-automatics. The 9mmP and the .45 caliber ACP cartridges were the rounds of choice. The 10mm Auto and .40 S&W rounds had not yet emerged. Even though the 9mm bullets of the time were not

The 15-round Beretta magazine has firepower advantages over a six-shot speed-loader meant for the revolver. The magazine also is a great deal easier to load in a poor light situation, according to reports from actual incidents.

The Safariland hoster is standard issue for deputies of LASD. They are not allowed to use personal holsters.

and the Heckler & Koch system was considered superior for this specialized work. This became the department's first official acceptance of a semi-auto handgun.

For SWAT activations, the H&K semi-auto 9mm pistol chosen to replace the revolver was the P7-M8. The Benelli shotgun replaced the standard-issue Ithaca Model 37. When Special Enforcement Bureau members were not on a SWAT call-out and were augmenting regular uniform patrol assignments, they had to revert back to the standard .38 revolver and Ithaca shotgun.

In 1987, after the military and the Los Angeles Police Department began switching to the Beretta 92F 9mm semi-auto pistol, the sheriff's department began giving serious thought to a change. The initial steps weren't easy; some department executives were not convinced the change was necessary.

After much debate, the department finally gave the stamp of approval, but not before a complete "system" of safety involving the pistol and holster could be found. This was not going to be a selective-use situation. The sheriff's department would mandate the exact pistol and holster that must be used at all times.

"The criteria in selecting a sidearm for everyday use in uniform patrol varies quite a bit. Revolvers, as opposed to semi-autos, are easier to teach people how to shoot and operate. They are less mechanical and routine maintenance is not as critical. To overcome a misfire, one only has to squeeze the trigger again," Fosselman points out.

With a semi-auto, one needs to check the magazine, operate the slide and check the safety. Reloading a revolver with speed-loaders is just about as fast as inserting a magazine into a semi-auto, if lighting conditions are good. But, you are adding only six rounds to your firepower versus up to 19 for some large-capacity semi-autos.

"In poor lighting conditions, reloading with a magazine is easier, because this can be accomplished by feel. With a revolver, the individual rounds in a speed-loader must line up with the empty cylinder; good lighting is helpful, otherwise

producing the desired results relative to expansion and penetration, they survived. Fortunately, ammunition suppliers began to conduct serious testing, along with the FBI, in an effort to develop a more effective 9mm round.

In 1982, two years before Los Angeles was to host the '84 Olympics, the sheriff's department's Special Enforcement Bureau was outfitted with a complete Heckler & Koch weapons system. Members of the SEB handle all SWAT call-outs

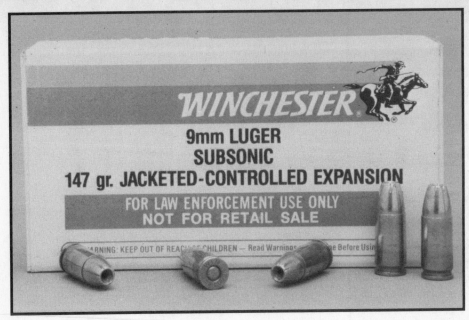

In 1990, after the FBI and the Los Angeles Sheriff's Dept. conducted extensive testing, the latter entity switched to the Winchester sub-sonic 147-grain, Jacketed Controlled Expansion round, with had good results.

this feat can be time consuming. The thought process to operate a revolver is much simpler. The shooter can remain focused on the target rather than directing his thoughts to the mechanical operation of the semi-automatic."

Fosselman's observation is that, "when looking at the semi-automatics, firepower or capacity wins hands down. The average officer with a large-capacity semi-auto like the Beretta 92F and a pair of magazines has around 45 rounds at this fingertips. The revolver user has only 18, unless carrying more than two speed-loaders. The semi-auto is less bulky and offers greater concealment than a revolver. And, if the semi-auto is not a double-action-only model, accuracy tends to increase after the first shot due to the semi-auto's single-action trigger mode."

In 1988, the Los Angeles County Sheriff's Department began issuing and conducting in-service conversion training with the Beretta 92F. A Safariland break-front holster was chosen. Two extra 15-round magazines were issued to each deputy, along with a double magazine pouch. The pouches could be worn either vertically or horizontally, depending on the deputy's wishes. Departmental regulations require that the magazine pouches be worn on the Sam Browne belt, opposite the side of the holster. A few problems developed on some of the pouches being worn horizontally. As a result, subsequent pouches were modified to fit only in the vertical position.

Initial Beretta conversion training consisted of a 16-hour training block. Once the 16-hour course was completed, the deputies could not revert back to their revolvers. The Beretta became their mandated duty sidearm.

Half of the first day was spent in the classroom learning how to assemble, disassemble, clean and maintain the new semi-automatic pistol and its magazines. The second half of that day was spent on the firing line for weapons familiarization, shooting and qualification. Today, a qualification score must be attained before the deputy is permitted to carry the Beretta as an on-duty or off-duty weapon.

The second day of training was spent at the sheriff's all-purpose outdoor range. Training consisted of shooting and reloading drills, as well as clearing a jammed handgun.

Various problems like stove-piped rounds and misfires were staged to create fairly realistic malfunction situations. Today, staged malfunctions are set up to occur while the shooter is running through a PPC course. The shooter has to clear the 9mm competently and once again engage the target successfully. All of the practical drills and the qualification courses are timed, so some expediency and weapon familiarization are necessary to pass.

The Beretta will not pick up a round from the magazine if it is not fully inserted into the magazine well. This stands to reason, since the slide will not engage a round between the magazine lips if it is not in the proper plane as the slide returns to battery.

The magazine release can be switched to accommodate right- or left-handed shooters. For either shooter, it is possible to hit the magazine release button inadvertently while using a two-handed combat grip. Should this occur, the magazine will drop anywhere from an eighth of an inch to completely out of the magazine well.

Because this could happen, training sessions grind the "tap, rack and lever up" message firmly into your brain. This means that, when a malfunction occurs, you first must tap the bottom of the magazine to ensure it is inserted completely into the magazine well. You then rack the slide to the rear manually by grasping it between your index and middle fingers and resting your thumb against the back of the slide below the rear sight.

When the slide is all the way back, you let it return on its own via the recoil spring. "Lever up" refers to pushing the ambidextrous safety to the off-safe position since it usually gets pushed into the safe position while racking the slide in the prescribed manner.

"During the past five years, over 6,000 sworn and reserve LASD deputies have been converted. Most of them like the Beretta, but some have reservations. Many old-timers — including yours truly — still like our old revolvers, and we use the Beretta daily simply as a matter of policy. The majority of the revolver diehards attribute liking the revolver to the fact that we have had an on-going relationship for several more years than those with the Beretta. Maybe with time, we'll

overcome that feeling," Fosselman concedes.

He questioned several deputies immediately after returning from their yearly PPC course training. Questions concerned their feelings toward the Beretta. When asked about the thought process required to get through the day's training using the Beretta, most agree that a semi-auto handgun requires more concentration. Knowing a staged malfunction is going to occur while running the PPC, deputies concentrate on the "tap, rack and lever-up" sequence, instead of sight picture and the target. They know it's bound to happen and due to time penalties assessed by the range staff, they must tap, rack and lever up in the proper order to avoid a penalty.

With a revolver, the thought process was much less demanding. If the hammer fell and went click instead of bang, one merely squeezed the trigger again and continued.

Pete Fosselman was working in the sheriff's public information bureau when the initial deputy-involved shootings utilizing the Beretta 92F started to occur, and he mentally noted the number of rounds fired in the confrontations. "Without a doubt, the number of rounds fired by deputy personnel was much higher than those deputy-involved shootings where revolvers were used.

"In revolver training, we were trained to 'double-tap' (shoot twice) and assess the situation, then double-tap again if necessary and so on. During Beretta training, time always was ticking during live-fire training and we were encouraged to shoot, shoot, shoot! At least, my class was rushed this way. If this held true for other classes, it only stands to reason that when the deputies got out onto the streets and needed to use deadly force, they reverted to the shoot, shoot, shoot training and fired more rounds.

"Our Homicide Bureau investigates all deputy-involved shootings. I requested some data regarding revolver versus

Above: The double magazine pouches fit vertically on the Sam Browne belt on opposite side from the leather holster. (Right) Monthly qualification is mandated and can be done in a three-stall indoor range.

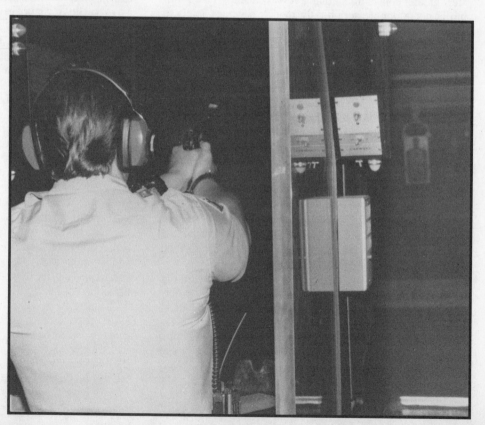

The Los Angeles County Sheriff's Department has 10 of these 40-foot trailers that have been turned into portable pistol ranges. They are moved weekly to various sheriff's facilities throughout the county for firing qualifications.

Beretta shootings. I was looking strictly for revolver-only or Beretta-only shootings. Throw out all the SWAT shootings or those in which a combination of revolver and/or shotgun and/or Beretta rounds were fired. I wanted to keep it simple and strictly look at one as opposed to the other."

Results were not as alarming as Fosselman expected, partly because the survey years used for the Beretta shootings were 1991 and 1992. The higher numbers of rounds fired on which he had made mental notes were 1987 and 1988, the inaugural years of using the Beretta.

Also, the '91-'92 two-year time frame was after some adjustments had been made in the training program. Beretta conversion training was expanded to 24 hours instead of 16. Monthly qualification for those issued Berettas was mandated, instead of the initial trimester qualification. These two factors alone would create more familiarity and confidence in this firearm.

In 1985 and 1986, deputies using revolvers fired a total of 340 rounds in 87 suspect verses deputy shootings. This averages out to 3.9 rounds fired per deputy. In 1991 and 1992, deputies using the Beretta semi-automatics fired a total of 742 rounds in 144 suspect vs. deputy shootings. This averages out to 5.2 rounds fired per deputy.

"From this simple survey — and I do mean simple — the numbers indicate that more rounds are fired with semi-autos than revolvers. Even though there's only a little over one round difference, there is still a difference."

To help accomplish the monthly qualification requirement, the department purchased several 40-foot trailers and converted them to three-stall indoor ranges. The trailers are moved from facility to facility on a weekly basis to give personnel the opportunity to qualify. Once the ranges are set up, sheriff's personnel can shoot 24 hours a day, thus eliminating overtime pay for personnel working odd shifts. The trailers are completely self-contained and the course of fire at these indoor ranges is the same as an outdoor ranges. To compensate for the shorter distance — 10 yards in the trailers rather than the 25 yards of the outdoor ranges — silhouette targets are reduced proportionately in size.

The standard course of fire is to load 15 rounds in each of two magazines for a total of 30 rounds. All courses of fire are timed. The first course is six rounds in 60 seconds. The next course is 12 rounds in 40 seconds, necessitating a magazine change after 9 rounds. The final course is to shoot the remaining 12 rounds in 30 seconds. Each course of fire is started from the double-action mode.

Department-issued 9mm ammunition selected initially for the Beretta use was the Federal 115-grain hollow-point. As the FBI experienced in their unfortunate and tragic Dade County, Florida, shootout, the Los Angeles Sheriff's Department also discovered that the light 115-grain round — even though it "eventually" proved fatal in several shootings — provided a large temporary cavity upon impact, but not enough penetration and too little knockdown.

Deputy Sheriff Phil Luna uses a car door for partial concealment, knowing it protects little against incoming rounds.

Through testing — largely attributed to the FBI's Wound Ballistics Workshop in Quantico, Virginia — researchers determined that larger, slower-velocity bullets produced more desirable results in stopping suspects than higher velocity lightweight bullets that had a tendency to fragment. As a result, the Winchester 147-grain sub-sonic JHP round was phased in around 1990 and the Federal 115-grain HP phased out.

This brings us back to the earlier mentioned apparent decline in the number of rounds fired in 9mm shootings shown in Fosselman's statistics, as opposed to the number of rounds he vividly recalls being fired before the adoption of the 147-grain sub-sonic rounds.

"If the original issue 115-grain round was not producing the stopping power needed to put a suspect down, and the suspect continued to advance when shot — and I know it happened — then it only seems reasonable to assume deputies would shoot more rounds to stop an aggressor.

"Since the issue round in 1991 and 1992 was the sub-sonic 147 grain, it would seem reasonable that my earlier mental notes of more rounds being fired during the late 1980s was possibly due to the 115-grain round's ineffective stopping power. I have nothing official on this subject; only observations, experiences and speculation on my part."

Muzzle flash from the Winchester sub-sonic 147-grain JHP is much greater than that of the Federal 115-grain hollowpoint. This can cause some serious distraction and a temporary loss of night vision when involved in night-time shooting.

"With over 6,000 Beretta 92F semi-auto pistols in use by the Los Angeles Sheriff's Department, I've been told there have been approximately one dozen broken trigger springs. This does not make the pistol inoperable, but should this happen during a gunfight, you must return the trigger forward manually to engage the sear and fire again. The department also has experienced a couple of broken firing pins. This is a simple item for an armorer to replace, but it immediately removes one from a gunfight. It can't be remedied on the spot like the trigger springs. But revolvers were known to break their firing pins occasionally, too."

In the aftermath of the Rodney King civil unrest in Los Angeles, many deputies wanted to have additional loaded magazines in their patrol bags. Loading a staggered magazine is time-consuming. By pre-loading additional spare magazines at a convenient time and place, they always would be ready for immediate use. This is an excellent idea — if one thinks 45 rounds will not be enough.

"My concern developed when several deputies purchased after-market magazines for their Beretta pistols, then started having problems with over 50 percent of them. Instead of buying Beretta factory magazines, they struck a deal with a local supplier to save a few bucks. Unfortunately, the few bucks saved could have cost them their lives."

The following problems were encountered in this situation:

The magazine springs were stiff and, oftentimes, no more than five rounds could be loaded without severe effort on the part of the loader. In some cases, the magazines were assembled incorrectly. The welded seams on the back sides of the magazines were not milled properly, and the exposed spot welds caused friction when the magazines were inserted into the magazine well. This often resulted in the magazine getting stuck, then it failed to "free fall" from the gun when the release button was pushed. In some cases, they had to be forced out of the magazine well by using a wooden dowel inserted through the ejection port.

In still other "bargain" magazines, the lips that grip the rounds at the top of the magazine were not machined or aligned properly. This prevented the magazine from being inserted far enough into the magazine well, thus preventing it from being locked into place. When the magazine isn't locked in place, the slide can fail to pick up a fresh round during the course of fire.

These instances of magazine failure were encountered only with the after-market magazines. None of these problems, to the best of reported knowledge, have been encountered with factory-supplied Beretta magazines. We know what they say — "caveat emptor'" or "let the buyer beware."

There you have it: a working deputy's opinions, observations and experiences on the handgun changeover of the largest sheriff's department in the nation.

"Even though I pointed out some pluses and minuses, remember that whichever sidearm or ammunition you're using, bullet placement is one of the most important aspects of a gun fight," Fosselman insists. "With that in mind, practice officer safety, wear your vest — and keep your head down!"

Above: Deputy Phil Luna can insert a fresh magazine of 9mm ammo into the magazine well of his Beretta 92F by feel. He does not have to see what he is doing should it be in the dark. (Left) Deputy John Rodriguez, wearing the recently approved campaign hat, talks to a citizen on the street. Note that he keeps his gun side away, the butt of the auto covered by his arm.

CHAPTER *Thirty*

A TIME FOR CHOICES

With Dozens Of Calibers Available, Why Settle For This Aged Cartridge?

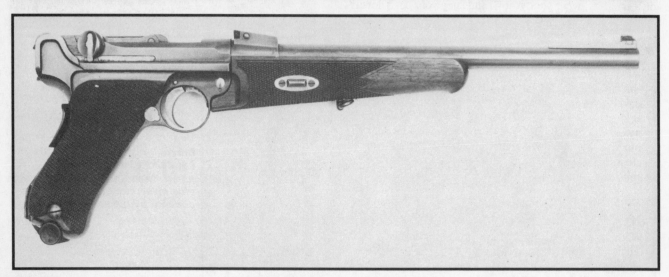

This long-barreled Luger was designed for use of the German military and even boasts swivels for a sling. It is not exactly the pistol one would choose today as a back-up gun. It is considered a prized item among arms collectors.

WITH SCORES of different handgun cartridges available, why choose the 9mm Parabellum? The answer to this question is as personal as each shooter's own desires, yet there are universal replies which can make sense for anyone — beginner, intermediate, expert or veteran.

Convenience rates high in recommending a 9mmP for shooters at any and all levels. With the possible exception of the .22 rimfire, there is no single cartridge on the face of the earth that is used more widely, nor available more extensively.

But simple access isn't the entire story. There are phenomena involved under the overall convenience umbrella which make the answer much more meaningful.

For example, because the 9mmP is so incredibly universal, it is a mass production proposition, both on the gun and ammunition fronts. Bottom line? The 9mmP is among the most inexpensive of all centerfire cartridges to shoot.

Further, because there are so incredibly many models and

Professional marksman Rick Kennereknecht tries out a Smith & Wesson Model 915 in 9mm Parabellum for accuracy.

sub-models of 9mmP handguns on the market, there are more guns within the financial reach of anyone at any level than any other kind.

By category of shooter and by application by the various shooters, here are some of the reasons why it makes sense to opt for the 9mmP when considering a handgun/cartridge combination.

BEGINNER

When it comes to anyone being introduced to a new activity, there are certain critical tests which much be passed if the neophyte is to enjoy the new activity enough to keep at it, or even become ardently involved with it. On the firearms front, it means using a firearm/ammunition combination that does not intimidate the new user. The 9mmP fills the bill well.

All too often, some shooters, enamored with the brute power of some kind of firearm/ammunition combination, decide to impress newcomers by showing them just how awesome such a rig can be. This is the Dirty Harry complex!

As much as such an exercise might fuel the mentor's machismo psyche, it too often causes the opposite reaction with the student. The 9mmP comes to the rescue. Although this is a potent little cartridge, neither its report nor its recoil are enough to intimidate any but the most recoil-sensitive people.

Beginner shooters also can find a handgun chambered for the 9mmP cartridge which fits their hands well enough to be controllable and enjoyable to shoot. Again, this factor by-passes the behemoth proportions of some firearms that can inhibit the development of operational familiarity.

If representing affordability on the gun front is good, then the ammunition picture has to be beautiful. Budget-priced ammo for the 9mmP is available just about anywhere and about anytime. That means someone who is just entering the shooting sports doesn't have to mortgage the ranch just to play the game. Oddly, something as simple as a few cents per round can be enough to keep many people from becoming shooters. To that end, the 9mmP comes to the rescue again.

Add the affordability of the gun and the ammunition together and the package looks even better — so good, in fact, that there is a likelihood a new shooter will stay with the sport long enough to become serious about it.

So what kind of 9mmP handgun is right for a newcomer to the shooting sports? It can be a tough question. Most 9mmP handguns are semi-autos, and semi-autos can be intimidating for those who are unfamiliar with firearms in general or handguns in particular.

One alternative could be for them to invest first in a 9mmP revolver. There are a number of them available and, as discussed elsewhere in this book, the 9mmP lends itself to use in revolvers quite well.

However, a quick reality check would indicate that newcomers to shooting are more likely to opt for a model that is

While the autoloading pistol seems the true home of the 9mmP cartridge, a number of revolvers — some of them custom reworks — have been outfitted to handle the round.

"on sale," or in some other way discounted in price to the extremely affordable level. New shooters cannot be blamed for some degree of trepidation, because they do not yet know whether they are going to enjoy shooting enough to make a larger investment.

Fortunately, there is a growing number of shooting facilities which offer specialized instruction for new shooters. This is good, not only from a safety standpoint, but also for the enjoyment levels that might be realized by the new shooters when they actually start putting rounds downrange.

Therefore, the best 9mmP with which to begin is the one that is at hand when one begins to shoot. No, that's not a cop-out. It happens to be true. Should the 9mmP at hand happen to be of the semi-auto persuasion, though, there are some bits of advice that might be in order.

First, learn and follow firearms safety procedures. Guns are not toys, and when misused they can wreck lives in a heartbeat. When used properly, they can offer a lifetime of

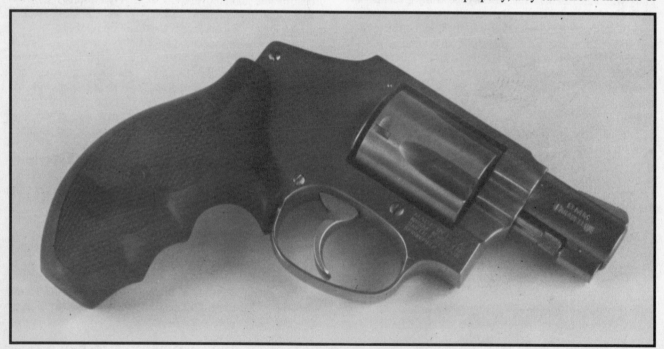

This Smith & Wesson Model 940 is chambered for the 9mm Parabellum, using half- or full-moon cylinder clips.

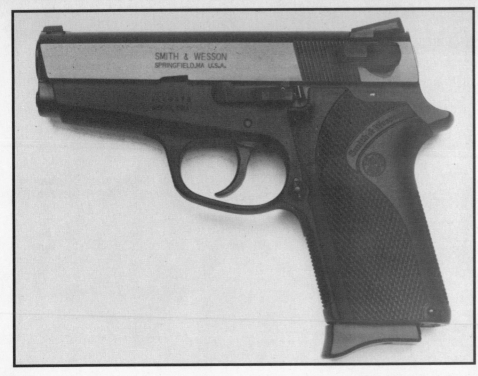

Left: Smith & Wesson's Model 3914LS, with fixed sights, is one of that maker's guns chambered for the venerable 9mmP round. (Below) Browning's BDM is a double-action pistol that has been chambered for 9mmP. It is designed primarily as a self-defense type of carry firearm.

fun. Within those safety parameters, it is a good idea for most newcomers to use the handgun as though it was a single-shot at first, even if it happens to be a semi-auto.

Single-loading cartridges into a 9mmP is simple, and assures the action will be open and safe after each shot. And, there are advantages to this procedure which transcend mere safety. This procedure forces new shooters to pay close attention to operating the action, and it also forces them to actually work the action every time the handgun is fired.

Such repeated working of the action contributes to familiarity with the firearm for the new shooter, and that is part of the object of initial practice. Once the shooter is more familiar with the pistol, it's time to load two rounds into the magazine and shoot it that way for at least a few hundred rounds. This is effective practice, because it helps the new shooter become familiar with the feel of a semi-auto as it operates as a semi-auto. Yet, the pistol is empty after every two shots, and that means there is no need for the shooter to try to hold onto a loaded firearm when the hand or arm begins to tire.

A person doesn't have to hang around shooting ranges for long to notice the roots of some of the most typical unsafe movements committed by new shooters. These are the shooters who, with a loaded firearm in hand, try to do something other than pull the trigger. Since they are not familiar with handling loaded firearms, they tend to look away and get involved in something else without paying terribly close attention to where the firearm is pointing.

Such activities are much more likely to happen if the new shooter is holding a pistol with many rounds in the magazine than if there is initially one, and then just two.

By the time a new shooter has put several hundred rounds downrange — one or two shots at a time maximum — there should be a degree of familiarity that will allow them to create an "instinctive" or subconscious tendency to handle the firearm in a safe manner. Ultimately, every shooter needs to develop such habits, and for newcomers, there is no time like

Above: The Beretta Model 92 is manufactured in half a dozen or more configurations, but all are chambered in 9mmP. (At left) Israel Military Industries has made a big thing of the heavy-weight, big-bore Desert Eagle pistols marketed in this and other countries, but they don't ignore guns chambered for the familiar "nine." They make them, too, meeting a demand.

at the beginning.

Next, it would serve the new shooter well to load no more than three or five shots into the handgun at a time while shooting informally. Actually, one can go entirely through a shooting career without loading any more ammo than that into a firearm at a time, so such advice is not really bad for intermediate or advanced shooters during informal sessions, either.

Regardless what kind of 9mmP handgun a new shooter might be using, it needs to be in a "safe" condition when it is not being used. For semi-autos, this means action open and the magazine removed from the gun. For revolvers, it means open cylinder and no ammo in the chambers. In the case of single-action 9mmP revolvers, make certain all chambers are clear and then leave the loading gate open.

INTERMEDIATE SHOOTERS

Most active shooters fall somewhere in the intermediate category. They have used firearms periodically, are fairly

The stainless steel Smith & Wesson Model 5946 was another entry in the 9mmP sweepstakes for a market share.

familiar with their operation and shoot rather infrequently and usually only informally. Whether someone is a good shot or not is not part of this discussion. Rather, the degree of familiarity and frequency of use are determinants in classification as intermediate.

Why would an intermediate shooter opt to get a 9mmP handgun? Assuming the shooter did not acquire a 9mmP as a beginner, there are many reasons why someone who shoots recreationally would be interested in having such a pistol.

Recreational shooting does not require the use of extremely expensive target equipment, and most 9mmP handguns on the market are general purpose pistols which are priced accordingly.

Also, intermediate shooters, as recreationalists, are shooting for the fun of it. This means the widespread availability of affordable ammunition for the 9mmP is particularly appropriate for this kind of shooter.

The specific choice of the proper 9mmP handgun for an intermediate shooter is more complex than for the beginner. The reason is that the intermediate shooter has had enough experience with firearms to be able to formulate an idea about what design and size rig he or she might really want to use.

As mentioned previously, this part of the selection process is entirely personal. Intermediate shooters should not rule out consideration of the more expensive models. By the time a shooter is at this level, he or she already has a commitment to the shooting sports. In fact, most of those in the intermediate category would likely be in the "frequent flier" advanced category if they had the time and money to do it.

Hence, shooters in this category can appreciate the features, construction and materials that separate the more expensive models from the basic handguns. And, that appreciation really should not be denied. After all, by the time a shooter has joined the intermediate ranks, he or she also has become serious about shooting.

For an intermediate shooter, it is worthwhile to consider the main line, substantial models available. It is also at the intermediate level that a shooter might want to reload ammunition — both as a cost-saving measure and as a way to expand the fun factor of the overall shooting sports.

The intermediate shooters would be well advised to investigate some of the full-size 9mmP handguns. Among them are some of the older collectible models. Again, at this level of shooting, one finds very many serious collectors. In fact, this is really the level of shooter which makes the entire sport and industry tick. It contains the largest numbers, and it also contains some of the most serious collectors who spend most of their time collecting and less time actually shooting.

As a measure of where one might fit into the spectrum, virtually all members of the military and virtually all law enforcement officers are, at most, intermediate shooters.

ADVANCED, FREQUENT SHOOTERS

Why would an advanced, frequent shooter want a 9mmP? For all of the right reasons, of course. Of all levels of shooter,

Smith & Wesson's Model 915 double-action auto was introduced in 1992. It has a 15-round magazine for 9mm. With a side-mounted decocking lever, four-inch barrel and weighing only 28.5 ounces, it has found favor with the author.

the fewest are in this category. These are the people who shoot, on average, at least once or twice a week all year long, and who shoot thousands of rounds of ammo every year. Not all are particularly good shots, but virtually all are credible shooters.

What this means is that the advanced, frequent shooters would be hard pressed not to have at least one 9mmP in their repertoire of handguns.

Again, regardless of shooting level, cost remains a consideration. And, for those who shoot very much, cost is also important. But more than that, those who shoot a lot generally keep current with developments within the sport and industry. This means that the rapid escalation in the popularity of the 9mmP over the past decade will have captured their curiosity, if not imagination.

TYPES OF SHOOTING

Having established that the 9mmP is, by definition, a prime candidate for any kind of informal shooting exercises, what about the more serious applications?

The 9mmP is used in some of the various target games, but not to the degree that it is used in real life situations. This is at least curious.

Somewhere in the development of shooting disciplines during the 20th Century, the 9mmP ended up taking a back seat to other cartridges for a number of reasons, some of which are even contradictory.

For example, the 9mmP is not used widely in some of the "practical" types of target shooting. Interestingly, this is due, in some instances, to the insistence of the architects of the disciplines that the 9mmP possesses insufficient power.

Yet, when law enforcement agencies alleged they were encountering larger and larger numbers of suspects, especially drug dealers, who were armed with high-capacity 9mmP firearms, they cried out that they were "out-gunned" and that they, too, needed to be armed with such weaponry. Very interesting.

The 9mmP is not exactly common when precision handgun target work is in progress. Other cartridges seem to have won that battle.

So what sorts of applications are accepted and proper for the 9mmP? Those which more or less call for the qualities that caused the cartridge to be designed in the first place.

The 9mmP is at home in the hands of more militaries around the world than any other single handgun cartridge. The 9mmP is found in the hands of more law enforcement agencies around the world than any other cartridge. And, within the past decade, the 9mmP has been finding itself more and more in more homes in a self-defense role.

What does all of this mean? The 9mmP and the handguns which shoot it are affordable, fun, handy for informal shooting and ready to serve in any of the many real life applications of firearms. Come to think of it, where else would any cartridge really want to be?